Brief Contents

M000280085

Finding What You Need

This brief book provides an overview of academic writing, help with editing, and a guide to research and documentation. You have many ways to find what you need in the book:

- **Use a table of contents.** Inside the front cover, a brief contents outlines the book at a glance. Inside the back cover, a detailed contents lists all the book's topics.
- **Use the documentation chapters.** Chapters 48–51 detail widely used styles for documenting sources: MLA, APA, Chicago, and CSE.
- **Use the glossaries.** "Commonly Misused Words" (p. 329) clarifies words and expressions that are often used incorrectly. "Grammar Terms" (p. 340) defines all the terms marked ° in the text.
- **Use a list.** "ESL Guide" (pp. 406–07) pulls together the book's material for students using English as a second language. "Editing Symbols" inside the back cover explains abbreviations often used to mark papers.
- **Use the index.** At the end of the book (p. 363), this alphabetical list includes all topics, terms, and problem words and expressions.
- **Use the elements of the page.**

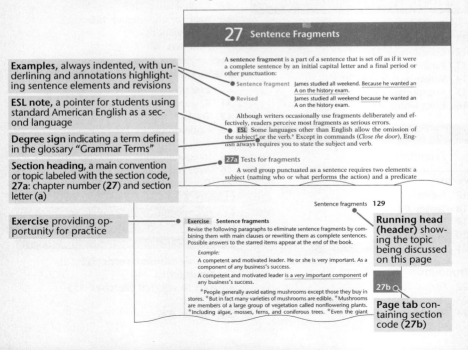

Examples, always indented, with underlining and annotations highlighting sentence elements and revisions

ESL note, a pointer for students using standard American English as a second language

Degree sign indicating a term defined in the glossary "Grammar Terms"

Section heading, a main convention or topic labeled with the section code, **27a:** chapter number (**27**) and section letter (**a**)

Exercise providing opportunity for practice

Running head (header) showing the topic being discussed on this page

Page tab containing section code (**27b**)

27 Sentence Fragments

A **sentence fragment** is a part of a sentence that is set off as if it were a complete sentence by an initial capital letter and a final period or other punctuation:

- Sentence fragment   James studied all weekend. Because he wanted an A on the history exam.
- Revised   James studied all weekend because he wanted an A on the history exam.

Although writers occasionally use fragments deliberately and effectively, readers perceive most fragments as serious errors.
- ESL Some languages other than English allow the omission of the subject or the verb.° Except in commands (*Close the door*), English always requires you to state the subject and verb.

27a Tests for fragments

A word group punctuated as a sentence requires two elements: a subject (naming who or what performs the action) and a predicate

Sentence fragments **129**

Exercise   Sentence fragments
Revise the following paragraphs to eliminate sentence fragments by combining them with main clauses or rewriting them as complete sentences. Possible answers to the starred items appear at the end of the book.

Example:
A competent and motivated leader. He or she is very important. As a component of any business's success.
A competent and motivated leader is a very important component of any business's success.

*People generally avoid eating mushrooms except those they buy in stores. *But in fact many varieties of mushrooms are edible. *Mushrooms are members of a large group of vegetation called nonflowering plants. *Including algae, mosses, ferns, and coniferous trees. *Even the giant

NINTH EDITION

The Little, Brown Essential Handbook

Jane E. Aaron

 Pearson

VP & Portfolio Manager: Eric Stano
Development Editor: Anne Ehrenworth
Marketing Manager: Nick Bolt
Program Manager: Rachel Harbour
Project Manager: Susan McIntyre, Cenveo Publishing Services
Cover Designer: Pentagram
Cover Illustration: Anuj Shrestha
Manufacturing Buyer: Roy L. Pickering, Jr.
Printer/Binder: LSC Communications/Crawfordsville
Cover Printer: Phoenix Color/Hagerstown

Student Edition ISBN 10: 0-134-51521-8
Student Edition ISBN 13: 978-0-134-51521-2

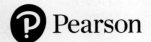 Pearson

www.pearsonhighered.com

Preface

This small book contains essential information about academic writing, the writing process, usage, grammar, punctuation, research writing, and source citation—all in a convenient, accessible format. With its cross-curricular outlook and straightforward presentation, *The Little, Brown Essential Handbook* helps students with writing tasks in a variety of disciplines.

The following description highlights as New the most significant additions and changes to this edition of *The Little, Brown Essential Handbook*.

A guide to academic writing

The handbook introduces the goals, requirements, and common types of academic writing, stressing the writing situation, the writing process, critical perspective, thesis and organization, drafting and revision, evidence, synthesis, and the use of sources.

- New The expanded Part 1 includes a new chapter on academic writing and more detailed chapters on analyzing the writing situation and writing as a process.
- New A full chapter on paragraphs discusses unity, coherence, development, introductions, and conclusions—all with relevant examples.
- New A new Part 2 presents writing in response to common academic assignments, including critical analysis, argument, literary analysis, informative writing, and oral presentations.
- New Eight annotated examples of student writing in varied genres appear throughout the handbook: a critical analysis of a visual, a proposal argument, a literary analysis paper, an informative essay, a research paper documented in MLA style, a research report documented in APA style, sample pages from a research paper documented in Chicago style, and a laboratory report documented in CSE style.
- New A revised chapter on presenting writing focuses on essential information related to document design, visuals, and other media.

A guide to research writing

The handbook helps students find sources; manage information; evaluate, synthesize, and cite sources; and avoid plagiarism.

- New The discussion of libraries' Web sites covers various ways that students may search for sources—catalog, databases, and research guides.
- New A revised discussion of keywords and subject headings helps students develop and refine their search terms.
- The discussion of evaluating sources—library, Web, and social media—helps students discern purposes and distinguish between reliable and unreliable sources. Case studies show the application of critical criteria to sample articles, Web documents, and a blog.

A guide to documentation

The extensive coverage of four documentation styles—MLA, Chicago, APA, and CSE—reflects each style's latest version, including the eighth edition of the *MLA Handbook* (2016).

- New Reorganized chapters for all four styles group sources by type, thus simplifying the process of finding appropriate models and clarifying differences among print, database, Web, and other sources.
- New Updated, annotated examples of key source types show students how to find the bibliographic information needed to cite each type.
- New Sample research papers show each style in the context of student work.
- For all styles, color highlighting makes authors, titles, dates, and other citation elements easy to grasp.

A guide to usage, grammar, and punctuation

The handbook's core reference material reliably and concisely explains basic concepts and common errors.

- New Exercises in connected discourse clarify and test important concepts. Answers to selected exercises appear at the end of the book.
- New Added examples on appropriate language show how to revise common texting shortcuts for academic writing.
- Explanations use minimal grammar terminology, omitting needless terms and defining essential terms, marked °, in "Grammar Terms" (pp. 340–51).

A uniquely accessible reference handbook

The newly redesigned book includes numerous features to help students find what they need and then use what they find.

- "Essential" learning objectives opening each of the handbook's seven parts give an overview of key content.
- Examples use color annotations and underlining or highlighting to connect instruction and application.
- Two glossaries extend the handbook's usefulness. "Commonly Misused Words" (pp. 329–39) clarifies words that are often confused and misused. "Grammar Terms" (pp. 340–51) defines every term used in the handbook.
- Material especially for writers using English as a second language, integrated throughout the handbook, is marked ESL and indexed at the back of the book (pp. 406–07).
- Brief and detailed contents inside the front and back covers make material easy to find.
- Dictionary-style headers in the index allow for quick scanning.

Writing

Essential
Writing

Academic writing

- Focus academic writing on a main idea, or thesis. (See opposite.)
- Gather appropriate evidence. (See opposite.)
- Develop a critical perspective. (See p. 4.)
- Balance your own and others' ideas. (See p. 5.)
- Conduct research and handle sources responsibly. (See p. 5.)
- Use academic language. (See p. 6.)

The writing situation

- Understand the requirements of your writing assignment. (See p. 7.)
- Analyze the writing situation: subject, purpose, audience, and genre. (See pp. 7, 8, and 9.)
- Know the deadline and the requirements for length and presentation. (See p. 9.)

The writing process

- Use discovery techniques to generate ideas for your writing. (See p. 10.)
- Develop a thesis statement for your writing. (See p. 11.)
- Organize your ideas. (See p. 12.)
- Draft and revise your writing. (See pp. 13 and 14.)
- Edit and proofread your writing. (See p. 16.)

Paragraphs

- Unify each paragraph around a central idea. (See p. 17.)
- Make each paragraph coherent. (See p. 18.)
- Develop the central idea of each paragraph. (See p. 18.)
- Write introductory and concluding paragraphs that set up and finish your writing. (See p. 23.)

Presenting writing

- Follow the format of the discipline you are writing in. (See p. 24.)
- Use visuals and other media appropriately. (See p. 24.)

1 Academic Writing

When you write in college, you work within a community of teachers and students who have specific aims and expectations. The basic aim of this community—whether in English, psychology, biology, or another discipline—is to contribute to and build knowledge through questioning, research, and communication. The differences among the disciplines lie mainly in the kinds of questions asked, the kinds of research done to find the answers, and the ways of communicating the answers. Many academic papers share the features discussed in this chapter.

1a Thesis

The **thesis** is the central idea to which all of an essay's general statements and specific information relate. It is the main point or claim that the entire work develops and supports with evidence.

In college writing, your thesis usually appears in a thesis statement that is explanatory or argumentative. An **explanatory thesis statement** makes a claim that promises to inform readers about something, whereas an **argumentative thesis statement** makes a claim that promises to convince readers of something:

Explanatory thesis statement	Military service teaches teamwork, discipline, and job-related skills that translate well to civilian life.
Argumentative thesis statement	Using a cellphone while driving should be outlawed because it causes accidents.

For more on developing a thesis statement, see pages 11–12.

1b Evidence

In academic writing, you support your thesis with **evidence**, such as facts that can be verified by observation and research, examples that illustrate and reinforce a point, and the opinions of subject-area experts based on their research and experience. You draw evidence from reading assignments, articles and other sources found through research, experiments, observations, interviews, and sometimes personal experience.

For more on evidence in arguments and literary analyses, see pages 43–44 and 54, respectively.

1c Critical perspective

Academic writing requires critical thinking, reading, and writing. **Critical** here does not mean "negative"; rather, it means "skeptical," "exacting," and "curious." When you read an essay or view an advertisement through a critical lens, you examine it closely in order to question and understand it. When you write critically about a work, you contribute ideas and information to the knowledge about it.

Three primary operations contribute to a critical perspective:

- **Analysis:** separating something (a text, a visual, a video) into its parts or elements in order to understand it. (For more on analysis, see pp. 37.)
- **Interpretation:** considering the meaning and significance of the work's elements and how they contribute to the work as a whole. Interpretation usually involves making inferences about a work's underlying **assumptions**—the creator's opinions, beliefs, or principles about what is, what could be, or what should be. (For more on interpretation and assumptions in critical analysis and argument, see pp. 37–38 and 44, respectively.)
- **Synthesis:** making connections among ideas and information and drawing conclusions. Synthesis often involves working with sources gathered through research. (For more on synthesis in critical analysis and research writing, see pp. 38 and 203–04, respectively.)

The following example, from the student research paper on pages 266–76, shows analysis, interpretation, and synthesis at work in a paragraph about environment-friendly (green) products and consumption. The paragraph uses a pattern common to academic writing: it opens with the writer's own idea, synthesizes evidence from sources analyzed by the writer (with source citations), and concludes with the writer's own interpretation of the information.

Writer's idea	Unfortunately, the growing popularity of green products has not reduced the environmental effects of consumption. The journalist David Owen notes that as eco-friendly and energy-efficient products have become more available, the "reduced costs stimulate consumption" (80). The author gives the example of home cooling: in the last fifty years, air conditioners have become much more affordable and energy efficient, but seven times more Americans now use them on a regular basis, for a net gain in energy use. At the same time, per-person waste production in the United States has risen by more than 20% (United States 10). Greener products may reduce our cost of consumption and even reduce our guilt about consumption, but they do not reduce consumption and its effects.
Evidence (quotation)	
Evidence (paraphrase)	
Evidence (paraphrase)	
Writer's interpretation and conclusion	

1d Balance

Academic writing balances views so that the presentation is reasonable and believable. If your thesis makes a significant, debatable claim, then others can supply evidence to support different views. Dealing with these views honestly, giving them their due, shows that you are responsible and open to dealing with readers' possible objections.

For more on opposing views in argument, see pages 45–47.

1e Responsible research and use of sources

Academic writing often requires you to conduct research and draw on sources in your writing. You are free to borrow from sources *if* you do so responsibly, not misrepresenting or distorting what sources say and not **plagiarizing**, or presenting sources' ideas and information as if they were your own.

ESL Cultures have varying definitions of a writer's responsibilities to sources. In some cultures, for instance, a writer need not cite sources that are well known. In the United States, however, you are obligated to cite all sources.

Responsible research

Responsible research starts with an open mind. You should be willing to explore and test your own views on your subject and consider the views of others. This mindset encourages you to treat other views fairly, whether or not you agree with them.

- **Use your own knowledge, experience, and opinions.** Gauge what you know and think about your subject so that you recognize how source information reinforces, contradicts, or expands your knowledge. See pages 175–78 for more on research strategy.
- **Consider others' positions and biases.** Seek multiple viewpoints, and evaluate sources carefully in order to identify and weigh other writers' biases and positions. See pages 193–203 for more on evaluating sources.
- **Treat sources fairly.** Take care not to misinterpret or alter an author's meaning when taking notes on sources. See pages 205–07 for more on summary, paraphrase, and quotation.

Responsible handling of sources

You can avoid plagiarism by keeping close track of the sources you consult and any ideas, words, and sentences you borrow from them.

1f

- **Track source information.** Record complete publication information for every source you consult: author, title, date, and so on. See pages 179–80 for what to record.
- **Carefully summarize, paraphrase, and quote sources.** Avoid plagiarism by marking other authors' ideas, words, and sentences when you summarize, paraphrase, and quote. See pages 205–07 for more on summary, paraphrase, and quotation and pages 212–18 for more on avoiding plagiarism.
- **Document sources.** Clearly cite the sources of borrowed ideas, words, and sentences, using the style of source citation preferred by the discipline in which you are writing. For lists of disciplines' style guides, see page 219. For documentation guidelines and samples, see pages 220–76 (MLA style), 277–302 (APA style), 303–17 (Chicago style), and 318–28 (CSE style).

1f Language

American academic writing relies on a dialect called **standard American English.** The dialect is also used in business, the professions, the media, and other sites of social and economic power where people of diverse backgrounds must communicate with one another. It is "standard" not because it is better than other forms of English, but because it is accepted as the common language, much as the dollar bill is accepted as the common currency.

Aim for these features when writing for academic audiences:

- **Conventional grammar and usage:** Follow the grammar and usage conventions of standard American English, described in guides such as this handbook.
- **Standard vocabulary:** Avoid words that only some groups understand, such as slang, an ethic or regional dialect, or another language.
- **Third-person point of view:** Generally prefer the third person (*he, she, it, they*), not the first (*I, we*) or the second (*you*).
- **Confident, neutral tone:** Write confidently, not timidly, and refrain from hostility or overt enthusiasm.

For more on academic language, see pages 81–87.

2 The Writing Situation

As an academic writer, you'll always communicate within a **writing situation**: the requirements and options that determine what and how you write.

2a Assignment

When you receive a writing assignment, study its wording and requirements:

- **What does your writing assignment tell you to do?** Words such as *discuss, report, describe,* and *analyze* ask you to explain something about your subject. Words such as *argue* and *evaluate* ask you to make a case for your opinion.
- **What kind of research is required?** An assignment may specify the kinds of sources you are expected to consult.
- **What other requirements do you have to meet?** When is the assignment due? How long should your writing be? What format does the assignment require—a printed paper? a digital project? an oral presentation?

2b Subject

Most writing assignments give at least some latitude for choice of subject. Consider the following questions to find your approach:

- **What subject do you want to know more about?** A good subject is one that interests you. Consider something that you are willing to learn more about, even something you care about.
- **Is your subject limited enough?** Choose a subject that you can cover in the space and time you have, or narrow a broad subject by breaking it into as many specific subjects as you can think of.
- **Is your subject suitable for the assignment?** Review the assignment to ensure that the subject fulfills the requirements.

2c Purpose

Your **purpose** in writing is your chief reason for communicating about your subject to readers.

For most academic writing, your general purpose will be mainly explanatory or mainly argumentative. If your purpose is **explanatory,** you will aim to clarify your subject so that readers understand it as you do. If your purpose is **argumentative**, you will aim to gain readers' agreement with a debatable idea about the subject. The following questions can help you think about your general purpose:

- **Does your assignment specify a purpose?** For instance, does it ask you to explain something or to argue a point?
- **What do want your work to accomplish?** What effect do you intend it to have on readers?
- **How can you best achieve your purpose?** Will research aid you in fulfilling the purpose of your writing?

Many writing assignments narrow the purpose by using a signal word such as the following:

- **Report:** Survey, organize, and objectively present the available evidence on the subject.
- **Summarize:** Concisely state the main points in a text, argument, theory, or other work.
- **Discuss:** Examine the main points, competing views, or implications of the subject.
- **Compare and contrast:** Explain the similarities and differences between two subjects. (See also p. 21.)
- **Define:** Specify the meaning of a term or a concept—distinctive characteristics, boundaries, and so on. (See also p. 20.)
- **Analyze:** Identify the elements of the subject and discuss how they work together. (See also pp. 20 and 37.)
- **Interpret:** Infer the subject's meaning or implications. (See also pp. 37–38 and 53.)
- **Evaluate:** Judge the quality or significance of the subject.
- **Argue:** Take a position on the subject and support your position with evidence. (See also pp. 41–48.)

2d Audience

The readers likely to see your work—your **audience**—will often be specified or implied in a writing assignment. When you write an editorial for the student newspaper, your audience consists of students, instructors, and administrators. When you post on your class blog, the audience consists of your classmates and instructor. When you write a formal paper, your audience consists of your instructor and perhaps your classmates. Use the following questions to adapt your writing to your readers:

- **Who will read your writing?** What can you assume your readers already know and think about your subject? What do you need to tell them so that they see the subject as you want them to?

- **What are readers' expectations?** For the type of writing you are doing, what evidence, organization, language, and format will readers look for? Will they expect you to present research and cite sources in your writing?
- **What is your appropriate role in relation to readers?** Do you want them to perceive you as an advocate, leader, scholar, friend, or something else?
- **What is an appropriate tone?** How formal or informal should your writing be? Should it be serious, calm, friendly, passionate, or something else?
- **What do you want readers to do or think after they read your writing?**

2e Genre

Writers express their ideas in familiar **genres**, or types of writing, such as essays, reports, and letters. In academic writing, the genre conventions help to further the aims of the disciplines, and they help to improve communication because the writer knows what readers expect and readers can predict what they will encounter in the writing. Be sure you understand any requirements relating to genre:

- **Is a particular genre being assigned?** An assignment that asks you to write, say, an analysis, an argument, or a report has specified the genre.
- **What are the conventions of the genre?** Your instructor and/or your textbook will probably outline the requirements for you.
- **Does the genre require research and citation of sources?** For example, if you are writing a research paper or report, you are expected to find, evaluate, integrate, and document sources in your writing.
- **What flexibility do you have?** Within their conventions, most genres still allow plenty of room for your own approach and voice.

See Chapters 6–10 for discussions of common academic genres, such as critical analysis and argument.

2f Deadline, length, and presentation

The due date, the amount of writing expected, and the format all affect your options:

- **When is the assignment due?** How will you apportion the work you have to do in the available time?
- **How long should your writing be?** If no length is assigned, what seems appropriate for your subject, purpose, and audience?
- **What format or method of presentation does the assignment require?** See pages 24–25 on academic formats and pages 61–65 on oral presentations.
- **How might you use headings, lists, illustrations, video, and other elements to achieve your purpose?** See pages 24–29.

3 The Writing Process

Like most writers, you may find writing sometimes easy but more often challenging. This chapter will help you anticipate the stages you'll cycle through as you work on a writing assignment. The stages are not fixed, however: writing is a recursive, or circular, process, and on any given project you may find that some other sequence helps you accomplish your goal.

3a Discovery of ideas

With a sense of your writing situation (Chapter 2), you can begin to gather ideas for writing. The following techniques can help you discover ideas and information about your subject:

- **Keep a journal.** On paper or on a device, record your responses, thoughts, observations, and reactions to what you read, see, hear, or experience.
- **Write freely.** Write without stopping for a set amount of time (say, ten minutes) or a certain length (say, one page), or brainstorm a list of ideas. Don't stop to edit your thoughts or your writing. Instead, let the process of writing down ideas generate new ones.
- **Draw your ideas.** Techniques such as clustering and idea mapping use free association and nonlinear drawing to produce ideas and show their relations. Start with your topic at a center point and then radiate outward with ideas suggested by the topic and with

further thoughts suggested by those ideas. Draw lines or arrows between related ideas.

- **Ask questions.** Ask the journalist's questions—who, what, when, where, why, and how—and write answers to them to help you look at your subject objectively and see fresh possibilities in it.
- **Observe your surroundings.** Intentionally observe and record what you see happening in a particular situation—for example, your commute on public transportation or the behavior of other students in the cafeteria or the library.
- **As appropriate, begin finding sources to support and extend your ideas.** See pages 175–78 for research tips.

3b The thesis statement

Your readers will expect your writing to be focused on and controlled by a main idea, or thesis. Often you will express the thesis in a one- or two-sentence **thesis statement** toward the beginning of your paper.

Functions of the thesis statement

As an expression of the thesis, the thesis statement serves four functions:

- **The thesis statement narrows your subject to a single, central idea** that you want readers to take away from the writing.
- **It claims something specific and significant about your subject,** a claim that requires support.
- **It conveys your purpose,** your reason for writing.
- **It often concisely previews the arrangement of ideas,** in which case it can also help show the way your writing is organized.

Development of the thesis statement

Your thesis may start out as a single, dominant question about your subject that you seek to answer. Let the question guide your planning and research, but allow it to change as you generate ideas and gather information. As your work continues, begin answering your question in a statement of your main idea. Like your question, this thesis may change as your ideas do, but eventually it will be the focus of your writing.

Following are pairs of starting questions and eventual thesis statements from various disciplines:

3c

Literature question	What makes the ending of Kate Chopin's "The Story of an Hour" believable?
Thesis statement	The ironic ending of "The Story of an Hour" is believable because it is consistent with the story's other ironies.
History question	How did eviction from its homeland in 1838 affect the Cherokee Nation of Native Americans?
Thesis statement	Disastrous as it was, the forced resettlement of the Cherokee did less to damage the tribe than did its allegiance to the Confederacy during the Civil War.
Psychology question	How common is violence between partners in dating relationships?
Thesis statement	The survey showed that dating violence may occur among one-fifth of college students, indicating a neglected area of social science research.
Biology question	Does the same physical exertion have the same or different effects on the blood pressure of men and women?
Thesis statement	After the same physical exertion, the average blood pressure of female participants increased significantly more than the average blood pressure of male participants.

Most of the thesis statements you write in college papers will be argumentative or explanatory. Of the preceding examples, the first two are argumentative: the writers mainly want to convince readers of something. The last two examples are explanatory: the writers mainly want to explain something to readers.

ESL   In some other cultures it is considered unnecessary or impolite for a writer to express an opinion or to state his or her main idea outright. When writing in American academic situations, you can assume that your readers expect a clear expression of what you think. They will not consider you rude if you give your opinion.

3c Organization

An effective paper has a recognizable shape—an arrangement of parts that guides readers, helping them to see how ideas and details relate to one another and contribute to the thesis.

Outlines

Some writers like to use an informal or a formal outline to organize their ideas and plan their writing before they start to draft. An informal outline includes key points and may suggest specific evidence. A formal outline uses letters and numbers with indentions to show the relative importance of ideas and their support. Either type can show patterns of general and specific ideas, suggest proportions, and highlight gaps and overlaps in coverage.

Below is the thesis statement and informal outline for the student paper on pages 48–51.

Thesis

This campus needs a program to increase awareness and prevention of cyberbullying and to support its victims.

Informal outline

Introduction
    Roommate's experience with cyberbullying
    New program needed on this campus (thesis)
Body
    Published research on cyberbullying
    Campus survey on cyberbullying
    Proposal for a new program on this campus
    Possible objections to proposed new program
Conclusion
    Argument for new approach to cyberbullying
    Summary of benefits of proposed new program

Structure

Many academic essays follow the pattern above in having an **introduction**, which presents the subject and often states the thesis; the **body**, which contains the substance of the paper; and a **conclusion**, which ties together the parts of the body and links them to the thesis.

Beyond this basic scheme, organization in academic writing varies widely depending on the discipline and the type of writing. Whatever framework you're using, develop your ideas as simply and directly as your purpose and content allow. And clearly relate sentences, paragraphs, and sections so that readers always know where they are in the paper's development.

3d First draft

Whenever in the process you write a first draft, try to compose freely so that you can work out what you want to say. Resist looking critically at your writing until you have a draft.

Here are some tips for getting started on a first draft:

- **Read over what you've already written**—notes, outlines, and so on— and immediately start your draft on whatever comes to mind.

3e

- **Imagine you're talking to a friend about what you're going to write,** and jot down what you would say.
- **Start writing the part that you understand best or feel most strongly about.** Using your outline, divide your work into chunks—say, one for the introduction, another for the first point, and so on. One of these chunks may call out to be written.
- **Keep going.** Skip over difficult spots, leave a blank if you can't find the right word, and use boldface or brackets to mark words, sentences, and paragraphs that you want to return to later.
- **If you must stop working, write down what you expect to do next.** Then you can more easily pick up where you stopped.

You may find it helpful to draft in sections, devoting a paragraph or more to each major point that supports your thesis. State the point clearly, and support it with facts, examples, expert opinions, and other evidence. This approach will keep you moving ahead while it also helps you focus on making your evidence work for your ideas.

3e Revision

Think of revision and editing as separate stages: in revision you deal with the underlying ideas, meaning, and organization of your writing; in editing you deal with the surface, with clarity, correctness, and the manner of expression.

Whenever possible, let a draft rest for a while to get some distance from it. The following tips can aid you in revising your draft.

- **Ask someone to respond to your draft.** A roommate, family member, classmate, or tutor in the writing center can call attention to what needs revising.
- **Read your draft in a new medium.** Typing a handwritten draft or reading a hard copy of a word-processed draft can reveal weaknesses that you didn't see in the original.
- **Listen to your draft.** Read the draft aloud to yourself or a friend, record and listen to it, or have someone read the draft to you.
- **Outline your draft.** Highlight the main points supporting the thesis, and write these sentences down separately in outline form. Then examine the outline for logical order, gaps, and digressions.
- **Use a revision checklist.** Don't try to review everything in your draft at once. Use the following checklist, reviewing the draft multiple times to check each item on the list.

Checklist for revising academic writing

Assignment (p. 7)

- How have you responded to the assignment for this writing?
- Do your subject, purpose, and genre meet the requirements of the assignment?

Purpose, audience, and genre (pp. 7–9)

- What is your purpose? Does it conform to the assignment?
- Who are your readers? Will your purpose be clear to them?
- How does your writing conform to the conventions of the genre you are writing in?

Thesis (pp. 3, 11–12)

- What is your thesis, or central claim?
- Where in the paper does your thesis become clear?

Development (pp. 17–22)

- What are the main points supporting the thesis?
- How well do the facts, examples, and other evidence support each main point?

Use of sources

- Have you used sources to support—not substitute for—your own ideas? (See pp. 5–6, 203–04.)
- Have you integrated borrowed material into your own sentences? (See pp. 204–12.)
- Have you fully cited each use of a source? (See pp. 218–19.)

Unity

- What does each paragraph contribute to the thesis?
- Within paragraphs, what does each sentence contribute to the paragraph's idea? (This paragraph idea is often expressed in a topic sentence, p. 17.)

Coherence

- Will the organization be clear to readers?
- How smoothly does the paper flow?
- Have you used transitions to link paragraphs and sentences? (See p. 18 and pp. 350–51 for a list of transitional expressions, such as *first, however,* and *in addition*.)

3f Editing and proofreading

Much of this book concerns editing—tightening or clarifying sentences, polishing words, repairing mistakes in grammar and punctuation. Leave this work until after revision so that your content and organization are set before you tinker with your expression. For editing guidelines, see the lists on pages 68 (effective sentences), 92 (grammatical sentences), 134 (punctuation), and 160 (spelling and mechanics).

Most writers find that they spot errors better on paper than on a computer screen, so edit a printout if you can. And be sure to proofread your final draft before you submit it, even if you have used a spelling checker or similar aid (see below).

Spelling checkers

A spelling checker can be a great ally: it will flag words that are spelled incorrectly and will usually suggest alternative spellings that resemble what you've typed. However, this ally has limitations:

- **The checker may flag a word that you've spelled correctly**, just because the word does not appear in its dictionary.
- **The checker may suggest incorrect alternatives.** Before you accept any highlighted suggestion from the checker, you should verify that the word is actually what you intend. Consult an online or printed dictionary when you aren't sure of the checker's recommendations.
- **Most important, a spelling checker will not flag words that appear in its dictionary but you have misused.** The paragraph in the following screen shot contains eleven errors that a spelling checker failed to catch. Can you spot all of them?

> The whether effects all of us, though it's affects are different for different people. Some people love a fare day with warm temperatures and sunshine. They revel in spending a hole day outside. Other people enjoy dark, rainy daze. They like to slow down and here they're inner thoughts. Most people agree, however, that to much of one kind of weather makes them board.

Grammar/style checkers

Grammar/style checkers can flag incorrect grammar or punctuation and wordy or awkward sentences. You may be able to customize a checker to suit your needs and habits as a writer—for instance, instructing it to look for problems with subject-verb agreement, passive verbs, or apostrophes in plural nouns.

Like spelling checkers, however, grammar/style checkers are limited:

- **They miss many errors** because they are not yet capable of analyzing language in all its complexity.
- **They often question passages that don't need editing,** such as an appropriate passive verb or a deliberate and emphatic use of repetition.

Each time a grammar/style checker questions something, you must determine whether a change is needed at all and what change will be most effective, and you must read your papers carefully on your own to find any errors the program missed.

4 Paragraphs

Paragraphs develop the main ideas that support the thesis of a piece of writing, and they break these supporting ideas into manageable chunks. For readers, paragraphs signal the movement between ideas and provide breathers from long stretches of text.

4a Paragraph unity

Each paragraph you write should be **unified** around a single idea. Often the idea is expressed in a **topic sentence** that appears at or near the start of the paragraph, though sometimes a topic sentence may come at the end. In the following example, the first sentence gives the topic of the paragraph, and the sentences that follow are focused on it.

> <u>Perhaps the simplest fact about sleep is that individual needs for it vary widely.</u> Most adults sleep between seven and nine hours, but occasionally people turn up who need twelve hours or so, while some rare types can get by on three or four. Rarest of all are those legendary types who require almost no sleep at all; respected researchers have recently studied three such people. One of them—a healthy, happy woman in her seventies—sleeps about an hour every two or three days. The other two are men in early middle age, who get by on a few minutes a

Topic sentence

Examples supporting topic sentence

4c

night. One of them complains about the daily fifteen minutes or so he's forced to "waste" in sleeping.

—Lawrence A. Mayer,
"The Confounding Enemy of Sleep"

Sometimes the main idea of a paragraph is not stated, particularly in description (see opposite). Even so, the sentences of the paragraph should all contribute to a single idea.

4b Paragraph coherence

When a paragraph is **coherent**, readers can see how it holds together: the sentences flow logically and smoothly from one to the next. The paragraph below contains connections within and between sentences:

- After the topic sentence, the writer gives two explanations and four sentences of examples.
- Words in green repeat or restate key terms or concepts, reminding readers what the topic is.
- Words in orange are transitional expressions° that forge specific connections between sentences and paragraphs.
- Phrases in purple are examples of parallelism°—the use of similar grammatical structures for similar elements of meaning within or among sentences.

Topic sentence	The ancient Egyptians were masters of preserving dead people's bodies by making mummies of them. Basically, mummification con-
Explanation 1: mummification	
Explanation 2: mastery of Egyptians	sisted of removing the internal organs, applying natural preservatives inside and out, and then wrapping the body in layers of bandages. And the process was remarkably effective. Indeed, mummies several thousand years old have been discovered nearly intact. Their skin, hair,
Specific examples of explanation 2	teeth, finger- and toenails, and facial features are still evident. Their diseases in life, such as smallpox, arthritis, and nutritional deficiencies, are still diagnosable. Even their fatal afflictions are still apparent: a middle-aged king died from a blow on the head; a child king died from polio. —Mitchell Rosenbaum (student), "Lost Arts of the Egyptians"

4c Paragraph development

An effective, well-developed paragraph provides the specific information that readers need and expect in order to understand and stay interested in what you say. Paragraph length can be a rough gauge of development: anything much shorter than 75 to 125 words may leave readers with a sense of incompleteness. The following

°Defined in "Grammar Terms," page 340.

patterns may help you develop ideas into paragraphs. (These patterns may also be used to develop entire essays.)

Narration

Narration retells a significant sequence of events, usually in the order of their occurrence (that is, chronologically). A narrator is concerned with the sequence of events and their importance to the whole story.

> Jill's story is typical for "recruits" to religious cults. She was very lonely in college and appreciated the attention of the nice young men and women who lived in a house near campus. They persuaded her to share their meals and then to move in with them. Between intense bombardments of "love," they deprived her of sleep and sometimes threatened to throw her out. Jill became increasingly confused and dependent, losing touch with any reality besides the one in the group. She dropped out of school and refused to see or communicate with her family. Before long she, too, was preying on lonely college students.
>
> —Hillary Begas (student),
> "The Love Bombers"

Topic sentence

Important events in chronological order

Description

Description details the sensory qualities of a person, scene, things, or feeling, using concrete and specific words to convey a mood, to illustrate an idea, or to achieve some other purpose.

> The sun struck straight upon the house, making the white walls glare between the dark windows. Their panes, woven thickly with green branches, held circles of impenetrable darkness. Sharp-edged wedges of light lay upon the windowsill and showed inside the room plates with blue rings, cups with curved handles, the bulge of a great bowl, the criss-cross pattern in the rug, and the formidable corners and lines of cabinets and bookcases. Behind their conglomeration hung a zone of shadow in which might be a further shape to be disencumbered of shadow or still denser depths of darkness.   —Virginia Woolf, *The Waves*

Specific record of sensory details

Unstated main idea: Sunlight barely penetrated the house's secrets.

Illustration or support

An idea may be developed with several specific examples, like those used by Lawrence A. Mayer in the paragraph on pages 17–18. Or it may be developed with a single extended example, as in this paragraph:

> Teaching teenagers to drive is a nerve-racking job. During his first lesson, one particularly inept student refused to drive faster than ten miles per hour, forcing impatient drivers behind

Topic sentence

Single detailed example

4c

the car to pass on a residential street with a speed limit of twenty-five and cyclists in the bike lanes. Making a left turn at a four-way stop, the student didn't await his turn and nearly collided with an oncoming car. A few moments later, he jumped the curb when turning right and had to slam on the brakes to avoid hitting a concrete barrier. For a driving instructor, every day is an exercise in keeping one's fear and temper in check.   —Jasmine Greer (student), "Driving School"

Definition

Defining a complicated, abstract, or controversial term often requires extended explanation. The following paragraph defines the professional middle class:

Topic sentence

General definition

Specific examples of who is and is not included in the definition

Before this story [of changes in America's middle class] can be told, I must first introduce its central character, the professional middle class. This class can be defined, somewhat abstractly, as all those people whose economic and social status is based on education, rather than on ownership of capital or property. Most professionals are included, and so are white-collar managers, whose positions require at least a college degree, and increasingly also a graduate degree. Not all white-collar people are included, though; some of these are entrepreneurs who are better classified as "workers." But the professional middle class is still extremely broad, and includes such diverse types as schoolteachers, anchorpersons, engineers, professors, government bureaucrats, corporate executives (at least up through the middle levels of management), scientists, advertising people, therapists, financial managers, architects, and, I should add, myself.

—Barbara Ehrenreich, *Fear of Falling: The Inner Life of the Middle Class*

Division or analysis

With division or analysis, you separate something into its elements to understand it better. The following paragraph identifies the elements of reality shows:

Topic sentence

Elements: carefully selected participants, created environments, planned scenes, designed wardrobes, edited footage

Reality TV shows are anything but "real." Participants are selected from thousands of applicants, and they have auditioned to prove themselves to be competent in front of a camera. The settings for the action are often environments created especially for the shows. Scenes that seem unscripted are often planned to capture entertaining footage. The wardrobes of the participants may be designed to enhance participants' "characters" and to improve their looks on camera. And footage is clearly edited to create scenes that seem authentic and tell compelling stories.

—Darrell Carter (student), "(Un)Reality TV"

Classification

When you sort many items into groups, you classify the items to see their relations more clearly. The following paragraph identifies three groups, or classes, of parents:

In my experience, the parents who hire daytime sitters for their school-age children tend to fall into one of three groups. The first group includes parents who work and want someone to be at home when the children return from school. These parents are looking for an extension of themselves, someone who will give the care they would give if they were at home. The second group includes parents who may be home all day themselves but are too disorganized or too frazzled by their children's demands to handle child care alone. They are looking for an organizer and helpmate. The third and final group includes parents who do not want to be bothered by their children, whether they are home all day or not. Unlike the parents in the first two groups, who care for their children whenever and however they can, these parents are looking for a permanent substitute for themselves.	Topic sentence
	Three groups: Alike in one way (all hire sitters)
	No overlap in groups (each has a different attitude)
	Classes arranged in order of increasing drama

—Nancy Whittle (student),
"Modern Parenting"

Comparison and contrast

Comparison and contrast may be used separately or together to develop an idea. One common way of organizing a comparison is **subject by subject**, first one subject and then the other. Another is **point by point**, with two subjects discussed side by side and matched feature for feature, as shown in the next example:

Arguing is often equated with fighting, but there are key differences between the two. Participants in an argument approach the subject to find common ground, or points on which both sides agree, while people engaged in a fight usually approach the subject with an "us-versus- them" attitude. Participants in an argument are careful to use respectful, polite language, in contrast to the insults and worse that people in a fight use to get the better of their opponents. Finally, participants in an argument commonly have the goal of reaching a new understanding or larger truth about the subject they're debating, while those in a fight have winning as their only goal.	Topic sentence
	Attitude: argument, flight
	Language: argument, flight
	Goal: argument, flight

—Erica Ito (student),
"Is an Argument Always a Fight?"

Cause-and-effect analysis

When you use analysis to explain why something happened or what did or may happen, then you are determining causes or effects. In the following paragraph, the author looks at the effects of consumerism:

Cause: consumerism	The consumerism of the postwar era [since World War II] has not been without its effects on the way we use our time. As people became accustomed to the material rewards of prosperity, desires for leisure time were eroded. They increasingly looked to consumption to give satisfaction, even meaning, to their lives. In both the workplace and the home, progress has repeatedly translated into more goods and services, rather than more free time. Employers channel productivity increases into additional income; housewives are led to use their labor-saving appliances to produce more goods and services. Consumerism traps us as we become habituated to the good life, emulate our neighbors, or just get caught up in the social pressures created by everyone else's choices. Work-and-spend has become a mutually reinforcing and powerful syndrome—a seamless web we somehow keep choosing, without even meaning to.
Effects: erosion of leisure time, emphasis on goods and services, higher incomes, labor-saving devices, habituation to the good life, work-and-spend syndrome	

—Juliet B. Schor,
The Overworked American

Process analysis

When you analyze how to do something or how something works, you explain a process. Paragraphs developed by process analysis are usually organized chronologically, as the steps in the process occur. The following example identifies a process, describes the equipment needed, and details the steps in the process:

Topic sentence	As a car owner, you waste money when you pay a mechanic to change the engine oil. The job is not difficult, even if you know little about cars. All you need is a wrench to remove the drain plug, a large, flat pan to collect the draining oil, plastic bottles to dispose of the used oil, and fresh oil. First, warm up the car's engine so that the oil will flow more easily. When the engine is warm, shut it off and remove its oil-filler cap (the owner's manual shows where this cap is). Then locate the drain plug under the engine (again consulting the owner's manual for its location) and place the flat pan under the plug. Remove the plug with the wrench, letting the oil flow into the pan. When the oil stops flowing, replace the plug and, at the engine's filler hole, add the amount and kind of fresh oil specified by the owner's manual. Pour the used oil into the plastic bottles and take it to a waste-oil collector, which any garage mechanic can recommend.
Equipment needed	
Steps in process	

—Anthony Andreas (student),
"Do-It-Yourself Car Care"

4d Introductory and concluding paragraphs

Introductions

An introduction draws readers into the world of your writing, focusing them on the topic and your perspective. To gain readers' attention, you have a number of options:

Ask a question.	Relate an incident.
Use a quotation.	Offer a surprising statistic or fact.
Give an opinion related to your thesis.	Provide background.
Outline a problem or dilemma.	Define a word central to your subject.

A very common introduction opens with a statement of your general subject, clarifies or limits the subject, and then asserts the point of the essay in the thesis statement. Here is an example:

> The Declaration of Independence is so widely regarded as a statement of American ideals that its origins in practical politics tend to be forgotten. Thomas Jefferson's draft was intensely debated and then revised in the Continental Congress. Jefferson was disappointed with the result. However, a close reading of both the historical context and the revisions themselves indicates that the Congress improved the document for its intended purpose. —Ann Weiss (student), "The Editing of the Declaration of Independence"

Statement about subject

Clarification of subject

Thesis statement

Conclusions

Your conclusion finishes off your writing, tells readers where you think you have brought them, and conveys the significance of your thesis. It may take one or more of the following approaches:

Summarize the paper.	Restate the thesis and reflect on its implications.
Recommend a course of action.	
Echo the approach of the introduction (but don't repeat the introduction).	Use a quotation.
	Give a compelling fact, detail, or example.

The following conclusion drives home the main point of the essay whose introduction appears above:

> The Declaration of Independence has come to be a statement of this nation's political philosophy, but that was not its purpose in 1776. Jefferson's passionate expression had to bow to the goals of

Echo of introduction

Restatement and elaboration of thesis

> the Congress as a whole to forge unity among the colonies and to
> win the support of foreign nations. —Ann Weiss (student),
> "The Editing of the Declaration of Independence"

Generally resist the temptation to make a broad, sweeping conclusion, to introduce a new point, or to apologize. End on a strong note that draws a reasonable conclusion based on the evidence you have presented.

Note Additional examples of effective introductions and conclusions appear in the sample papers on pages 39, 48, 55, 58, and 266.

5 Presenting Writing

Presenting your writing gives you a chance to display your hard work in an attractive, readable format.

5a Academic formats

Many academic disciplines prefer specific formats for students' papers. This book details the following formats:

- **MLA** used in English, foreign languages, and some other humanities, illustrated on the facing page and discussed in detail on pages 264–65.
- **APA,** used in the social sciences and some natural sciences, discussed on pages 294–95.
- **Chicago,** used in history, art history, religion, and some other humanities, discussed on page 315.
- **CSE,** used in some natural and applied sciences (pp. 324–25).

You can make your work accessible and attractive by taking care with margins, line spacing, type fonts, lists, headings, and visuals, as shown in the example opposite. Your instructors may want you to use a different style. Ask them for their preferences.

5b Visuals and other media

When they are used responsibly, visuals and other media can often make a point more efficiently and effectively than words can. Tables and figures (such as graphs and charts) usually present data.

Torres 1

Mia Torres
Mr. O'Donnell
English 131
14 March 2016

Identification: writer's name, instructor's name, course title, date.

Double-spaced throughout.

Title centered.

Standard type font and size (reduced here).

Creating the Next Generation of Smokers

Parents warn their children not to smoke. Schools teach kids and teens about the dangers. States across the country have enacted smoking bans, making it illegal for adults to smoke in restaurants, bars, workplaces, and public buildings. Yet despite these efforts, smoking among teens and young adults continues, and it does so in part because the film industry creates movies that promote smoking.

Margins of 1'' on all sides of each page.

According, to the organization Smoke Free Movies, a group based in the School of Medicine at the University of California, San Francisco, tobacco companies and film makers collaborate to promote smoking in the following ways:

Indentions mark paragraph breaks.

- Celebrities smoke in movies, giving the illusion that smoking is something they endorse.
- Movies portray smoking as glamorous, healthful, and socially respectable.
- Tobacco companies pay filmmakers to show their products (4–5).

Stopping young people's exposure to images of smoking in movies requires stopping each of these activities.

List highlights like items and uses parallel wording.

Smoking Celebrities

Despite proof that showing smoking in movies encourages young people to start smoking, more than half of movies feature well-known stars smoking (Fox). As fig. 1 shows, cigarettes often figure prominently, with the cigarette held close to the celebrity's head so that it is an integral part of the shot.

Heading serves as signpost. Headings should be worded consistently—for instance, all phrases or all questions.

Introduction to visual explains its meaning and purpose.

Fig. 1. The actress Scarlett Johansson in *Black Dahlia*, one of many movies released each year in which characters smoke. From *Daily Mail*, 18 Sept. 2006, www.dailymail.co.uk/article-1602474.html.

Caption allows visual to be read independently from the text.

Images, audio, and video can explain processes, represent what something looks and sounds like, or show a sequence of events.

Visuals

Visuals can support print or electronic documents. They include tables, pie charts, bar charts, line graphs, infographics, diagrams, flowcharts, and images such as photographs, maps, fine art, advertisements, and cartoons. (See the box on next two pages.)

Video and audio

Links to video and audio are sometimes appropriate in digital writing projects. You might explain a process with a video of how

(text continues on p. 28)

5b

Types of visuals

Tables

Tables present raw data to show how variables relate to one another or how two or more groups contrast. Place a descriptive title above the table, and use headings to label rows and columns.

Table 1
Public- and private-school enrollment of US students, 2014

	Number of students (in millions)	Percentage in public school	Percentage in private school
All students	49.7	89	11
Kindergarten through grade 8	35.0	88	12
Grades 9-12	14.7	91	9

Source: Data from *Digest of Education Statistics: 2014*, National Center for Education Statistics, 2015, nces.ed.gov/tables/dt13_205.asp.

Diagrams and flowcharts

Diagrams show concepts visually, such as the structure of an organization or the way something works or looks.

Fig. 4. *MyPlate,* a graphic representation of daily food portions recommended for a healthy diet. From *ChooseMyPlate.gov*, US Dept. of Agriculture, 2011, www.choosemyplate.gov.

Images

Photographs, maps, paintings, advertisements, and cartoons can be the focus of critical analysis or can support points you make.

Fig. 5. View from the *Cassini* spacecraft, showing Saturn and its rings. From *Cassini-Huygens: Mission to Saturn and Titan*, NASA, Jet Propulsion Laboratory, 24 Feb. 2015, nasa.gov/multimedia/imagegallery/137.html.

Pie charts

Pie charts show the relations among the parts of a whole, adding up to 100%. Use a pie chart when shares of data are the focus. Make each pie slice proportional to its share of the whole, and label each slice.

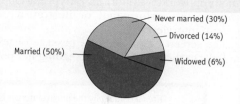

Fig. 1. Marital status in 2014 of adults age 18 and over. Data from Pew Research Center, 4 Nov. 2014, www.pewresearch.org/data-trend/society-and-demographics/marriage/.

Bar charts

Bar charts compare groups or time periods. Use a bar chart when relative size is important. On the vertical scale, start with a zero point in the lower left and label the values being measured. On the horizontal scale, label the groups being compared.

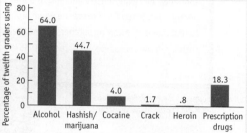

Fig. 2. Lifetime prevalence of use of alcohol, compared with other drugs, among twelfth graders in 2015. Data from *Monitoring the Future: A Continuing Study of American Youth*, U of Michigan, 12 Dec. 2015, www.monitoringthefuture.org/data/2015data-drugs.

Line graphs

Line graphs compare many points of data to show change over time. On the vertical scale, start with a zero point in the lower left and label the values being measured. On the horizontal scale, label the range of dates. Label the data lines, and distinguish them with color, dots, or dashes.

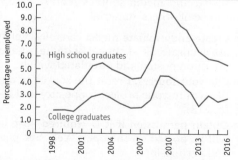

Fig. 3. Unemployment rates of high school graduates and college graduates, 1998-2016. Data from *Economics News Release*, US Dept. of Labor, Bureau of Labor Statistics, 1 Apr. 2016, www.bls.gov/news.release/empsit.t04.htm.

(continued from p. 25)

5b

something works, support an interpretation of a play with a video of a scene from a performance, or illustrate a profile of a person by linking to an interview.

The screen below shows a passage of text from an online paper that links to the poet Rita Dove reading her poem "American Smooth."

Often a reading by the poet reinforces both the sound and the meaning of the poem. In Rita Dove's "American Smooth," two people move self-consciously through an intricate dance, smiling and holding their bodies just so, when suddenly they experience a moment of perfection: they nearly float. When Dove reads the poem aloud, she builds to that moment, allowing listeners to feel the same magic (https://www.youtube.com/watch?v=RKJKWYQyBOM).

Courtesy of the Poetry Foundation
Jeff Malet Photography/Newscom

Responsible use of visuals and other media

Visual and media sources require care to ensure accuracy and honest use of others' material.

- **Create and evaluate media carefully.** Verify that the data you use are accurate. Be skeptical of digital images—altered photographs are often posted and circulated widely.
- **Cite your sources.** Credit the source of any data, visual, or media file within your project (opposite) and at the end of your project (p. 218).
- **Obtain permission if it is required**—for instance, if your project will be posted on the open Web. See pages 217–18 on copyright and permissions.

Effective use of visuals and other media

Follow these guidelines when using media in academic writing:

- **Focus on a purpose.** Ensure that any media relate directly to points in your writing and are appropriate for your audience. Otherwise, readers may find the media distracting, irrelevant, or confusing.

- **Explain audio and video links in online projects.** Whether you link to photographs, sound, or video, refer to them in your text and tell the audience how the media relate to your ideas and what you intend them to show.
- **Connect visuals to your text.** Direct readers to visuals with references in your text—for instance, "See fig. 2"—and explain each visual's significance. Number and label tables separately from other figures (Table 1, Table 2, and so on; Fig. 1, Fig. 2, and so on).
- **Provide a caption for each visual.** The caption performs two functions: it explains the visual briefly, and it cites the source of the data or the entire visual, as shown in the following example.

Fig. 2. Lifetime prevalence of use of alcohol, compared with other drugs, | Explanation
among twelfth graders in 2015. Data from *Monitoring the Future: A* | Source
Continuing Study of American Youth, U of Michigan, 12 Dec. 2015, | information
www.monitoringthefuture.org/data/2015data-drugs.

For examples of figure captions, see pages 26–27. For a table title and source note, see page 26.

Note Each discipline has a slightly different style for crediting sources of visuals. The example above and those in the illustrations on pages 26–27 reflect MLA style.

5c Readers with vision loss

Your audience may include readers who have low vision, problems with color perception, or difficulties processing visual information. If so, consider adapting your design to meet these readers' needs. Here are a few pointers:

- **Use large type fonts.** Most guidelines call for 14 points or larger.
- **Use standard type fonts.** Avoid decorative fonts with unusual flourishes, even in headings.
- **Avoid words in all-capital letters.**
- **Avoid relying on color alone to distinguish elements.** Label elements, and distinguish them by position or size.
- **Use contrasting colors.** To make colors distinct, choose them from opposite sides of the color spectrum—violet and yellow, for instance, or orange and blue.

5c

- **Use red and green selectively.** To readers who are red-green color-blind, these colors will appear in shades of gray, yellow, or blue.
- **Use only light colors for tints behind type.** Make the type itself black or a very dark color.

Common Academic Assignments

Common Academic Assignments

Critical analysis

- Use techniques of critical reading and viewing. (See opposite.)
- Summarize the main points of texts, visuals, and other works. (See p. 35.)
- Use analysis, interpretation, and synthesis to develop a critical analysis. (See p. 36.)

Argument

- Know the elements of argument: subject, claims, evidence, and assumptions. (See p. 42.)
- Develop an argument by making rational, emotional, and ethical appeals, responding to opposing views, and organizing effectively. (See p. 45.)

Literary analysis

- Read literary works critically. (See p. 52.)
- Develop and support a literary analysis using evidence from the work. (See p. 53.)

Informative writing

- Write an informative essay to explain a situation, compare and contrast ideas or things, describe a process, and so on. (See p. 57.)
- Write a report to explain research you have conducted. (See p. 59.)
- Write a lab report to explain an experiment and results. (See p. 60.)

Oral presentations

- Plan and organize a presentation. (See p. 61.)
- Prepare visual aids. (See p. 62.)
- Practice and deliver the presentation. (See p. 64.)

Sample Student Writing

- Critical analysis (p. 39)
- Proposal argument (p. 48)
- Literary analysis (p. 55)
- Informative essay (p. 58)
- Research paper in MLA style (p. 265)

- Research report in APA style (p. 296)
- Research paper in Chicago style (p. 316)
- Lab report in CSE style (p. 325)

6 Critical Analysis

Critical thinking, reading, and writing will enable you to develop and express thoughtful perspectives on both written texts (such as articles, short stories, and social-media posts) and visual or multimedia texts (such as advertisements, photographs, and videos). Analyzing such works and crafting responses involve the techniques discussed in this chapter.

6a Critical reading and viewing

A first step in critical analysis involves careful reading or viewing of a work.

Previewing the material

Often it's worthwhile to step back and consider a work as a whole, forming expectations and even some preliminary questions before reading or examining it closely. This preview will make your reading more informed and fruitful.

- **Assess the work as a whole.** What type of work are you looking at—a scholarly essay, a magazine article, an advertisement, a diagram, a social-media post, or something else? How simple or complex is the work?
- **Learn about the author or creator.** Use a Web search to trace the author if one is given. What seems to have been the author's or creator's purpose for the work?
- **Check the facts of publication.** Does the date of publication suggest that the work is current or historical? Who is the publisher? For a Web publication, who or what sponsors the site—a corporation? a nonprofit organization? a government body?
- **Consider your preliminary response.** What do you already know about the topic of the work? What questions do you have about the topic or the work's approach to it? What biases of your own—for instance, curiosity, boredom, or familiarity—might influence your reading of the work?

Reading and viewing

Critical reading is more than a one-step process. At first, you want to understand what the author or creator actually says or shows and begin to form your impressions. Focus on the following as you read or view the work:

6a

- **Determine the purpose of the work.** Is the work mainly explanatory, conveying information, or is it argumentative, trying to convince readers of something or to persuade them to act? What information or point of view does the work seem intended to get across?
- **Think about the intended audience for the work.** What expectations does the writer or creator seem to have for readers' knowledge, interests, and attitudes?
- **Consider the content, form, and organization of the work.** How do the work's content and apparent purpose and audience relate to its form—for instance, an article, a Web site, or an advertisement—and its organization?

Rereading and annotating

After the first reading, plan on at least one other. This time read *slowly.* Your main concern should be to grasp the content and how it is constructed. That means rereading a paragraph if you didn't get the point or using a dictionary to look up words you don't know. Use the following tips to highlight and annotate a work:

- **Distinguish main and supporting points.** In a written text, mark the central idea (the thesis), the main idea of each paragraph or section, and the evidence supporting ideas. In a visual, identify elements that convey main and supporting ideas.
- **Note important words or symbols** In written texts, know the meanings of key terms. In visuals, consider whether words or symbols add information, focus your attention, or alter your impression.
- **Distinguish between facts and opinions.** Especially when reading a written or visual argument, mark opinions as well as the facts on which the opinions are based. Keep an eye out for fallacies—errors in argument—as you read (see p. 46).
- **Add your own comments.** In the margins or separately, note links to other readings or visuals, ideas from class discussions, questions to explore further, possible topics for your writing, and points you find especially strong or weak.

The illustration on the facing page shows the notes that a student, Richard Oliva, made on an advertisement for *Teach.org.*

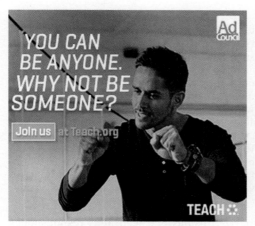

Guy in photo: Eyes focused ahead (on students?). Caught in mid-speech. Clenched hands = intense, engaged, passionate.

Large, white type highlights message. 1st sentence: what kids hear growing up. 2nd sentence: a challenge to be "someone" important, like a celebrity.

"Join us": direct invitation to be like this guy.

What is Teach.org? Recruits new teachers?

Advertisement for *Teach.org*

6b Summarizing

Once you have grasped the content and structure of a work, a good way to comprehend it and to see its strengths and weaknesses is to **summarize** it—that is, distill it to its main points in your own words. Following is a method of summarizing, which can be used for visuals as well as texts:

- **State the main idea.** Write a sentence or two capturing the central idea of the work.
- **Support the main idea.** Write a full paragraph (or more, if needed) that begins with the central idea and supports it with sentences that summarize sections or elements of the work. The paragraph should concisely and accurately state the thrust of the entire work.
- *Use your own words.* By writing, you recreate the meaning of the work in a way that makes sense for you. You also avoid plagiarism.
- *Cite the source.* If you use a summary in writing that you do for others, including assignments in your college courses, always cite the source.

Summarizing even a passage of text can be tricky. Here we'll look at attempts to summarize the following material from an introductory biology textbook.

Original text

As astronomers study newly discovered planets orbiting distant stars, they hope to find evidence of water on these far-off celestial bodies, for water is the substance that makes possible life as we know it here on Earth. All organisms familiar to us are made mostly of water and live in an environment dominated by water. They require water more than any other substance. Human beings, for example, can survive for quite a few weeks without food, but only a week or so without water. Molecules of water participate in many chemical reactions necessary to sustain life. Most cells are surrounded by water, and cells themselves are about 70–95% water. Three-quarters of Earth's surface is submerged in water. Although most of this water is in liquid form, water is also present on Earth as ice and vapor. Water is the only common substance to exist in the natural environment in all three physical states of matter: solid, liquid, and gas.   —Neil A. Campbell and Jane B. Reece, *Biology*

The first attempt to summarize this passage accurately restates ideas in the original, but it does not pare the passage to its essence:

Draft summary

Astronomers look for water in outer space because life depends on it. It is the most common substance on Earth and in living cells, and it can be a liquid, a solid (ice), or a gas (vapor).

The work of astronomers and the three physical states of water add color and texture to the original, but they are asides to the key concept that water sustains life because of its role in life. The following revision narrows the summary to this concept:

Revised summary

Water is the most essential support for life—the dominant substance on Earth and in living cells and a component of life-sustaining chemical processes.

Note Summarizing is also an important skill in writing a research paper. See page 205.

6c Writing a critical analysis

Many academic writing assignments ask for critical analysis, or critique, in which you write critically about texts, visuals, or media. As you form a response to a work, you integrate its ideas and information to come up with your own conclusions. As you write your response, you support your ideas about the work by citing evidence from it.

Deciding how to respond

When an assignment asks you to respond directly to a text or visual, you might take one of the following approaches to decide on your position:

- **Agree with and extend the ideas expressed in the work,** exploring related ideas and providing additional examples.
- **Agree with some of the ideas but disagree with others.**
- **Disagree with one or more ideas.**
- **Explain how the work achieves a particular effect,** such as balancing opposing views or conveying a mood.
- **Analyze the overall effectiveness of the work**—for example, how well a writer supports a thesis with convincing evidence or whether an advertisement succeeds in its unstated purpose.

6c

Forming a critical response

Forming a critical response involves understanding both what the author or creator actually says or shows *and* what he or she does not say outright. At this stage, you are concerned with the purpose or intention of the author and with how he or she carries it out. Developing a response involves three operations: analyzing, interpreting, and synthesizing.

Analysis

When you analyze, you separate a work into its parts or elements in order to understand it. For instance, an analysis of the *Teach.org* ad on page 35 might focus on the point of view and intensity of the photograph as well as the direct appeal to readers in the text of the ad: *You can be anyone* and *Join us.*

The following questions can guide your analysis:

- **What are its important elements?**
- **What elements are most interesting?**
- **What elements can you ignore?**

Interpretation

When you interpret a work, you look more deeply at the elements or parts you've analyzed to consider their meaning and significance and how they contribute to the work as a whole.

Interpretation usually requires you to infer the work's **assumptions**—the creator's opinions or beliefs about what is, what could be, or what should be. For example, you might infer the following about the *Teach.org* ad on page 35: *The creators of the* Teach.org *ad assume that viewers want careers that make them feel important.* Like many

6c

assumptions, this one is not stated outright in the *Teach.org* ad. Creators may judge that their audience already understands and accepts their assumptions; they may not even be aware of their assumptions; or they may leave their assumptions unstated because they fear that the audience will disagree. (For more on assumptions in argument, see p. 44.)

The questions below can guide your interpretation of a work:

- Why are the elements or parts you have identified significant to the work?
- How do these elements or parts contribute to the work's meaning or its effect?
- How do these elements contribute to the work as a whole?
- What assumptions does the work's creator seem to make?

Synthesis

When you synthesize, you make connections among ideas and information and draw conclusions of your own. Depending on your assignment, you may make connections among the elements of the work itself, between the work and similar works, or between the work and the larger context of history, culture, and other forces. The following questions can guide you:

- How does the work function as a whole?
- How does the work compare to other texts, visuals, or media?
- How does the work fit into the context of other works by the same author or creator?
- What other factors have influenced the work, such as cultural currents, historical events, or political and economic forces?

With synthesis, you create something different from what you started with. For example, when student Richard Oliva visited the Web site of *Teach.org* to research the ad on page 35, he learned that the ad was part of a larger campaign to attract young people to careers in teaching. This knowledge, combined with his critical reading and interpretation of the ad, helped him write the critical analysis paper on pages 39–41. (For more on synthesis in the context of research writing, see pp. 203–04.)

Shaping a critical analysis

The following tips can help you shape your critical response into focused, well-organized writing:

- Make sure your writing has a point—a central idea, or thesis, that focuses your response, usually stated in the introduction. (For more on developing a thesis, see pp. 11–12.)

- **Include a very brief summary of the work if readers may be unfamiliar with your subject or the context of the work.** A summary should come toward the beginning of your essay, either in the introduction or shortly after. Keep any summary short: your job is not just to report what the text says or the visual shows; it is to *respond* to the work from your own critical perspective.
- **Center each body paragraph on an idea of your own that supports your thesis.** Generally state the idea outright, in your own voice.
- **Support the paragraph idea with evidence from the work**—quotations, paraphrases, descriptive details, and examples. Synthesize your perspective on the work with evidence from the work and possibly also the support of research sources. (See p. 4 for a sample paragraph.)
- **Conclude each paragraph with your interpretation of the evidence.** As a general rule, avoid ending paragraphs with evidence from the work or from sources; instead, end with at least a sentence that explains what the evidence shows. (See p. 4 for a sample paragraph.)
- **Write a conclusion.** Conclude your critical analysis by wrapping up your main points and reminding readers of your thesis.
- **Document sources you used in your paper.** Acknowledge the text or visual you are analyzing as well as any sources you consulted, using citations in the text that refer to a list of sources at the end of the paper. This book details four styles of documentation in Chapters 48–51.

6d Sample critical analysis

The following essay responds to the *Teach.org* advertisement on page 35. In the paper, the writer reproduces the ad and interprets its significance. He cites his sources using MLA style (Chapter 48).

Note A visual is a source just as a written work is, and like a written work it must be acknowledged. The student cites the *Teach .org* ad in a caption and in his list of works cited. If the paper were published online, the writer would also need to seek the copyright owner's permission to use the ad (see pp. 217–18).

Being Someone

"You can be anyone." Most children hear it repeatedly from parents, teachers, coaches, and other adults. Now this encouragement is part of an advertising campaign from *Teach.org* aimed at recruiting 100,000 college undergraduates to be teachers by 2021 ("Community"). The Web ad in fig. 1,

Introduction

Background information on the ad campaign

created by the nonprofit Ad Council is typical of the campaign in encouraging viewers to consider teaching and to learn more at the *Teach.org* Web site.

Thesis statement

Through its photography and direct appeals in four lines of text, the ad leads viewers to identify with a teacher and to imagine themselves becoming teachers.

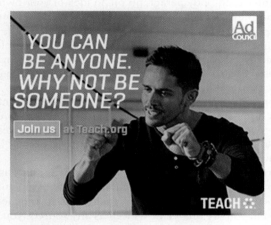

Caption giving the ad's main idea and source

Fig. 1. An advertisement for *Teach.org* encouraging viewers to consider becoming teachers. From "Teacher Recruitment," *Ad Council*, 2014, www.adcouncil.org/Our-Campaigns/Education/Teacher-Recruitment.

First main point

Evidence for first point: analysis of photo

Conclusion of first point: Oliva's interpretation

The main element in the ad is a photograph that fills the frame. The image is of a young-looking man intent on what is in front of him, something he sees but the viewer does not. He is caught in mid-speech, looking down at what viewers eventually assume to be his students, and his clenched hands indicate that he is passionate about what he is saying. He is engaged in what he is doing, which viewers soon learn is teaching. Clearly he finds teaching interesting and fulfilling.

Second main point

Evidence for second point: analysis of message

The next most important element in the ad is four lines of large white type next to the man: "You can be anyone. Why not be someone?" These lines of text explain the photograph and make readers connect to it at an emotional level. "You can be anyone" will resonate with the target audience, college students, particularly those who have been encouraged by the adults in their lives to make the most of their educations. Some viewers will almost hear those familiar words being spoken to them and will be reminded of their dreams of becoming firefighters, doctors, architects, musicians, and, yes, teachers.

The following question—"Why not be someone?"—draws the viewer back to the man in the photo. The question could easily read, "Why not be someone like this guy?" Standing alone, he is in charge of a class and is independent— he's not sitting in a cubicle, wearing a suit, or appeasing a boss. "Why not be someone?" also means "Don't be just anyone. Be important." In this way, the ad taps into today's celebrity-obsessed culture, connecting to the desire many people have to become famous or unforgettable in some way.

> Evidence for second point: analysis of message
>
> Conclusion of second point: Oliva's interpretation

The final element of the ad that stands out is the orange "Join us at Teach. org." This invitation pulls together the image of the man and the first two sentences, making viewers see that the man is a teacher. Those who haven't yet chosen a career path should see "Join us" as encouragement to explore teaching at the *Teach.org* Web site. The words challenge them to put their desire to be "someone" to good use by pursuing the worthwhile career of teaching.

> Third main point
>
> Evidence for third point: analysis of message

Taken together, the elements of the ad make a strong emotional appeal to viewers to identify with the man in the photo—a person who has chosen teaching over other careers, who has a job that is respected and significant, and who enjoys his work. "This can be you," the ad seems to say, effectively appealing to viewers' sense of themselves and their futures.

> Conclusion of third point: Oliva's interpretation
>
> Conclusion

[New page.]

Works Cited

> Works cited in MLA style

"Community." *Teach.org*, 2014, www.teach.org/community.

"Teacher Recruitment." *Ad Council*, 2014, www.adcouncil.org/
Our-Campaigns/Education/Teacher-Recruitment.

—Richard Oliva (student)

7 Argument

Argument seeks to persuade readers, moving them to action or convincing them to think as you do. Written arguments contain an arguable thesis statement—a claim that reasonable people can disagree over—with support for its main points and usually an acknowledgment of opposing views. Arguments often, but not always, involve research.

7a Argument assignments

When you receive an assignment, determine the type of argument you are being asked to write. Following are some common types:

- **A proposal argument** defines a problem, gives a solution, explains how the solution can be implemented, and responds to possible objections to the solution. (See pp. 48–51 for a proposal argument that cites sources.)
- **A position argument** seeks to convince readers to agree with a position on a debatable issue, such as lowering the drinking age or requiring military service. A position argument introduces the issue, conveys the position in a thesis statement, makes and supports claims about the issue, and responds to opposing views. (One type of position argument is literary analysis, described in Chapter 8.)
- **An evaluation argument** judges whether something is good or effective. A common type of evaluation argument is critical analysis, described in Chapter 6. Reviews of movies, books, television shows, exhibits, and so on are also evaluation arguments.
- **A research paper** often develops an argumentative thesis statement, draws on and cites multiple sources to support the thesis, and synthesizes the writer's and the sources' views. (See Chapters 41–47 on research writing and pp. 266–76 for a sample research paper that makes an argument.)

7b Elements of argument

An argument you read or write has four main elements: a subject, claims, evidence, and assumptions.

Subjects for argument

An argument starts with a subject and an opinion about the subject. For instance, you might think that your school should do more to conserve energy or to involve students in clubs and other activities. Your initial subject and opinion should meet several requirements:

- **It can be disputed:** reasonable people can disagree over it.
- **It *will* be disputed:** it is controversial.
- **It is narrow enough:** it can be researched and argued in the space and time available.

Claims in argument

Claims are statements that require support. In an argument the thesis statement makes the central claim that you want readers to accept or act on. This claim is what the argument is about. Then in the body of the argument, supporting claims back up this central claim.

The thesis statement

A thesis statement is always an **opinion**—that is, a judgment based on facts and arguable on the basis of facts. Depending on the type of argument you are writing, it may be one of the following:

- **A claim about past or present reality,** such as *Academic cheating increases with students' economic insecurity.*
- **A claim of value,** such as *The new room fees are unfair given the condition of the dorm.*
- **A recommendation for a course of action,** such as *The campus can relieve traffic congestion by improving bus service and rewarding bus riders.*

Supporting claims

The body of an argument consists of specific claims that support the thesis statement. Supporting claims may be opinions (see above) as well as facts, examples, and appeals to beliefs (see below).

Evidence in argument

Evidence backs up your claims and shows their validity. You will find it in your reading assignments, in sources you discover through research, and sometimes in your own experience. Several kinds of evidence commonly support arguments:

- **Facts,** statements whose truth is generally known, is verifiable, or can be inferred from verifiable facts: *Full-time students pay up to $15,200 a semester in tuition. Over their lifetimes, college graduates earn almost twice as much as high school graduates.*
- **Statistics,** facts expressed as numbers: *Of those polled, 22% prefer a flat tax.*
- **Examples,** specific instances of the point being made: *Some groups, such as children and teens, would benefit from this policy.*
- **Expert opinions,** the judgments formed by authorities on the subject based on their own examination of the facts: *Affirmative action is necessary to right the injustices of the past, a point argued by Howard Glickstein, a past director of the US Commission on Civil Rights.*
- **Appeals to readers' beliefs or needs,** statements that ask readers to accept a claim in part because they already accept it as true without out evidence: *The run-down dorm makes the school seem a second-rate institution.*

The following questions can help you determine what support your assignment will need:

- **What kinds of evidence will best support your thesis?** Depending on the discipline you're writing in and the kind of paper you're working on, you'll use a mix of facts, examples, expert opinions, and appeals to support your ideas.
- **Does your assignment require research?** Will you need to consult sources or conduct interviews, surveys, or experiments?
- **Even if research is not required, what information do you need to develop your subject?** How will you obtain it?

Finding evidence is only part of the argument process. You must also ensure that what you find is reliable. Ask these questions about your evidence:

- **Is it accurate**—trustworthy, exact, and undistorted?
- **Is it relevant**—authoritative, current, and pertinent to your subject?
- **Is it representative**—true to its context, neither under- nor over-representing any element of the sample it's drawn from?
- **Is it adequate**—plentiful and specific?

ESL Research serves different purposes in some other cultures than it does in the United States. For instance, students in some cultures may be expected to consult only well-known sources and to adhere closely to the sources' ideas. In US colleges and universities, students are expected to look for relevant and reliable sources, whether well known or not, and to use sources mainly to support their own ideas.

Assumptions in argument

An **assumption** is a stated or unstated belief, principle, or opinion about what is, what could be, or what should be. In argument, assumptions tie evidence to claims: the assumption explains why a particular piece of evidence is relevant to a particular claim. For example:

Claim	The college needs a new chemistry lab.
Evidence (in part)	The testimony of chemistry professors.
Assumption	Chemistry professors are reliable evaluators of the present lab's quality.

Assumptions are always present in arguments, even when they are not stated. In writing an argument, you need to recognize your own assumptions. If you think that readers may not agree with an assumption, you should state it forthrightly and establish its validity.

7c Writing an argument

With your subject and claims in mind and your evidence gathered, you are ready to begin writing. Argument papers all include the same parts, but the organization can vary depending on the type of argument.

Introduction

Running a paragraph or two, the introduction establishes the significance of the subject and provides background. The introduction generally includes the thesis statement. If readers are likely to resist the thesis statement, you may want to put it later in the paper, after the evidence. (For more on developing a thesis, see pp. 11–12.)

7c

Body paragraphs

The body paragraphs of your argument develop the claims supporting the thesis and respond to readers' possible objections. Drawing on relevant evidence, you appeal to readers' reason and emotions, and you present yourself as someone worth listening to.

Appeals

In presenting claims and the evidence to support them, you'll make three kinds of appeals to readers:

- A *rational* appeal calls on readers' sense of logic. It requires reasonable claims and sound evidence to support the claims.
- An *emotional* appeal calls on readers' feelings. You strengthen support for your claims by encouraging readers to feel empathy, pride, pity, anger, or some other emotion.
- An *ethical* appeal is the sense you give of being reasonable, fair, and competent.

See the box on the next page for examples of **fallacies**, or errors in argument. Fallacies result from faulty reasoning, which undercuts a rational appeal, or from an inappropriate emotional appeal, which raises an irrelevant emotional issue.

Response to opposing views

Your arguable thesis is certain to have opponents—people for whom the evidence leads to different conclusions. Acknowledging opposing views and treating them fairly make you more credible as a writer, strengthen your ethical appeal, and strengthen your entire argument. Before or while you draft your essay, list for yourself all the opposing views you can think of. You'll find them in your research, by talking to others, and by thinking critically about your own ideas.

Avoiding fallacies

Fallacies are errors in argument that either evade the issue of the argument or treat the argument as if it were much simpler than it is.

Evasions

- **Begging the question:** treating an opinion that is open to question as if it were already proved or disproved. *The college library's expenses should be reduced by cutting subscriptions to useless databases.* (Begged questions: Are some of the library's databases useless? Useless to whom?)

- **Red herring:** introducing an irrelevant issue to distract readers. *A campus speech code is essential to protect students, who already have enough problems coping with rising tuition.* (Speech codes and tuition costs are different subjects.)

- **Appealing to fear or pity:** ignoring the real issue by stirring up irrelevant emotions in readers. *She should not have to pay taxes because she is an elderly widow with no relatives or friends.* (Appeals to readers' pity. Should age and loneliness, rather than income, determine a person's tax obligation?)

- **Snob appeal:** appealing to readers' wish to be like people who are more famous, intelligent, rich, and so on. *Alec Baldwin carries a Capitol One credit card, and so should you.* (A celebrity's endorsement does not guarantee the worth of a product, a service, an idea, or anything else.)

- **Bandwagon:** appealing to readers' wish to be part of the group. *As everyone knows, marijuana use leads to heroin addiction.* (What is the evidence?)

- **Argument ad populum ("to the people"):** appealing to readers' shared values or even prejudices. *Any patriotic American will support the President's decision.* (But is the decision a good one?)

- **Argument ad hominem ("to the man"):** attacking the opponent instead of the argument. *The scientist has undergone treatment for emotional problems, so his pessimism about nuclear waste should be ignored.* (Do the scientist's previous problems negate his views about nuclear waste?)

Oversimplifications

- **Hasty generalization (jumping to a conclusion):** making a claim based on inadequate evidence. *From the way the management handled Ms. Jackson's complaint, we can assume that the company does not intend to listen to its employees.* (One experience does not demonstrate the company's intention.)

- **Reductive fallacy:** oversimplifying the relation between causes and effects. *Poverty causes crime.* (If so, then why do people who are not poor commit crimes? And why aren't all poor people criminals?)

- **Post hoc fallacy:** assuming that *A* caused *B* because *A* preceded *B*. *In two months in office, the mayor has allowed crime to increase 12%.* (The increase is probably due to conditions existing before the mayor took office.)

- **Either/or fallacy (false dilemma):** reducing a complicated question to two alternatives. *Unless we mandate drug testing in the workplace, productivity will continue to decline.* (Productivity is not necessarily dependent on drug testing.)

A common way to address opposing views is to state them, refute those you can, grant the validity of others, and demonstrate why, despite their validity, the opposing views are less compelling than your own.

A somewhat different approach, developed by the psychologist Carl Rogers, emphasizes the search for common ground. In a **Rogerian argument** you start by showing that you understand readers' views and by establishing points on which you and readers can agree and disagree. Creating a connection in this way can be especially helpful when you expect readers to resist your argument, because it encourages them to hear you out as you make your argument.

Organization

You may want to experiment with different ways of organizing the body of your argument. For instance, you can give your strongest claims first or last in the body, depending on how you anticipate readers will respond to your argument. You can state claims directly or let the evidence build to them. You can address the opposition claim by claim or address all opposing views near the beginning or end of your paper. Following are four effective schemes for organizing claims, evidence, and opposing views in the body of an essay.

A common scheme
Claim 1 and evidence
Claim 2 and evidence
Claim X and evidence
Response to opposing views

A variation
Claim 1 and evidence
Response to opposing views
Claim 2 and evidence
Response to opposing views
Claim X and evidence
Response to opposing views

The Rogerian scheme
Common ground and concession to opposing views
Claim 1 and evidence
Claim 2 and evidence
Claim X and evidence

The problem-solution scheme
The problem: claims and evidence
The solution: claims and evidence
Response to opposing views

Conclusion

Usually one paragraph, the conclusion often restates the thesis, summarizes the supporting claims, and makes a final appeal to readers. In a Rogerian argument, the conclusion often states the thesis as a solution to the problem discussed, giving ground and inviting readers to do the same.

Citation of sources

Be sure to document any sources you consulted. Use citations in the text of your paper to refer to a list of sources at the end of the paper. This book details four styles of documentation in Chapters 48–51.

7d Sample proposal argument

7d

As you read the following student essay, notice the structure, the relation of claims and supporting evidence (including illustrations), the kinds of appeals, and the response to opposing views. The writer cites the sources she consulted in MLA style (Chapter 48).

Awareness, Prevention, Support:

A Proposal to Reduce Cyberbullying

Introduction: identification of the problem

My roommate and I sat in front of her computer staring at the vicious message under her picture. She quickly removed the tag that identified her, but the comments already posted on the photo proved that the damage was done. While she slept, my roommate had become the victim of a cyberbully. She had joined an increasing number of college students who are targeted in texts, e-mails, social-networking sites, and other Web sites that broadcast photographs, videos, and comments. My roommate's experience alerted me that our campus needs a program aimed at awareness and prevention of cyberbullying and support for its victims.

Thesis statement: proposal for a solution to the problem

Evidence of the problem: published research

Although schoolyard bullying typically ends with high school graduation, cyberbullying continues in college. According to data gathered by researchers at the Massachusetts Aggression Reduction Center (MARC) of Bridgewater State College, cyberbullying behavior decreases when students enter college, but it does not cease. Examining the experiences of first-year students, the researchers found that 8% of college freshmen had been cyberbullied at college and 3% admitted to having cyberbullied another student (Englander et al. 217-18). In a survey of fifty-two freshmen, I found further evidence of cyberbullying on this campus. I asked two questions: (1) Have you been involved in cyberbullying as a victim, a bully, or both? (2) If you answered "no" to the first question, do you know anyone who has been involved in cyberbullying as a victim, a bully, or both? While a large majority of the students I surveyed (74%) have not been touched by cyberbullying, more

Evidence of the problem: student's own research

than one-fourth (26%) have been involved personally or know someone
who has, as shown in fig. 1. Taken together, the evidence demonstrates that
cyberbullying is significant in colleges and specifically on our campus.

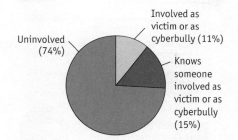

Fig. 1 Involvement in cyberbullying among fifty-two first-year students.

7d

Pie chart show-
ing results
of student's
research

The proposed "Stop Cyberbullying" program aims to reduce the behavior through a month-long campaign of awareness, prevention, and support
modeled on the college's "Alcohol Awareness Month" program. The program
can raise awareness of cyberbullying by explaining what cyberbullying is and
by informing students about the college's code of conduct, which prohibits
cyberbullying behavior but which few people read. The program can work to
prevent cyberbullying by appealing to students to treat those around them
respectfully. And, with the participation of the counseling department, the
program can provide support for victims, their friends, and others involved in
the behavior.

Explanation
of proposed
solution:
goals of the
program

If adopted, the program can use online and print media to get the
message out to the entire college community. For instance, an extensive bro-
chure distributed to first-year students and available through the counseling
center can describe cyberbullying and how it violates the college's code
of conduct, give strategies for avoiding it, and provide resources for help.
During the month-long campaign, flyers posted on campus (see fig. 2) can
also raise awareness of the problem, and brief postings to the college's Web
site, *Facebook* page, and *Twitter* feed can reach students who take online and
hybrid classes as well as those in traditional classes.

Explanation
of proposed
solution:
specific actions

Fig. 2 Sample flyer for proposed "Stop Cyberbullying" program.

Visual evidence of program publicity

Anticipation of objection: code of conduct does enough

Because this college already has a code of conduct in place and because the state has recently enacted anti-bullying legislation that includes cyberbullying, some students and administrators may contend that enough is being done to deal with the problem. To the administration's credit, the code of conduct contains specific language about online behavior, but promises of punishment for proven allegations do not address several aspects of the problem.

Response to objection: anonymity of cyberbullies

First, cyberbullies are sometimes anonymous. To accuse another student of cyberbullying, the victim needs to know the identity of the bully. While postings on *Facebook* are attached to real names, most college gossip sites are anonymous. On such sites, a cyberbully can post photographs, videos, and aggressive messages under the cover of anonymity.

Response to objection: invisibility of the problem

Second, even when the identities of cyberbullies are known, the bullying is often invisible to those in a position to take action against it. According to Ikuko Aoyama and Tony L. Talbert at Baylor University, cyberbullying occurs frequently in groups of people who know each other and who attack and retaliate: students are rarely "pure bullies" or "pure victims" but instead are often part of a "bully-victim group" (qtd. in Laster). Moreover, even if students want to separate from bullying groups, Englander and her coauthors found that they probably will not report cyberbullying incidents to authorities because they generally believe that administrators are unlikely to do anything (221). Thus counselors and administrators who may be interested in helping students to cope are often unaware of the problem.

Third, conduct codes rarely affect cyberbullying. While some cyberbullying has resulted in tragedy, many aggressive incidents do not rise to the level of punishable offenses ("Cyberbullying"). More often they consist of a humiliating photograph or a mean message—hurtful, to be sure, but not necessarily in violation of the law or the code of conduct. Indeed, the hurdles to getting recourse through official channels are fairly high.

Response to objection: conduct codes ineffective

Given its hidden nature and the inability of punitive measures to stop it, cyberbullying needs another approach—namely, a program that teaches students to recognize and regulate their own behaviour and provides help when they find themselves in a difficult situation. This program will not heal the wound suffered by my roommate, nor will it prevent all cyberbullying. But if adopted, the program will demonstrate to the college community that the administration is aware of the problem, eager to prevent it, and willing to commit resources to support students who are affected by it.

Conclusion

[New page.]

Works cited in MLA style

Works Cited

"Cyberbullying Goes to College." *Bostonia*, Boston U, Spring 2009, www.bu.edu/bostonia/spring09/bully/.

Englander, Elizabeth, et al. "Cyberbullying and Information Exposure: User-Generated Content in Post-Secondary Education." *International Journal of Contemporary Society*, vol. 46, no. 2, Oct 2009, pp. 213-20, www.uef.fi/c/document_library/get_file?uuid=113358&p_I_id=144412.

Laster, Jill. "Two Scholars Examine Cyberbullying among College Students." *The Chronicle of Higher Education*, 6 June 2010, chronicle.com/article/2-Scholars-Examine/65766/.

8 Literary Analysis

Works of literature include novels, short stories, poems, plays, and forms of creative nonfiction. Writing about a literary work requires close reading of the text with particular attention to the words, in order to form an interpretation of meaning. Evidence for the interpretation is mainly quotations from or paraphrases of the work. Literary analysis also sometimes draws on secondary sources.

8a Reading literary works

In reading literature, you face the question of meaning. Readers often disagree over the meanings of works of literature, in part because the works do not say how they should be understood. Further, readers bring different experiences to their reading and thus understand texts differently. In analyzing literature, you can offer only your interpretation of the meaning rather than *the* meaning. Your interpretation must be supported by evidence from the work itself that other readers find at least plausible if not convincing.

Writing while reading

You will become more engaged in reading literature if you write while you read. Here are some tips for reading closely:

- **Underline or highlight passages that especially interest you.**
- **Annotate the margins or use sticky notes.** Add remarks like *Nice detail* or *This narrator seems unreliable* or *Not believable*.
- **Keep a reading journal.** A journal is useful for developing and storing your reflections on what you read, such as an answer to a question you posed in the margin or a response to something said in class.

Analyzing literary elements

One reason interpretations of meaning differ is that readers approach literary works differently. For instance, some approaches focus on the cultural context of a work, others stress readers' responses to the work, and still others view the work as something to be analyzed in itself.

Despite their differences, most critical approaches discuss the following conventional elements of literary works:

- **Plot: patterns of events and relationships.** Plot is essentially what happens in a work. Even a poem has a plot—for instance, a change in mood from grief to resignation.
- **Characters: people the author creates,** including the narrator of a story or the speaker of a poem.
- **Point of view: the perspective or attitude of the speaker in a poem or the voice who tells a story.** The point of view may be first person (a participant, using *I*) or third person (an outsider, using *he, she, it, they*). A first-person narrator may be a major or a minor character in the narrative and may be **reliable** or **unreliable** (unable to report events wholly or accurately). A third-person narrator may be **omniscient** (knows what goes on in all characters' minds), **limited** (knows what goes on in the mind of only one or two characters), or **objective** (knows only what is external to the characters).
- **Tone: the narrator's or speaker's attitude,** perceived through the words (for instance, joyful, bitter, confident).
- **Imagery: word pictures or details involving the sense of sight, sound, touch, smell, and taste.**
- **Symbolism: concrete things standing in for larger and more abstract ideas.** For instance, the American flag may symbolize freedom, or a wilted flower may symbolize death.
- **Setting: the place and time where the action happens.**
- **Form: The shape and structure of the work.**
- **Themes: the main ideas about human experience suggested by the work as a whole.** A theme is neither a plot (what happens) nor a subject (such as death or marriage). Rather, it is what the author says with that plot about that subject. For instance, a theme of Agha Shahid Ali's poem "Postcard from Kashmir" (p. 55) is the experience of having more than one home.

8b Writing a literary analysis

A literary analysis is a type of argument, a claim you make and support about your interpretation of a work's meaning or effect.

Finding your interpretation

As you read and take notes, seek patterns in the work such as recurring images, symbols, or events. Such patterns can help you see themes both in the work itself and in your ideas about it. During this process, begin to formulate the main point you want to make about the work. Eventually, this main point will be the thesis statement of your essay—the specific idea that you develop and argue with evidence from the work. (For more on developing a thesis, see pp. 11–12).

Using evidence from the text

To support your interpretation, quote and paraphrase the work you are analyzing, a primary source. Depending on your assignment, you may also draw on secondary sources, such as other critics' views of the work or a biography of the author.

Follow the guidelines below when quoting from literary works, and see the sample paper on the following pages for examples.

- **Use quotations to support your assertions.** Quotations provide evidence for your ideas and let readers hear the voice of the work.
- **Specify how each quotation supports your idea.** For instance, *The poet depicts fate as a burden:* "..."
- **Indicate any editing of quotations.** Use ellipsis marks (...) to indicates deletions from quotations (pp. 154–56). Use brackets to indicate additions to or changes in quotations (p. 156).
- **Cite sources in MLA style.** Use citations within the text of your paper to refer to a list of works cited at the end (Chapter 48).

Shaping the analysis

The following tips can help you shape your interpretation into a focused, well-organized essay.

- **Make sure your interpretation has a point**—a central idea, or thesis, that you will argue in the paper, usually stated in the introduction. (For more on developing a thesis, see pp. 11–12.)
- **Include a short summary if readers may be unfamiliar with the work.** Summarize the plot of the work only briefly, and place the summary near the start of the essay. Devote the essay to analysis, not summary. (See pp. 35–36 for more on summarizing.)
- **Center each body paragraph on an idea of your own that supports your interpretation.** Generally state the idea in a topic sentence.
- **Support each paragraph idea with evidence from the work.** Introduce quotations and paraphrases so that readers see clearly how they relate to your ideas.
- **Use present-tense verbs to describe both the author's work and the action in the work**—for example, *The poem's speaker imagines his home* and *The author compares the two characters*.
- **Write a conclusion,** wrapping up your main points and connecting to your thesis.
- **Use MLA style to document the work and any other sources you consulted.** Citations in the text refer to a list of all the works you used in writing the paper. (See Chapter 48 on MLA style).

8c Sample literary analysis

A poem and a student paper on the work appear below and on the following pages. The student makes an argument for a particular interpretation of the poem, developing a thesis and supporting her ideas with quotations from and some paraphrases of the poem. The student also draws on secondary sources (other critics' views), which test or further support her own views. She cites the poem and these secondary sources in MLA style.

8c

Poem

Agha Shahid Ali

Postcard from Kashmir

Kashmir shrinks into my mailbox,
my home a neat four by six inches.
I always loved neatness. Now I hold
the half-inch Himalayas in my hand.

This is home. And this the closest   5
I'll ever be to home. When I return,
the colors won't be so brilliant,
the Jhelum's waters so clean,
so ultramarine. My love
so overexposed.   10

And my memory will be a little
out of focus, in it
a giant negative, black
and white, still undeveloped.

Literary research paper on poetry

Jessie Glenn

Professor Narracci

English 101

14 March 2016

Past and Future in

Agha Shahid Ali's "Postcard from Kashmir"

Most literary critics interpret Agha Shahid Ali's "Postcard from Kashmir" as a longing for a lost home, a poetic expression of the heartbreak of exile. For instance, Maimuna Dali Islam describes the speaker's futile effort "to capture his homeland" (262). However, such a reading of the poem seems too narrow.

Introduction naming author/ title and summarizing other interpretations

Thesis state-
ment: student's
interpretation

"Postcard from Kashmir" does evoke the experience of being displaced from a beloved home, but the speaker does not seem to feel an intense loss. Instead, he seems to reflect on his position of having more than one home.

Summary of
poem

Ali's brief poem consists of three stanzas and divides into two parts. In the first half, the speaker examines a postcard he has received from his former home of Kashmir (lines 1-6). In the second half, the speaker looks forward, imagining how Kashmir will look the next time he sees it and assuming that the place will be different from the idealized view of the postcard and his memory

Background
information

(6-14). The geography is significant. Kashmir has been in the news for many years as the focus of territorial conflict, often violent, among the bordering nations of India, Pakistan, and China. Many residents of the region have been killed, and many have left the region. One of the exiles was Ali: he moved to the United States in 1976 and lived here until his death in 2001, but he also

In-text citations
in MLA style

regularly visited his family in Kashmir (Benvenuto 261, 263).

Critic's inter-
pretation

In the context of Kashmir, the literary theorist Jahan Ramazani concludes that the poem "dramatizes the . . . condition" of losing one's homeland to

First point sup-
porting thesis

political turmoil (12). Yet several lines in the poem suggest that the speaker is not mourning a loss but musing about having a sense of home both in Kashmir

Quotations
from poem

and in the United States. This sense is evident in the opening stanza: "Kashmir shrinks into my mailbox, / my home a neat four by six inches" (1-2), with "my mailbox" conveying his current residence as home and "my home" referring to Kashmir. The dual sense of home is even more evident in the lines "This is home. And this the closest / I'll ever be to home" (5-6). Although Maimuna Dali Islam

Critic's inter-
pretation

assumes that "This" in these lines refers to the Kashmir pictured on the postcard (262), it could also or instead refer to the home attached to the mailbox.

Second point
supporting
thesis

The speaker also seems to perceive that his dual sense of home will continue into the future. The critics do not mention that the second half of the poem is written in the future tense. Beginning with "When I return" (6), the speaker makes it clear that he expects to find himself in Kashmir again, and he imagines how things will be, not how they were. Islam takes the image on the

Quotation
from secondary
source

postcard as proof that "there is a place that can be captured in a snapshot" (263), but the poem's speaker compares photography to memory, character- izing both as flawed and deceptive with terms such as "overexposed" (10) and "out of focus" (12). He acknowledges that the place won't be like the photo- graph: "the colors won't be so brilliant, / the Jhelum's waters so clean, / so ultramarine" (7-9). Kashmir still exists, but not as any photograph or memory has recorded it. And the speaker's relationship to his original home, his "love" (9), is changing with the place itself.

    In "Postcard from Kashmir" the speaker reflects on home and displacement as he gazes into a representation of his past and considers the future. If the poem mourns a loss, as the critics suggest, it is a loss that has not happened yet, at least not completely. More convincingly, the poem captures a moment when the two homes and the past, present, and future all meet.

[New page.]

Conclusion restating critics' and student's interpretations

Works Cited

Works cited in MLA style

Ali, Agha Shahid. "Postcard from Kashmir." *The Half-Inch Himalayas,* Wesleyan
    UP, 1987, p. 1.

Benvenuto, Christine. "Agha Shahid Ali." *The Massachusetts Review,* vol. 43,
    no. 2, Summer 2002, pp. 261-63.

Islam, Maimuna Dali. "A Way in the World of an Asian American Existence:
    Agha Shahid Ali's Transimmigrant Spacing of North America and India
    and Kashmir." *Transnational Asian American Literature: Sites and
    Transits,* edited by Shirley Lim et al., Temple UP, 2006, pp. 257-73.

Ramazani, Jahan. *The Hybrid Muse: Postcolonial Poetry in English.* U of
    Chicago P, 2001.

9 Informative Writing

Informative writing seeks to teach readers about a subject. When you write to inform, you explore a subject in depth and provide information that readers may not know. Common types of informative writing assignments include essays, research reports, and lab reports.

9a Writing an informative essay

    Depending on the assignment, you may focus an informative essay on a nonpersonal subject or on an aspect of your own experience. Among other options, you might explain the subject, compare and contrast it with something else, or describe how it works. The following tips can help you shape an informative essay:

- **Make sure your writing has a point**—a central idea, or thesis, that focuses your essay, usually stated in the introduction. (For more on developing a thesis, see pp. 11–12.)
- **Use each body paragraph to present points and evidence that support and develop your thesis statement.** Depending on the assignment, evidence may come from research or from your personal experience or observations. Conclude each paragraph with your own idea about the evidence.
- **Write a conclusion.** Conclude an informative essay by summarizing your main points and referring back to your thesis.
- **Document any sources you consulted.** Use citations in the text to refer to a list of sources at the end of the paper. This book details four styles of documentation in Chapters 48–51.

9b Sample informative essay

The following student essay seeks to inform readers about who benefits from the income generated by college football. The writer did not conduct research, instead drawing on information commonly known by the game's followers, so he does not cite sources.

Who Benefits from the Money in College Football?

Introduction establishing subject of essay

Anyone who follows Division 1-A college football cannot fail to notice the money that pours into every aspect of the sport—the lavish stadiums, corporate sponsorships, televised games, and long playoff tournament. The

Informative thesis statement

money may seem to flow to everyone, but in reality it doesn't. Although college football is a multimillion-dollar industry for the schools, conferences, and television networks, the benefits do not extend to the players.

Paragraph idea, linked to thesis statement

Colleges and universities are major players in the for-profit football industry. A vibrant football program attracts not only skilled coaches and talented players but also wealthy, sports-minded donors who give money for

Paragraph developed with evidence supporting its idea

state-of-the art stadiums and facilities. These great facilities in turn attract fans, some of whom are willing to pay high ticket prices to watch games in luxurious sky boxes and thus generate more profits for the schools' athletic departments.

Paragraph idea, linked to thesis statement

The athletic conferences to which the schools belong—such as the Big Ten, the Atlantic Coast Conference, and the Pac-12—reap financial rewards from college football. Each conference maintains a Web site to post schedules and scores, sell tickets and merchandise, and promote interest in its teams. However, the proceeds from ticket and merchandise sales surely pale in comparison to the money generated by the College Football Playoff—the three-week-long post-season football extravaganza. Each game not only is televised but also carries the name of a corporate sponsor that pays for the privilege of having its name attached to a game.

Paragraph developed with evidence supporting its idea

Like the schools and athletic conferences, the television networks profit from football. Networks sell advertising slots to the highest bidders for every televised game during the regular season and the College Football Playoff, and they work to sustain fans' interest in football by cultivating viewers on the Web. For instance, one network generates interest in up-and-coming high school players through *Scout.com*, a Web site that posts profiles of boys being recruited by colleges and universities and that is supported, at least in part, through advertising and paid subscriptions.

Paragraph idea, linked to thesis statement

Paragraph developed with evidence supporting its idea

Amid these money-making players are the actual football players, the young men who are bound by NCAA rules to play as amateurs and to receive no direct compensation for their hours of practice and field time. They may receive scholarships that cover tuition, room and board, uniforms, medical care, and travel. Yet these payments are a small fraction of the millions of dollars spent on and earned from football.

Transition and new paragraph idea, linked to thesis statement

Paragraph developed with evidence supporting its idea

Many critics have pointed out the disparity between players' rewards and the industry's profits. Recent efforts to unionize the players and file lawsuits on their behalf have caused schools, conferences, and the NCAA to make some concessions in scholarship packages and rules. However, these changes do not fundamentally alter a system in which the big benefits go to everyone but the players.

Conclusion echoing thesis statement and summarizing

—Terrence MacDonald (student)

9c Writing a research report (APA style)

A research report explains research you have conducted yourself or your attempt to replicate some else's research. In APA style, the leading guide for the social sciences, a formal research report typically contains the elements described below and illustrated in the sample paper on pages 296–302.

- **Title page:** provides the title, your name, the course title, the instructor's name, and the date.
- **Abstract:** in 120 words or fewer, summarizes your subject, research method, findings, and conclusions. Although the abstract

will come at the start of your paper, you should write it last, after you have completed the report.

- **Introduction:** presents the problem you researched, your method, the relevant background (such as published research on the subject), and the purpose of your research.
- **Method section:** provides a detailed discussion of how you conducted your research, including a description of the research subjects, any materials or tools you used (such as questionnaires), and the procedure you followed. You may want to break the method section down into subsections labeled with headings.
- **Results section:** summarizes the data you collected, explains how you analyzed the data, and presents the data in detail, often in tables, graphs, or charts.
- **Discussion section:** interprets the data and presents your conclusions. When the discussion is brief, you may combine it with the Results section.
- **References:** an alphabetical list of all the sources you cited in the report. (See Chapter 49 on APA style.)

9d Writing a lab report (CSE style)

Scientists write to explain experimental methods and results. They formulate hypotheses that they test by gathering data from experiments or observation, generally in a controlled laboratory setting but also in the natural world.

A lab report explains the procedure and results of an experiment or observation that you conducted. A formal report typically contains the elements described below and illustrated in the sample paper on pages 325–28.

- **Title page:** provides the title, your name, the course title, the instructor's name, and the date.
- **Abstract:** in 120 words or fewer, summarizes the subject, research method, findings, and conclusions. Although the abstract will come at the start of your paper, you should write it last, after you have completed the report.
- **Introduction (or Objective) section:** states the problem, explains why you conducted the experiment, and summarizes the background, such as previous studies of the problem.
- **Method (or Procedure) section:** explains how you conducted the experiment, including any statistical analysis.
- **Results section:** explains your major findings, including any unexpected results, and summarizes any data you present in graphs and tables.

- **Discussion section:** interprets the results and explains how they relate to the goals of the experiment. This section also describes new hypotheses that other researchers might test as a result of the experiment. If the section is brief, you may combine it with the Results in a section with the heading Conclusions.
- **References:** a list of all the sources you cited in the report. (See Chapter 51 on CSE style.)

10 Oral Presentations

Speaking to a group can produce anxiety, even for those who are experienced at it. This chapter shows you how to present your work to a listening audience.

10a Organizing a presentation

Give your oral presentation a recognizable shape so that listeners can see how ideas and details relate to each other.

The introduction

The beginning of an oral presentation should try to accomplish three goals:

- **Gain the audience's attention and interest.** Begin with a question, an unusual example or statistic, or a short, relevant story.
- **Put yourself in the speech.** Demonstrate your expertise, experience, or concern to gain the interest and trust of your audience.
- **Introduce and preview your topic and purpose.** By the time your introduction is over, listeners should know what your subject is and the direction you'll take to develop your ideas.

Your introduction should prepare your audience for your main points but not give them away. Think of it as a sneak preview of your speech, not the place for an apology such as *I wish I'd had more time to prepare ...* or a dull statement such as *My speech is about....*

Supporting material

Just as you do when writing, you should use facts, statistics, examples, and expert opinion to support the main points of your oral presentation. In addition, you can make your points more memorable with vivid description, well-chosen quotations, true or fictional stories, and analogies.

The conclusion

You want your conclusion to be clear, of course, but you also want it to be memorable. Remind listeners of how your topic and main idea connect to their needs and interests. If your speech is motivational, tap an emotion that matches your message. If your speech is informational, give some tips on how to remember important details.

10b Using visual aids

You can supplement an oral presentation with visual aids such as posters, models, slides, or videos.

- **Use visual aids to underscore your points.** Short lists of key ideas, illustrations such a graphs or photographs, and objects such as models can make your presentation more interesting and memorable. But use visual aids judiciously: a constant flow of illustrations or objects will bury your message.
- **Match visual aids and setting.** An audience of five people may be able to see a photograph and share a chart; a classroom or an audience of a hundred will need projected images.
- **Coordinate visual aids with your message.** Time each visual to reinforce a point you're making. Tell listeners what they're looking at. Give them enough viewing time so that they don't mind turning their attention back to you.
- **Show visual aids only while they're needed.** To regain your audience's attention, remove or turn off any aid as soon as you have finished with it.

Many speakers use *PowerPoint, Prezi,* or other software to project main points, key images, video, or other elements. To use such software effectively, follow the guidelines with the samples on the next page and also these tips:

- **Don't put your whole presentation on screen.** Select key points and distill them to as few words as possible. Use slides as quick, easy-to-remember summaries or ways to present examples. For a twenty-minute presentation, plan to use approximately ten slides.
- **Use a simple design.** Avoid turning your presentation into a show about the software's many capabilities and special effects.
- **Make text readable.** The type should be easy to see for viewers in the back of the room, whether the lights are on or not.
- **Use a consistent design.** For optimal flow through the presentation, each slide should be formatted similarly.

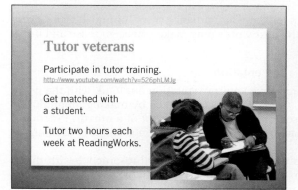

First slide, introducing the project and presentation.

Simple, consistent slide design focusing viewers' attention on information, not software features.

Later slide, including a title and brief points to be explained by the speaker.

Link to video about the project's activities.

Photograph reinforcing the project's activities.

- **Add relevant images and media.** Presentation software allows you to play images, audio, and video as part of your speech. Before you add them, however, be sure each has a point so that you don't overload the presentation. See pages 24–29 on choosing and using visuals and other media.
- **Review all your slides before the presentation.** Make sure they are complete, consistent, and easy to read. Proofread each slide.
- **Pace your presentation and your slides.** If a section of your presentation doesn't have a slide keyed to it, insert a blank slide to project during that section.
- **Cite your sources.** Include a brief source note on any slide that contains borrowed material, such as a quotation or paraphrase from a source. Add a complete list of works cited on a slide at the end of the presentation.

10c Delivering a presentation

Choosing a method of delivery

You can deliver an oral presentation in several ways:

- **Impromptu, without preparation:** Make a presentation without planning what you will say. Impromptu speaking requires confidence and excellent general preparation.
- **Extemporaneously:** Prepare notes to glance at but not read from. This method allows you to look and sound natural while ensuring that you don't forget anything,
- **Speaking from a text:** Read aloud from a written presentation. You won't lose your way, but you may lose your audience. Avoid reading for an entire presentation.
- **Speaking from memory:** Deliver a prepared presentation without notes. You can look at your audience every minute, but the stress of retrieving the next words may make you seem tense and unresponsive.

Practicing before a presentation

Take time to rehearse your presentation out loud, with the notes you will be using. Gauge your performance by making an audio- or videotape of yourself or by practicing in front of a mirror. Practicing out loud will also tell you if your presentation is running too long or too short.

If you plan to use visual aids, you'll need to practice with them, too. Your goal is to eliminate glitches (slides in the wrong order, missing charts) and to weave the visuals seamlessly into your presentation.

Engaging your audience

You can take steps to help your audience pay attention to your presentation:

- **Speak loudly, slowly, and clearly enough for your audience to hear you.** Rehearse in advance so that you are confident that your audience can understand you.
- **If you are able, stand up to deliver your presentation.** Step out from behind any lectern or desk and gesture as appropriate.
- **Don't talk to the computer or the projection.** Move away from both, and face the audience.
- **Make eye contact.** Above all, look directly into your listeners' eyes as you speak. Doing so conveys your honesty, your confidence, and your control of the material.

Dealing with stage fright

Many people report that speaking in front of an audience is their number-one fear. Even many experienced and polished speakers have some anxiety about delivering an oral presentation, but they let this nervous energy propel them into working hard on each presentation. Several techniques can help you reduce anxiety:

- **Use simple relaxation exercises.** Deep breathing or tensing and relaxing your stomach muscles can ease some of the physical symptoms of speech anxiety—stomachache, rapid heartbeat, and shaky hands, legs, and voice.
- **Think positively.** Instead of worrying about the mistakes you might make, concentrate on how well you've prepared and practiced your presentation and how significant your ideas are.
- **Don't avoid opportunities to speak in public.** Practice and experience build speaking skills and offer the best insurance for success.

Essential
Effective Sentences

Emphasis

- Make subjects and verbs of sentences focus on key actors and actions. (See opposite.)
- Stress main ideas by placing them first or last in a sentence. (See p. 70.)
- Link equally important ideas with coordination. (See p. 71.)
- De-emphasize less important ideas with subordination. (See p. 72.)

Conciseness

- Use the active voice to focus on key actors and actions. (See p. 73.)
- Cut empty words and unneeded repetition. (See p. 73.)
- Avoid unneeded *there is* and *it is* constructions. (See p. 75.)
- Tighten word groups to their essence, and combine sentences where appropriate. (See p. 75.)

Parallelism

- Use parallel constructions to show the equivalence of elements that are connected by *and, or, not only ... but also,* and similar words. (See p. 77.)
- Use parallelism in lists, headings, and outlines. (See p. 78.)

Variety and details

- Vary sentence lengths and structures to stress your main ideas and hold readers' attention. (See p. 79.)
- Provide details that make your sentences clear and interesting. (See p. 80.)

Appropriate words

- Use language appropriate for your writing situation. (See pp. 81–84.)
- Avoid sexist and other biased language. (See pp. 85–87.)

Exact words

- Choose words that are suited to your meaning and are concrete and specific. (See pp. 88–89.)
- Make words correct in idiom and also fresh, not clichéd. (See p. 89.)

11 Emphasis

Emphatic writing leads readers to see your main ideas immediately, without having to puzzle out meanings or importance. Besides the following strategies for achieving emphasis, see also the discussions of conciseness (p. 73) and variety (p. 79).

11a Subjects and verbs

The heart of every sentence is its subject° and its predicate verb.° The subject is the person or thing that acts, and the verb is what the subject does: *Children* [subject] *grow* [predicate verb]. When these elements do not identify the key actor and action in the sentence, readers must find that information elsewhere and the sentence may be wordy and unemphatic. In the following sentences, the subjects and verbs are underlined:

> Unemphatic The intention of the company was to expand its workforce. A proposal was also made to diversify the backgrounds and abilities of employees.

These sentences are unemphatic because their key ideas do not appear in their subjects and verbs. Revised, the sentences are not only clearer but also more concise:

> Revised The company intended to expand its workforce. It also proposed to diversify the backgrounds and abilities of employees.

The unemphatic constructions shown below and on the next page usually drain meaning from the subject and verb of a sentence.

Nouns made from verbs

Nouns made from verbs can obscure the key actions of sentences and add words. These nouns include *intention* (from *intend*), *proposal* (from *propose*), *decision* (from *decide*), *expectation* (from *expect*), *persistence* (from *persist*), *argument* (from *argue*), and *inclusion* (from *include*).

> Unemphatic After the company made a decision to hire more workers with disabilities, its next step was the construction of wheelchair ramps and other facilities.

°Defined in "Grammar Terms," page 340.

69

| Revised | After the company <u>decided</u> to hire more workers with disabilities, it next <u>constructed</u> wheelchair ramps and other facilities. |

Weak verbs

Weak verbs don't express much action. They include *made* and *was* in the last example on the previous page. Such verbs tend to stall sentences just where they should be moving, and they often bury key actions:

| Unemphatic | The company <u>is</u> now the leader among businesses in complying with the 1990 Americans with Disabilities Act. Its officers <u>make</u> speeches on the act to business groups. |
| Revised | The company now <u>leads</u> other businesses in complying with the 1990 Americans with Disabilities Act. Its officers <u>speak</u> on the act to business groups. |

Passive voice

Verbs in the passive voice° state actions received by, not performed by, their subjects. Thus the passive de-emphasizes the true actor of the sentence, sometimes omitting it entirely. Generally, use the active voice,° in which the subject performs the verb's action. (See p. 103 for more on passive and active voice.)

| Unemphatic | The 1990 <u>law is seen</u> by most businesses as fair, but the <u>costs</u> of complying <u>have</u> sometimes <u>been objected to</u>. |
| Revised | Most <u>businesses see</u> the 1990 law as fair, but <u>some</u> have <u>objected to</u> the costs of complying. |

11b Sentence beginnings and endings

The beginning and ending of a sentence are the most emphatic positions, and the ending is usually more emphatic than the beginning. To emphasize information, place it first or last, reserving the middle for incidentals.

| Unemphatic | Education remains the single best means of economic advancement, despite its shortcomings. |
| Revised | Education remains, despite its shortcomings, the single best means of economic advancement. |

Generally, readers expect the beginning of a sentence to contain information that they already know or that you have already introduced. They then look to the ending for new information. In the following unemphatic passage, the second and third sentences both begin with new topics (highlighted in green), while the old topics from the first sentence (education and controversy) appear at the end.

Unemphatic   Education often means controversy these days, with rising costs and constant complaints about its inadequacies. But the value of schooling should not be obscured by the controversy. The single best means of economic advancement, despite its shortcomings, remains education.

In the revision below, the old information begins each sentence and new information ends the sentence.

Revised   Education often means controversy these days, with rising costs and constant complaints about its inadequacies. But the controversy should not obscure the value of schooling. Education remains, despite its shortcomings, the single best means of economic advancement.

11c Coordination

Use coordination to show that two or more elements in a sentence are equally important in meaning:

- **Link two complete sentences (main clauses°) with a comma and a coordinating conjunction°:** *and, but, or, nor, for, so, yet.*

  Independence Hall in Philadelphia is now restored, but fifty years ago it was in bad shape.

- **Link two main clauses with a semicolon alone or a semicolon and a transitional expression°** such as *however, indeed,* and *therefore.*

  The building was standing; however, it suffered from decay and vandalism.

- **Within clauses, link words and word groups with a coordinating conjunction** such as *and, but, or,* and *nor.*

  The people and officials of the nation were indifferent to Independence Hall or took it for granted.

- **Link main clauses, words, or phrases° with a correlative conjunction°** such as *not only ... but also* and *either ... or.*

  People not only took the building for granted but also neglected it.

Notes A string of main clauses connected by *and* implies that all ideas are equally important and creates a dull, plodding rhythm. Use subordination (next page) to revise such excessive coordination. See also page 79.

°Defined in "Grammar Terms," page 340.

Two punctuation errors, the comma splice and the fused sentence, can occur when you link main clauses. See pages 130–32.

11d Subordination

Use **subordination** to indicate that some elements in a sentence are less important than others for your meaning. Usually, the main idea appears in the main clause° and supporting information appears in subordinate structures:

- **Use a subordinate clause° beginning with a subordinating word** such as *although, because, before, if, since, that, when, where, which,* and *who* (*whom*).

  Although production costs have declined, they are still high. [Stresses that costs are still high.]

  Costs, which include labor and facilities, are difficult to control. [Stresses that costs are difficult to control.]

- **Use a phrase.°**

  Despite some decline, production costs are still high.
  Costs, including labor and facilities, are difficult to control.

- **Use a single word.**

  Declining costs have not matched prices.
  Labor costs are difficult to control.

Generally, subordinate clauses give the most emphasis to secondary information, phrases give less, and single words give the least.

Note A subordinate clause or a phrase is not a complete sentence and should not be set off and punctuated as one. See pages 127–29 on sentence fragments.

Exercise   Coordination and subordination for emphasis

The following paragraph consists entirely of simple sentences. Use coordination and subordination to combine sentences in the ways you think most effective to emphasize main ideas. Possible answers to starred sentences appear at the end of the book.

Example:

The storm dumped two feet of snow. It caused car accidents. It knocked out electricity. It shut down businesses and schools.

Dumping two feet of snow, the storm caused car accidents, knocked out electricity, and shut down businesses and schools.

°Defined in "Grammar Terms," page 340.

*Sir Walter Raleigh personified the Elizabethan Age. *That was the period of Elizabeth I's rule of England. *The period occurred in the last half of the sixteenth century. *Raleigh was a courtier and poet. *He was also an explorer and entrepreneur. *Supposedly, he gained Queen Elizabeth's favor. *He did this by throwing his cloak beneath her feet at the right moment. *She was just about to step over a puddle. There is no evidence for this story. It does illustrate Raleigh's dramatic and dynamic personality. His energy drew others to him. He was one of Elizabeth's favorites. She supported him. She also dispensed favors to him. However, he lost his queen's goodwill. Without her permission he seduced one of her maids of honor. He eventually married the maid of honor. Elizabeth died. Then her successor imprisoned Raleigh in the Tower of London. Her successor was James I. The king falsely charged Raleigh with treason. Raleigh was released after thirteen years. He was arrested again two years later on the old treason charges. At the age of sixty-six he was beheaded.

12 Conciseness

Concise writing makes every word count. Conciseness is not the same as brevity: detail and originality should not be cut along with needless words. Rather, the length of an expression should be appropriate to the thought.

12a Focusing on the subject and verb

Using the subjects° and verbs° of your sentences for the key actors and actions will tighten sentences. See pages 69–70 for a discussion of these ways of stressing the subject and verb:

- **Avoid nouns made from verbs,** such as *intention* (from *intend*) and *decision* (from *decide*).
- **Strengthen weak verbs,** such as *is* and *make*.
- **Rewrite the passive voice as active**—for instance, changing *The star was seen* by astronomers to *Astronomers saw* the star.

12b Cutting empty words

Cutting words that contribute nothing to your meaning will make your writing move faster and work harder.

°Defined in "Grammar Terms," page 340.

> Wordy   In my opinion, the council's proposal to improve the nature of the city center is inadequate for the reason that it ignores pedestrians.
>
> Concise The council's proposal to improve the city center is inadequate because it ignores pedestrians.

The underlining in the wordy example above highlights these kinds of empty words:

- **Phrases that add nothing to meaning:**

all things considered	in a manner of speaking
a person by the name of	in my opinion
as far as I'm concerned	last but not least
for all intents and purposes	more or less

- **Abstract or general words that pad sentences (and usually require additional words such as *of* and *the*):**

area	element	kind	situation
aspect	factor	manner	thing
case	field	nature	type

- **Word groups that mean the same thing as single words:**

For	Substitute
at all times	always
at the present time	now
at this point in time	now
for the purpose of	for
due to the fact that	because
because of the fact that	because
in the final analysis	finally

12c Cutting unneeded repetition

Repeating or restating key words from sentence to sentence can link the sentences and emphasize information the reader already knows (see p. 18). But unnecessary repetition weakens sentences and paragraphs.

> Wordy   Many unskilled workers without training in a particular job are unemployed and do not have any work.
>
> Concise Many unskilled workers are unemployed.

Be especially alert to phrases that say the same thing twice. In the following examples, only the underlined words are needed:

circle around	the future to come
consensus of opinion	important essentials
continue on	repeat again
cooperate together	return again
few in number	square [round] in shape
final completion	surrounding circumstances

12d Tightening modifiers

Modifiers° can be expanded or contracted depending on the emphasis you want to achieve. When editing your sentences, consider whether any modifiers can be tightened without loss of emphasis or clarity.

Wordy   The weight-loss industry faces new competition from lipolysis, which is a cosmetic procedure that is noninvasive.

Concise   The weight-loss industry faces new competition from lipolysis, a noninvasive cosmetic procedure.

12e Revising *there is* and *it is*

Sentences beginning *there is* or *it is* (called expletive constructions°) are sometimes useful to emphasize a change in direction, but usually they just add needless words.

Wordy   There is a completely noninvasive laser treatment that makes people thinner by rupturing fat cells and releasing the fat into the spaces between cells. It is the expectation of some doctors that the procedure will replace liposuction.

Concise   A completely noninvasive laser treatment makes people thinner by rupturing fat cells and releasing the fat into the spaces between cells. Some doctors expect that the procedure will replace liposuction.

12f Combining sentences

Often the information in two or more sentences can be combined into one tight sentence.

Wordy   People who receive fat-releasing laser treatments can lose inches from their waists. They can also lose inches from their hips and thighs. They do not lose weight. The released fat remains in their bodies.

Concise   People who receive fat-releasing laser treatments can lose inches from their waists, hips, and thighs; but they do not lose weight because the released fat remains in their bodies.

°Defined in "Grammar Terms," page 340.

Exercise Concise writing

Make the following paragraph more concise. Combine sentences when doing so reduces wordiness. Possible answers to starred sentences appear at the end of the book.

Example:

The preschool teacher education training program involves active interaction with children of a young age and intensive peer interaction in the form of role plays.

<u>Training for preschool teachers</u> involves <u>interaction</u> with children and <u>role playing with peers</u>.

*If sore muscles after exercising are a problem for you, there are some measures that can be taken by you to ease the discomfort. *It is advisable to avoid heat for the first day of soreness. *The application of heat within the first twenty-four hours can cause an increase in muscle soreness and stiffness. *In contrast, the immediate application of cold will help to reduce inflammation. Blood vessels are constricted by cold. Blood is kept away from the injured muscles. There are two ways the application of cold can be made: you can take a cold shower or use an ice pack. Inflammation of muscles can also be reduced with aspirin, ibuprofen, or another anti-inflammatory medication. When healing is occurring, you need to take it easy. A day or two after overdoing exercise, it is advisable for you to get some light exercise and gentle massage.

13 Parallelism

Parallelism matches the form of your sentence to its meaning: when your ideas are equally important, or parallel, you express them in similar, or parallel, grammatical form.

The air is dirtied by <u>factories belching smoke</u> and <u>vehicles spewing exhaust</u>.

Parallelism can also link the sentences of a paragraph:

<u>Pulleys are ancient machines</u> for transferring power. Unfortunately, <u>they are also inefficient machines</u>.

13a Parallelism with *and, but, or, nor, yet*

The coordinating conjunctions° *and, but, or, nor,* and *yet* connect elements of the same kind and importance. These conjunctions aways signal a need for parallelism.

The industrial base was shifting and shrinking.

Politicians seldom acknowledged the problem or proposed alternatives.

Industrial workers were understandably disturbed that they were losing their jobs and that no one seemed to care.

| Nonparallel | The reasons that steel companies kept losing money were that their plants were inefficient, high labor costs, and foreign competition was increasing. |
| Revised | The reasons that steel companies kept losing money were inefficient plants, high labor costs, and increasing foreign competition. |

13b

Notes Parallel elements match in structure, but they need not match word for word. In the preceding example, each element consists of at least one modifier° and a noun,° but two of the elements also include an additional modifier.

Be careful not to omit needed words in parallel structures.

| Nonparallel | Given training, workers can acquire the skills and interest in other jobs. [Idiom dictates different prepositions with *skills* and *interest*.] |
| Revised | Given training, workers can acquire the skills for and interest in other jobs. |

13b Parallelism with *both … and, either … or,* and so on

Correlative conjunctions° stress equality and balance between elements. The correlative conjunctions include *both … and, either … or, neither … nor, not only … but also,* and *whether … or.* Parallelism confirms the equality between elements: the words after the first and second connectors must match.

| Nonparallel | Huck Finn learns not only that human beings have an enormous capacity for folly but also enormous dignity. [The first element includes *that human beings have*; the second element does not.] |
| Revised | Huck Finn learns that human beings have not only an enormous capacity for folly but also enormous dignity. [Moving *not only* makes the two elements parallel.] |

°Defined in "Grammar Terms," page 340.

13c Parallelism with lists, headings, and outlines

The items in a list or an outline should be parallel. Parallelism is essential in the headings that divide a paper into sections (see p. 25).

13c

Nonparallel	Revised
Changes in Renaissance England	Changes in Renaissance England
1. Extension of trade routes	1. Extension of trade routes
2. Merchant class became more powerful	2. Increased power of the merchant class
3. The death of feudalism	3. Death of feudalism
4. Upsurging of the arts	4. Upsurge of the arts
5. Religious quarrels began	5. Rise of religious quarrels

Exercise   Parallelism

Revise the following paragraph as needed to create parallelism for grammar and coherence. Add or delete words or rephrase as necessary. Possible answers to sentences 1–3 appear at the end of the book.

Example:

After emptying her bag, searching the apartment, and she called the library, Sasha realized she had lost the book.

After emptying her bag, searching the apartment, and calling the library, Sasha realized she had lost the book.

1 The ancient Greeks celebrated four athletic contests: the Olympic Games at Olympia, the Isthmian Games were held near Corinth, at Delphi the Pythian Games, and the Nemean Games were sponsored by the people of Cleonae. 2 Each day the games consisted of either athletic events or holding ceremonies and sacrifices to the gods. 3 Competitors participated in running sprints, spectacular chariot and horse races, and running long distances while wearing full armor. 4 The purpose of such events was to develop physical strength, demonstrating skill and endurance, and sharpening the skills needed for war. 5 The athletes competed to achieve great wealth and for gaining honor both for themselves and their cities. 6 Exceptional athletes received financial support from patrons, poems and statues by admiring artists, and they even got lavish living quarters from their sponsoring cities. 7 With the medal counts and flag ceremonies, today's Olympians sometimes seem to be proving their countries' superiority as well as to demonstrate individual talent.

14 Variety and Details

To make your writing interesting as well as clear, use varied sentences that are well textured with details.

14a Varied sentence lengths and structures

Sentences generally vary from about ten to about forty words, with an average of fifteen to twenty-five words. If your sentences are all at one extreme or the other, your readers may have difficulty locating main ideas and seeing the relations among them.

- **Long sentences.** Break a sequence of long sentences into shorter, simpler ones that stress key ideas.
- **Short sentences.** Combine a sequence of short sentences with coordination (p. 71) and subordination (p. 72) to show relationships and stress main ideas.

A good way to focus and hold readers' attention is to vary the structure of sentences so that they do not all follow the same pattern.

Varied sentence structures

A long sequence of main clauses° can make all ideas seem equally important and create a plodding rhythm, as in the unvaried passage below. You want to emphasize your key subjects and verbs, moving in each sentence from old information to new (see pp. 70–71). Subordinating less important information (bracketed in the revised passage) can help you achieve this emphasis.

Unvaried

The moon is now drifting away from the earth. It moves away about one inch a year. This movement is lengthening our days, and they increase about a thousandth of a second every century. Forty-seven of our present days will someday make up a month. We might eventually lose the moon altogether. Such great planetary movement rightly concerns astronomers, but it need not worry us. It will take 50 million years.

Revised

The moon is now drifting away from the earth [about one inch a year.] [At a thousandth of a second every century,] this movement is lengthening our days. Forty-seven of our present days will someday make up a month, [if we don't eventually lose the moon altogether.] Such great planetary

°Defined in "Grammar Terms," page 340.

movement rightly concerns astronomers, but it need not worry us. It will take 50 million years.

Varied sentence beginnings

An English sentence often begins with its subject, which generally captures old information from a preceding sentence (see pp. 70–71). In the following example, *He* captures *lawyer*:

The defendant's lawyer was determined to break the prosecution's witness. He relentlessly cross-examined the stubborn witness for a week.

However, an unbroken sequence of sentences beginning with the subject quickly becomes monotonous:

Monotonous

The defendant's lawyer was determined to break the prosecution's witness. He relentlessly cross-examined the witness for a week. The witness had expected to be dismissed in an hour and was visibly irritated. She did not cooperate. She was reprimanded by the judge.

Beginning some of these sentences with other expressions improves readability and clarity:

Revised

The defendant's lawyer was determined to break the prosecution's witness. For a week he relentlessly cross-examined the witness. Expecting to be dismissed in an hour, the witness was visibly irritated. She did not cooperate. Indeed, she was reprimanded by the judge.

Varied word order

Occasionally, to achieve special emphasis, reverse the usual word order of a sentence.

A dozen witnesses testified, and the defense attorney barely questioned eleven of them. The twelfth, however, he grilled. [Compare normal word order: *He grilled the twelfth, however.*]

14b Details

Relevant details such as facts and examples create the texture and life that keep readers alert and help them grasp your meaning. For instance:

Flat

Constructed after World War II, Levittown, New York, comprised thousands of houses in two basic styles. Over the decades, residents have altered the houses so dramatically that the original styles are often unrecognizable.

Detailed

Constructed <u>on potato fields</u> after World War II, Levittown, New York, comprised <u>more than 17,000</u> houses in <u>Cape Cod and ranch</u> styles. Over the decades, residents have <u>added expansive columned porches, punched dormer windows through roofs, converted garages to sun porches, and otherwise</u> altered the houses so dramatically that the original styles are often unrecognizable.

Exercise Variety

The following paragraph consists entirely of simple sentences that begin with their subjects. Use the techniques discussed in this chapter to vary the sentences. Delete, add, change, and rearrange words to make the paragraph more readable and to make important ideas stand out clearly. Possible answers to starred sentences appear at the end of the book.

Example:

The tornado left extensive damage. It tore the roof off a school. It destroyed nearly a hundred homes. Few injuries were reported.

<u>Although few injuries were reported</u>, the tornado left extensive damage, <u>tearing the roof off a school and destroying nearly a hundred homes</u>.

*The Italian volcano Vesuvius had been dormant for many years. *It then exploded on August 24 in the year AD 79. *The ash, pumice, and mud from the volcano buried two busy towns. *Herculaneum is one. *The more famous is Pompeii. *Both towns lay undiscovered for many centuries. *Herculaneum and Pompeii were discovered in 1709 and 1748, respectively. The excavation of Pompeii was the more systematic. It was the occasion for initiating modern methods of conservation and restoration. Herculaneum was simply looted of its most valuable finds. It was then left to disintegrate. Pompeii appears much as it did before the eruption. A luxurious house opens onto a lush central garden. An election poster decorates a wall. A dining table is set for breakfast.

15 Appropriate Words

Appropriate words suit your writing situation—your subject, purpose, and audience. In most college and career writing you should rely on what's called **standard American English**, the dialect of English normally expected and used in school, business, the professions, government, and the communications media. (For more on its role in academic writing, see p. 6.)

The vocabulary of standard American English is huge, allowing expression of an infinite range of ideas and feelings; but it does exclude words that only some groups of people use, understand, or find inoffensive. The types of words are discussed in this chapter. Whenever you doubt a word's status, consult a dictionary. A label such as *nonstandard, slang,* or *colloquial* tells you that the word is not generally appropriate in academic or business writing.

15a Dialects other than Standard English

15b

Like many countries, the United States includes scores of regional, social, and ethnic groups with their own distinct dialects, or versions of English. Standard American English is one of those dialects, and so are African American Vernacular English, Appalachian English, and Creole. All the dialects of English share many features, but each also has its own vocabulary, pronunciation, and grammar.

If you speak a dialect other than standard English, you are probably already adept at moving between your dialect and standard English in speech and writing. Dialects are not wrong in themselves, but forms imported from one dialect into another may still be perceived as unclear or incorrect. When standard English is expected, such as in academic and public writing, edit your work to revise expressions in your dialect that you know (or have been told) differ from standard English. These expressions may include *theirselves, hisn, them books,* and others labeled "nonstandard" by a dictionary. They may also include certain verb forms, as discussed on pages 94–96.

Your participation in the community of standard American English does not require you to abandon your own dialect. You may want to use it in writing you do for yourself, such as journals, notes, and drafts, which should be composed as freely as possible. You may want to quote it in an academic paper, as when analyzing or reporting conversation in dialect. And, of course, you will want to use it with others who speak it.

15b Shortcuts of texting and other electronic communication

Rapid communication by e-mail and text or instant messaging encourages some informalities that are inappropriate for academic writing. If you use these media frequently, you may need to proofread your academic papers especially to identify and revise errors such as the following:

- **Sentence fragments.** Make sure every sentence has a subject and a predicate. (See pp. 127–29.)

Not   Observed the results.

But   Researchers observed the results.

- **Missing punctuation.** Between and within sentences, use standard punctuation marks. Check especially for missing commas within sentences and missing apostrophes in possessives and contractions. (See pp. 135–39 and 144–46.)

Not   The dogs bony ribs visible through its fur were evidence of neglect.

But   The dog's bony ribs, visible through its fur, were evidence of neglect.

- **Missing capital letters.** Use capital letters at the beginnings of sentences, for proper nouns and adjectives, and in titles. (See pp. 165–67.)

Not   scholars have written about abraham lincoln more than any other american.

But   Scholars have written about Abraham Lincoln more than any other American.

- **Nonstandard spellings and abbreviations.** Write out most words, avoiding forms such as *2* for *to* or *too*, *b4* for *before*, *bc* for *because*, *ur* for *you are* or *you're*, and *+* or *&* for *and*. (See pp. 161–63 and 170–71.)

Not   Students + tutors need to meet b4 the third week of the semester.

But   Students and tutors need to meet before the third week of the semester.

15c Slang

Slang is the insider language used by a group, such as musicians or football players, to reflect common experiences and to make technical references efficient. The following example is from an essay on the slang of "skaters" (skateboarders):

> Curtis slashed ultra-punk crunchers on his longboard, while the Rube-man flailed his usual Gumbyness on tweaked frontsides and lofty fakie ollies.
>
> —Miles Orkin, "Mucho Slingage by the Pool"

Though valuable within a group, slang is often too private or imprecise for academic or business writing.

15d Colloquial language

Colloquial language is the everyday spoken language, including expressions such as *go nuts, get along with, a lot, kids* (for *children*), and *stuff* (for possessions or other objects). Colloquial language suits informal writing, and an occasional colloquial word can help you achieve a desired emphasis in otherwise formal writing. But most colloquial language is not precise enough for academic, public, and professional writing.

15e Technical words and jargon

All disciplines and professions rely on specialized language, often called jargon, that allows members to communicate precisely and efficiently with each other. Chemists, for instance, have their *phosphatides,* and literary critics have their *subtexts.* Use the terms of a discipline or profession when you are writing within it. However, when you are writing for a nonspecialist audience, avoid unnecessary technical terms and carefully define the terms you must use.

15f Indirect and pretentious writing

Small, plain, and direct words are usually preferable to big, showy, or evasive words. Take special care to avoid the following:

- **Euphemisms** are presumably inoffensive words that substitute for words deemed potentially offensive or too blunt, such as *passed away* for *died* or *misspeak* for *lie.* Use euphemisms only when you know that blunt, truthful words would needlessly hurt or offend members of your audience.
- **Double talk** (at times called **doublespeak** or weasel words) is language intended to confuse or to be misunderstood: the *revenue enhancement* that is really a tax, the *biodegradable* bags that still last decades. Double talk has no place in honest writing.
- **Pretentious writing** is fancy language that is more elaborate than its subject requires. Choose your words for their exactness and economy. The big, ornate word may be tempting, but pass it up. Your readers will be grateful.

Pretentious Hardly a day goes by without a new revelation about the devastation of the natural world, and to a significant extent our dependence on the internal combustion engine is the culprit. Respected scientific minds coalesce around the argument that carbon dioxide emissions, such as those from automobiles imbibing gasoline, are responsible for a gradual escalation in temperatures on the earth.

Revised Much of the frequent bad news about the environment can be blamed on the internal combustion engine. Respected scientists argue that carbon dioxide emissions, such as those from gas-powered cars, are warming the earth.

15g Sexist and other biased language

Even when we do not mean it to, our language can reflect and perpetuate hurtful prejudices toward groups of people. Such biased language can be obvious—words such as *nigger, honky, mick, kike, fag, dyke,* and *broad.* But it can also be subtle, generalizing about groups in ways that may be familiar but that are also inaccurate or unfair.

Biased language reflects poorly on the user, not on the person or persons whom it mischaracterizes or insults. Unbiased language does not submit to false generalizations. It treats people respectfully as individuals and labels groups as they wish to be labeled.

Stereotypes of race, ethnicity, and other characteristics

A **stereotype** characterizes and judges people simply on the basis of their membership in a group: *Men are uncommunicative. Women are emotional. Liberals want to raise taxes. Conservatives are affluent.*

In your writing, avoid statements about the traits of whole groups that may be true of only some members. Be especially cautious about substituting such statements for the evidence you should be providing instead.

> Stereotype Elderly drivers should have their licenses limited to day-time driving only. [Asserts that all elderly people are poor night drivers.]
>
> Revised Drivers with impaired night vision should have their licenses limited to daytime driving only.

Some stereotypes have become part of the language, but they are still potentially offensive.

> Stereotype The administrators are too blind to see the need for a new gymnasium.
>
> Revised The administrators do not understand the need for a new gymnasium.

Sexist language

Sexist language distinguishes needlessly between men and women in matters such as occupation, ability, behavior, temperament, and maturity. It can wound or irritate readers and indicates the writer's thoughtlessness or unfairness. The following guidelines can help you eliminate sexist language from your writing.

- **Avoid demeaning and patronizing language**—for instance, identifying women and men differently or trivializing either gender.

Sexist	Dr. Keith Kim and Lydia Hawkins collaborated.
Revised	Dr. Keith Kim and Dr. Lydia Hawkins collaborated.
Revised	Keith Kim and Lydia Hawkins collaborated.

Sexist	Ladies are entering almost every occupation formerly filled by men.
Revised	Women are entering almost every occupation formerly filled by men.

■ Avoid occupational or social stereotypes that assume a role or profession is exclusively male or female.

Sexist	A doctor should commend a nurse when she provides his patients with good care.
Revised	A doctor should commend a nurse who provides good care for patients.

■ Avoid using *man* or words containing *man* to refer to all human beings. Some alternatives:

businessman	businessperson
chairman	chair, chairperson
congressman	representative in Congress, legislator
craftsman	craftsperson, artisan
layman	layperson
mankind	humankind, humanity, human beings, people
manpower	personnel, human resources
policeman	police officer
salesman	salesperson

Sexist	Man has not reached the limits of social justice.
Revised	Humankind [or Humanity] has not reached the limits of social justice.

Sexist	The furniture consists of manmade materials.
Revised	The furniture consists of synthetic materials.

■ Avoid the generic *he,* the male pronoun used to refer to more than just males. (See also p. 114.)

Sexist	The newborn child explores his world.
Revised	Newborn children explore their world. [Use the plural for the pronoun and the word it refers to.]
Revised	The newborn child explores the world. [Avoid the pronoun altogether.]
Revised	The newborn child explores his or her world. [Substitute male and female pronouns.]

Use the last option sparingly—only once in a group of sentences and only to stress the singular individual.

Inappropriate labels

Labels for groups of people can be shorthand stereotypes and can be discourteous when they ignore readers' preferences. Although sometimes dismissed as "political correctness," sensitivity in applying labels hurts no one and helps gain your readers' trust and respect.

- Avoid labels that (intentionally or not) insult the person or group you refer to. A person with emotional problems is not a *mental patient*. A person using a wheelchair is not *wheelchair-bound*.
- Use names for racial, ethnic, and other groups that reflect the preferences of each group's members, or at least many of them. Examples of current preferences include *African American* or *black* and *people with disabilities* (rather than *the disabled* or *the handicapped*). But labels change often. To learn how a group's members wish to be labeled, ask them directly, attend to usage in reputable periodicals, or check a recent dictionary.
- Identify a person's group only when it is relevant to the point you're making. Consider the context of the label: Is it a necessary piece of information? If not, don't use it.

`15g`

Exercise   Appropriate words

Rewrite the following paragraph as needed for standard American English, focusing on inappropriate slang, pretentious language, and biased language. Consult a dictionary to determine whether particular words are appropriate and to find suitable substitutes. Possible answers to sentences 1–5 appear at the end of the book.

Example:

If negotiators lose their cool during contract discussions, they may mess up chances for a settlement.

If negotiators <u>become upset</u> during contract discussions, they may <u>harm</u> chances for a settlement.

1 Vaccinations to prevent serious diseases have been a huge deal for public health since they became widely available in the 1920s. 2 Diseases such as polio, measles, and whooping cough that used to sicken and kill many children have been pronounced mostly dead.

3 However, measles is making a comeback because some moms do not vaccinate their kids. 4 Measles is a serious and highly contagious affliction of the body, causing victims to exhibit multiple symptoms including high fever, cough, vomiting, diarrhea, and full-body rash. 5 Despite

tons of evidence to the contrary, some overprotective mothers claim that the measles vaccine, which is combined with vaccines for mumps and rubella, causes autism. 6 Other anti-vaccine types buy into the idea that vaccines are not necessary because other children's vaccinations will protect their children from coming into contact with disease. 7 But they are at odds with respected scientific and medical professionals, who coalesce around evidence showing that vaccines are not effective at eradicating disease unless 95% of the population receives these life-saving injections.

8 To immunize a child, a doctor must discuss the necessary vaccines with the child's mother. 9 If she agrees to the vaccines, he orders the shots while the child is in the office for a checkup. 10 A nurse typically administers vaccines, and she gives the shots quickly to minimize the pain.

16 Exact Words

To write clearly and effectively, you will want to find the words that fit your meaning exactly and convey your attitude precisely.

16a The right word for your meaning

One key to helping readers understand you is to use words according to their established meanings.

- Consult a dictionary whenever you are unsure of a word's meaning.
- Distinguish between similar-sounding words that have widely different meanings.

Inexact   Older people often suffer infirmaries [places for the sick].

Exact   Older people often suffer infirmities [disabilities].

Some words, called **homonyms**, sound exactly alike but differ in meaning: for example, *principal/principle* or *rain/reign/rein*. (Many homonyms and near-homonyms are listed in "Commonly Misused Words," p. 329.)

- Distinguish between words with related but distinct meanings.

Inexact   Television commercials continuously [unceasingly] interrupt programming.

Exact   Television commercials continually [regularly] interrupt programming.

- Distinguish between words that have similar basic meanings but different emotional associations, or *connotations*.

It is a <u>daring</u> plan. [The plan is bold and courageous.]
It is a <u>reckless</u> plan. [The plan is thoughtless and risky.]

Many dictionaries list and distinguish such **synonyms**, words with approximately, but often not exactly, the same meanings.

16b Concrete and specific words

Clear, exact writing balances abstract and general words, which outline ideas and objects, with concrete and specific words, which sharpen and solidify.

16c

- **Abstract words** name qualities and ideas: *beautiful, management, culture, freedom, awesome.* **Concrete words** name things we can know by our five senses of sight, hearing, touch, taste, and smell: *sleek, humming, rough, bitter, musty.*
- **General words** name classes or groups of things, such as *buildings, weather,* or *birds,* and they include all the varieties of the class. **Specific words** limit a general class, such as *buildings,* by naming one of its varieties, such as *skyscraper, Victorian courthouse, ranch house,* or *hut.*

Abstract and general statements need development with concrete and specific details. For example:

Vague   The size of his hands made his smallness real. [How big were his hands? How small was he?]

Exact   Not until I saw his delicate, doll-like hands did I realize that he stood a full head shorter than most other men.

16c Idioms

Idioms are expressions in any language that do not fit the rules for meaning or grammar—for instance, *put up with, plug away at, make off with.*

Because they are not governed by rules, idioms usually cause particular difficulty for people learning to speak and write a new language. But even native speakers of English can confuse idioms involving prepositions,° such as *agree <u>on</u> a plan, agree <u>to</u> a proposal,* and *agree <u>with</u> a person* or *occupied <u>by</u> a person, occupied <u>in</u> study,* and *occupied <u>with</u> a thing.*

When in doubt about an idiom, consult your dictionary under the main word (*agree* and *occupy* in the examples). (See also p. 97 on verbs with particles.)

°Defined in "Grammar Terms," page 340.

16d Clichés

Clichés, or **trite expressions**, are phrases so old and so often re-peated that they have become stale. Examples include *better late than never, beyond the shadow of a doubt, face the music, green with envy, ladder of success, point with pride, sneaking suspicion,* and *wise as an owl*.

Clichés may slide into your drafts. In editing, be wary of any ex-pression you have heard or used before. Substitute fresh words of your own, or restate the idea in plain language.

16d

Exercise   Exact words

In the following paragraph, revise any word that is used incorrectly or is a cliché. Consult a dictionary if you are uncertain of a word's precise mean-ing. Answers to sentences 1–4 appear at the end of the book.

Example:

Lucy and Kiara are going to New York and Chicago, <u>respectfully</u>, for summer internships.

Lucy and Kiara are going to New York and Chicago, <u>respectively</u>, for summer internships.

1 The acclaimed writer Maxine Hong Kingston sites her mother's sto-ries about ancestors and ancient Chinese customs as the sources of her first two books, *The Woman Warrior* and *China Men*. 2 One of her moth-er's fabrications, about a pregnant aunt who was ostracized by villagers, shook the young Kingston to her core. 3 The aunt gained avengeance by drowning herself in the village water supply. 4 Kingston made the aunt infamous by giving her immortality in *The Woman Warrior*. 5 Two of Kingston's progeny, her great-grandfathers, are the focal points of *China Men*. 6 Both men led rebellions against suppressive employers: a sugar-cane farmer and a railroad-construction engineer. 7 Kingston's razor-sharp writing infers her contradiction of racism and sexism both in the China of the past and in the United States of the present. 8 She was re-warded many prizes for these distinguished tomes.

PART 4

Grammatical Sentences

Grammatical Sentences

This list focuses on the grammatical errors that most often confuse or distract readers. See "Detailed Contents" inside the back cover for a complete guide to this part.

Verbs

- Use the correct forms of irregular verbs such as *has broken* [not *has broke*]. (See opposite.)

- Use helping verbs where required, as in *she has been* [not *she been*]. (See opposite.)

- Use consistent verb tense, as in *While she was jogging, she tripped* [not *trips*]. (See p. 99.)

- Make verbs agree with their subjects, as in *The list of items is* [not *are*] *long*. (See p. 105.)

Pronouns

- Make pronouns agree with the words they refer to, as in *Each of the women had her* [not *their*] *say*. (See p. 112.)

- Make pronouns refer clearly to the words they substitute for, avoiding uncertainties such as *Jill thanked Tracy when she* [Jill or Tracy?] *arrived*. (See p. 115.)

- Use pronouns consistently, avoiding shifts such as *When one enters college, you encounter new ideas*. (See p. 117.)

Modifiers

- Place modifiers close to the words they describe, as in *Trash cans without lids invite animals* [not *Trash cans invite animals without lids*]. (See p. 124.)

- Make each modifier clearly modify another word in the sentence, as in *Jogging, she pulled a muscle* [not *Jogging, a muscle was pulled*]. (See p. 125.)

Sentence faults

- Make every sentence complete, with its own subject and verb: *But first she called the police.* [Not *But first called the police.*] *New stores open weekly.* [Not *New stores weekly.*] (See p. 127.)

- A freestanding subordinate clause is not a complete sentence: *Jamal stayed home because he was sick.* [Not *Jamal stayed home. Because he was sick.*] (See p. 128.)

- Within sentences, link main clauses correctly. (See pp. 130–32.)

  Use a comma and a coordinating conjunction: *Cars jam the roads, and they add to smog.*

  Use a semicolon: *Many students attended the rally; the room was packed.*

  Use a semicolon and a transitional expression: *The snow fell heavily; however, it melted quickly.*

VERBS

17 Verb Forms

Verb forms may give you trouble when the verb is irregular, when you omit certain endings, or when you need to use helping verbs.

17a Sing/sang/sung and other irregular verbs

Most verbs are regular: their past-tense form° and past participle° end in -d or -ed:

> Today the birds migrate. [Plain form° of verb.]
> Yesterday the birds migrated. [Past-tense form.]
> In the past the birds have migrated. [Past participle.]

About two hundred **irregular verbs** in English create their past-tense form and past participle in some way other than adding -d or -ed.

> Today the birds fly. They begin migration. [Plain form.]
> Yesterday the birds flew. They began migration. [Past-tense form.]
> In the past the birds have flown. They have begun migration. [Past participle.]

You can find a verb's forms by looking up the plain form in a dictionary. For a regular verb, the dictionary will give the -d or -ed form. For an irregular verb, the dictionary will give the past-tense form and then the past participle. If the dictionary gives only one irregular form after the plain form, then the past-tense form and past participle are the same (*think, thought, thought*).

17b Helping verbs

Helping verbs combine with some verb forms to indicate time and other kinds of meaning, as in *can run, might suppose, will open, was sleeping, had been eaten.* The main verb° in these phrases is the one that carries the main meaning (*run, suppose, open, sleeping, eaten*).

Required helping verbs

Standard American English requires helping verbs in the situations listed on the next page.

■ **The main verb ends in -ing:**

Archaeologists <u>are</u> conducting fieldwork all over the world. [Not *Archaeologists conducting*....]

■ **The main verb is *been* or *be*:**

Many <u>have</u> been fortunate in their discoveries. [Not *Many been*....]
Some <u>could</u> be real-life Indiana Joneses. [Not *Some be*....]

■ **The main verb is a past participle,°** such as *given, talked, begun,* or *thrown*:

The researchers <u>have</u> given interviews on radio and TV. [Not *The researchers given*....]

In these examples, omitting the helping verb would create an incomplete sentence, or **sentence fragment** (p. 127).

Combinations of helping and main verbs ESL

Helping verbs and main verbs combine in specific ways.

Note The main verb in a verb phrase (the one carrying the main meaning) does not change to show a change in subject or time: *she has <u>sung</u>, you had <u>sung</u>.* Only the helping verb may change, as in these examples.

Form of *be* + present participle

Create the progressive tenses° with *be, am, is, are, was, were,* or *been* followed by the main verb's present participle° (ending in *-ing*).

Faulty   She <u>is work</u> on a new book.
Revised She <u>is working</u> on a new book.

Faulty   She <u>has been work</u> on it for several months.
Revised She <u>has been working</u> on it for several months.

Note Verbs that express mental states or activities rather than physical actions do not usually appear in the progressive tenses. These verbs include *adore, appear, believe, belong, have, hear, know, like, love, need, see, taste, think, understand,* and *want.*

Faulty   She <u>is wanting</u> to understand contemporary ethics.
Revised She <u>wants</u> to understand contemporary ethics.

Form of *be* + past participle

Create the passive voice° with *be, am, is, are, was, were, being,* or *been* followed by the main verb's past participle° (usually ending in *-d* or *-ed* or, for irregular verbs, in *-t* or *-n*).

°Defined in "Grammar Terms," page 340.

Faulty   Her last book <u>was complete</u> in four months.
Revised   Her last book <u>was completed</u> in four months.

Faulty   It <u>was bring</u> to the President's attention.
Revised   It <u>was brought</u> to the President's attention.

Note Only transitive verbs° (verbs that take objects) may form the passive voice.

Faulty   A philosophy conference <u>was occurred</u> that week. [*Occur* is not a transitive verb.]
Revised   A philosophy conference <u>occurred</u> that week.

Form of *have* + past participle

To create one of the perfect tenses,° use the main verb's past participle preceded by a form of *have,* such as *has, had, have been,* or *will have had.*

Faulty   Some students <u>have complain</u> about the lab.
Revised   Some students <u>have complained</u> about the lab.

Faulty   Money <u>has</u> not <u>been spend</u> on the lab in years.
Revised   Money <u>has</u> not <u>been spent</u> on the lab in years.

Form of *do* + plain form

Always with the plain form° of the main verb, three forms of *do* serve as helping verbs: *do, does, did.*

Faulty   Safety concerns <u>do exists.</u>
Revised   Safety concerns <u>do exist.</u>

Faulty   Didn't the lab <u>closed</u> briefly last year?
Revised   Didn't the lab <u>close</u> briefly last year?

Modal + plain form

Most **modal** helping verbs combine with the plain form of the main verb to convey ability, possibility, necessity, and other meanings. The modals include *be able to, be supposed to, can, could, had better, have to, may, might, must, ought to, shall, should, used to, will,* and *would.*

Faulty   The lab equipment <u>may causes</u> injury.
Revised   The lab equipment <u>may cause</u> injury.

Faulty   The school <u>ought to replaced</u> it.
Revised   The school <u>ought to replace</u> it.

Note When a modal combines with another helping verb, the main verb generally changes from the plain form to a past participle:

°Defined in "Grammar Terms," page 340.

| Faulty | The equipment <u>could have fail</u>. |
| Revised | The equipment <u>could have failed</u>. |

17c Verb + gerund or infinitive ESL

A **gerund** is the *-ing* form of a verb used as a noun (*Smoking kills*). An **infinitive** is the plain form° of the verb plus *to* (*Try <u>to quit</u>*). Gerunds and infinitives may follow certain verbs but not others. And sometimes the use of a gerund or an infinitive with the same verb changes the meaning of the verb.

Either gerund or infinitive

A gerund or an infinitive may follow certain verbs with no significant difference in meaning: *begin, can't bear, can't stand, continue, hate, hesitate, like, love, prefer, start.*

The pump began <u>working</u>. The pump began <u>to work</u>.

Meaning change with gerund or infinitive

A gerund and an infinitive have quite different meanings when they follow four verbs: *forget, remember, stop,* and *try.*

The engineer stopped <u>watching</u> the pump. [She no longer watched.]
The engineer stopped <u>to watch</u> the pump. [She stopped in order to watch.]

Gerund, not infinitive

Do not use an infinitive after these verbs: *admit, adore, appreciate, avoid, consider, deny, detest, discuss, dislike, enjoy, escape, finish, imagine, keep, mind, miss, practice, put off, quit, recall, resent, resist, risk, suggest, tolerate, understand.*

| Faulty | She suggested <u>to check</u> the pump. |
| Revised | She suggested <u>checking</u> the pump. |

Infinitive, not gerund

Do not use a gerund after these verbs: *agree, ask, assent, beg, claim, decide, expect, have, hope, manage, mean, offer, plan, pretend, promise, refuse, say, wait, want, wish.*

| Faulty | She decided <u>checking</u> the pump. |
| Revised | She decided <u>to check</u> the pump |

Noun or pronoun + infinitive

Some verbs may be followed by an infinitive alone or by a noun° or pronoun° and an infinitive: *ask, beg, choose, dare, expect, help,*

°Defined in "Grammar Terms," page 340.

need, promise, want, wish, would like. A noun or pronoun changes the meaning.

> The man expected to wait.
> He expected his friends to wait.

Some verbs *must* be followed by a noun or pronoun before an infinitive: *advise, allow, cause, challenge, command, convince, encourage, forbid, force, hire, instruct, order, permit, persuade, remind, require, teach, tell, warn.*

> He told his friends to wait.

Do not use *to* before the infinitive when it comes after one of the following verbs and a noun or pronoun: *feel, have, hear, let, make* ("force"), *see, watch.*

> He watched his friends leave without him.

17d Verb + particle ESL

Some verbs consist of two words: the verb itself and a **particle**, another word that changes the meaning of the verb, as in *Look up the answer* (research the answer) or *Look over the answer* (check the answer). Many of these two-word verbs, also called idioms, are defined in dictionaries. (For more on idioms, see p. 89.)

Some two-word verbs may be separated in a sentence; others may not.

Inseparable two-word verbs

Verbs and particles that may not be separated by any other words include the following: *catch on, get along, give in, go out, grow up, keep on, look into, run into, run out of, speak up, stay away, take care of.*

> Faulty   Children grow quickly up.
> Revised Children grow up quickly.

Separable two-word verbs

Most two-word verbs that take direct objects° may be separated by the object.

> Parents help out their children.
> Parents help their children out.

If the direct object is a pronoun,° the pronoun *must* separate the verb from the particle.

°Defined in "Grammar Terms," page 340.

Faulty   Parents <u>help out</u> them.
Revised Parents <u>help</u> them <u>out</u>.

The separable two-word verbs include the following: *call off, call up, fill out, fill up, give away, give back, hand in, help out, look over, look up, pick up, point out, put away, put back, put off, take out, take over, try on, try out, turn down.*

Exercise **Verb forms**

Supply a correct form for each verb and helping verb in brackets. If you are unsure of a verb's forms, consult a print or online dictionary. Answers to sentences 1–7 appear at the end of the book.

Example:

For three seasons, Sam [have] [lead] her team to the championship game.
For three seasons, Sam <u>has led</u> her team to the championship game.

1 In less than a decade, the world population [have] [grow] by two-thirds of a billion people. 2 Recently it [break] the 7.4 billion mark. 3 Population experts [have] [paint] pictures of a crowded future, predicting that the world population [may] [hit] 9.6 billion by the year 2050. 4 The supply of food, clean water, and land [be] of particular concern. 5 Even though the food supply [rise] in the last decade, the share to each person [fall]. 6 At the same time the water supply [sink] in size and quantity. 7 Changes in land use [run] nomads and subsistence farmers off their fields, while the overall number of species on the earth [shrink] by 20%.

8 Yet not all the news [be] bad. 9 Some countries [be] [begin] to explore how technology [can] [help] the earth and all its populations. 10 Population control [have] [find] adherents all over the world. 11 Crop management [have] [take] some pressure off lands with poor soil, allowing their owners to produce food, while genetic engineering [promise] to replenish food supplies that [have] [decline]. 12 Some new techniques for waste processing [have] [prove] effective. 13 Land conservation programs [be] [give] endangered species room to reproduce and thrive.

18 Verb Tenses

The **tense** of a verb expresses the time its action occurred. Definitions and examples of the verb tenses appear on pages 349–50. The following are the most common trouble spots.

18a Uses of the present tense (*sing*)

The present tense has several distinctive uses:

Action occurring now
We define the problem differently.

Habitual or recurring action
Banks regularly undergo audits.

A general truth
The earth is round.

Discussion of literature, film, and so on
Huckleberry Finn has adventures we all envy.

Future time
Funding ends in less than a year.

18b Uses of the perfect tenses (*have/had/will have sung*)

18c

The perfect tenses° generally indicate an action completed before another specific time or action. The present perfect tense° also indicates action begun in the past and continued into the present.

present perfect
The dancer has performed here only once.

past perfect
The dancer had trained in Asia before his performance here ten years ago.

future perfect
He will have danced here again by the end of the year.

18c Consistency in tense

Within a sentence, the tenses of verbs and verb forms need not be identical as long as they reflect actual changes in time: *Ramon will graduate from college twenty years after his father arrived in America.* In speech we often shift tenses even when they don't reflect changes in time. But in writing, such needless shifts in tense will confuse or distract readers.

Inconsistent tense	Immediately after Booth shot Lincoln, Major Rathbone threw himself upon the assassin. But Booth pulls a knife and plunges it into the major's arm.
Revised	Immediately after Booth shot Lincoln, Major Rathbone threw himself upon the assassin. But Booth pulled a knife and plunged it into the major's arm.

°Defined in "Grammar Terms," page 340.

18d Sequence of tenses

When the tenses in a sentence are in **sequence**, the verbs in the main clause° and the subordinate clause° relate appropriately for meaning. Problems with tense sequence often occur with the past tense and past perfect tense.°

Faulty   When researchers tried *(past)* to review the study, many of the original participants died *(past)*.

Revised   When researchers tried *(past)* to review the study, many of the original participants had died *(past perfect)*. [The deaths had occurred before the review.]

Faulty   Because other participants refused *(past)* interviews, the review had been terminated *(past perfect)*.

Revised   Because other participants refused *(past)* interviews, the review was terminated *(past)*. [The refusal occurred before the termination.]

Other tense-sequence problems occur with the distinctive verb forms of **conditional sentences**, in which a subordinate clause begins with *if, when,* or *unless* and the main clause states the result.

Faulty   If voters have *(present)* more confidence, they would vote *(would + verb)* more often.

Revised   If voters had *(past)* more confidence, they would vote *(would + verb)* more often.

See the next page for more on conditional sentences.

Exercise   Verb tenses

In the following paragraph, change the tenses of the verbs as needed to maintain consistent past tense and to correct tense sequence. If a sentence is correct as given, mark the number preceding it. Answers to sentences 1–3 appear at the end of the book.

Example:

Jehan was the first to learn that her team makes the playoffs.
Jehan was the first to learn that her team made the playoffs.

1 The 1960 presidential race between Richard M. Nixon and John F. Kennedy was the first to feature a televised debate. 2 Despite his extensive political experience, Nixon perspires heavily and looks haggard and uneasy in front of the camera. 3 By contrast, Kennedy was

projecting cool poise and providing crisp answers that make him seem fit for the office of President. 4 Some commentators grasped that night that election campaigns have changed forever, with TV playing a major role. 5 The public responded positively to Kennedy's image. 6 His poll ratings shoot up, while Nixon's take a corresponding drop. 7 In the end the popular vote was close, but Kennedy wins the election and the image war.

19 Verb Mood

The **mood** of a verb indicates whether a sentence is a statement or a question (*The theater needs help. Can you help the theater?*), a command (*Help the theater*), or a suggestion, desire, or other nonfactual expression (*I wish I were an actor*).

19a Subjunctive mood: *I wish I were*

The **subjunctive mood** expresses a suggestion, request, or requirement, or it states a condition that is contrary to fact (that is, imaginary or hypothetical).

- **A suggestion, request, or requirement often includes a verb such as** *ask, insist, urge, require, recommend, or suggest*. After the verb, a subordinate clause° beginning with *that* contains the substance of the request or requirement. For all subjects, the verb in the *that* clause is the plain form°:

  plain form
  Rules require that every donation <u>be</u> mailed.

- **A contrary-to-fact clause states an imaginary or hypothetical condition and usually follows** *wish* **or starts with** *if* **or** *unless*. For a present contrary-to-fact clause, use the verb's past-tense form° (for *be*, use the past-tense form *were* for all subjects):

  past
  I wish I <u>were</u> able to donate money to the theater.

  past   past
  If the theater <u>were</u> in better shape and <u>had</u> more money, its future would be assured.

°Defined in "Grammar Terms," page 340.

For a past contrary-to-fact clause, use *had* plus the verb's past participle°:

had + past participle
The theater would be better funded if it <u>had been</u> better managed last year.

Note Do not use *would* or *could* in a contrary-to-fact clause beginning with *if*:

| Not | Many people would have helped if they <u>would have</u> known. |
| But | Many people would have helped if they <u>had</u> known. |

19b Consistency in mood

Shifts in mood within a sentence or among related sentences can be confusing. Such shifts occur most frequently in directions.

| Inconsistent mood | Dissolve the crystals in the liquid. Then <u>you should heat</u> the solution to 120°C. [The first sentence is a command, the second a statement.] |
| Revised | Dissolve the crystals in the liquid. Then <u>heat</u> the solution to 120°C. [Consistent commands.] |

19b

Exercise   Verb mood

Revise the following paragraph with appropriate subjunctive verb forms. If a sentence is correct as given, mark the number preceding it. Answers to sentences 1 and 2 appear at the end of the book.

Example:
The parents insist that their child is tutored.
The parents insist that their child <u>be</u> tutored.

1 If John Hawkins would have known of all the dangerous side effects of smoking tobacco, would he have introduced the plant to England in 1565? 2 In promoting tobacco, Hawkins noted that if a Florida Indian man was to travel for several days, he would have smoked tobacco to satisfy his hunger and thirst. 3 Early tobacco growers in the United States feared that their product would not gain acceptance unless it was perceived as healthful, so they spread Hawkins's story. 4 But local governments, more concerned about public safety and morality than health, passed laws requiring that colonists smoked tobacco only if they were five miles from any town. 5 To prevent decadence, in 1647 Connecticut passed a law mandating that one's smoking of tobacco was limited to once a day in one's own home.

°Defined in "Grammar Terms," page 340.

20 Verb Voice

The **voice** of a verb tells whether the subject° of the sentence performs the action (**active voice**) or is acted upon (**passive voice**).

Active voice She wrote the book. [The subject *performs* the action.]

Passive voice The book was written by her. [The subject *receives* the action.]

20a Active voice

The active voice always names the actor in a sentence. It is usually clearer, more concise, and more forthright than the passive voice.

Weak passive The library is used by both students and teachers for studying and research, and the plan to expand it has been praised by many.

Strong active Both students and teachers use the library for studying and research, and many have praised the plan to expand it.

20b Passive voice

The passive voice places emphasis on the action, not the actor.

Actor unknown or unimportant

The passive voice is useful when the actor is not known and when the actor is not important or is less important than the object of the action.

The Internet was established in 1969 by the Department of Defense. The network has been extended both nationally and internationally. [In the first sentence the writer wishes to stress the Internet. In the second sentence the actor is unknown or too complicated to name.]

After the solution had been cooled to 10°C, the acid was added. [The person who cooled and added, perhaps the writer, is less important than the actions. Passive sentences are common in scientific writing.]

Actor in background

The passive voice can be useful when naming the actor is undesirable. Particularly in sensitive correspondence, this use of the passive can avoid offending readers because a specific actor is not named.

The residents of the shelter were turned away from your coffee shop.

°Defined in "Grammar Terms," page 340.

20c Consistency in voice

A shift in voice (and subject) within or between sentences can be awkward or even confusing.

Inconsistent subject and voice	Blogs cover an enormous range of topics. Opportunities for people to discuss their interests are provided on these sites.
Revised	Blogs cover an enormous range of topics and provide opportunities for people to discuss their interests.

Exercise Verb voice

In the following paragraph, rewrite passive sentences into the active voice, adding new sentence subjects as needed. Possible answers to sentences 1–5 appear at the end of the book.

Example:
Following the interview, the candidate was offered the job.
Following the interview, the company offered the candidate the job.

1 Water quality is determined by many factors. 2 Suspended and dissolved substances are contained in all natural waters. 3 The amounts of the substances are controlled by the environment. 4 Some dissolved substances are produced by pesticides. 5 Other substances, such as sediment, are deposited in water by fields, livestock feedlots, and other sources. 6 The bottom life of streams and lakes is affected by sediment. 7 Light penetration is reduced by sediment, and bottom-dwelling organisms may be smothered. 8 The quality of water in city systems is measured frequently. 9 Some contaminants can be removed by treatment plants. 10 If the legal levels are exceeded by pollutants, the citizens must be notified by city officials.

21 Agreement of Subject and Verb

A subject° and its verb° should agree in number°—singular with singular, plural with plural.

Many Japanese Americans live in Hawaii and California.
    subject   verb

Daniel Inouye was the first Japanese American in Congress.
  subject   verb

°Defined in "Grammar Terms," page 340.

21a -s ending for noun *or* verb, but not both

An *-s* or *-es* ending does opposite things to nouns and verbs: it usually makes a noun *plural*, but it always makes a present-tense verb *singular*. Thus if the subject noun is plural, it will probably end in *-s* or *-es* and the verb will not. If the subject is singular, it will not end in *-s* and the verb will.

Singular noun	Plural noun
The boy plays.	The boys play.
The bird soars.	The birds soar.
The street is busy.	The streets are busy.
The town has a school.	The towns have a school.
The bus does not [or doesn't] run.	The buses do not [or don't] run.

ESL Most noncount nouns—those that do not form plurals—take singular verbs: *That information is helpful.* (See pp. 122–23 for more on noncount nouns.)

21b Words between subject and verb

The survival of hibernating frogs in freezing temperatures is [not are] fascinating.

A chemical reaction inside the cells of the frogs stops [not stop] the formation of ice crystals.

Phrases beginning with *as well as, together with, along with,* and *in addition to* do not change the number of the subject.

The president, together with the deans, has [not have] agreed to improve the computer labs.

21c Subjects with *and*

Frost and Roethke were American poets who died in the same year.

Note When *each* or *every* precedes the compound subject, the verb is usually singular:

Each man, woman, and child has a right to be heard.

21d Subjects with *or* or *nor*

When parts of a subject are joined by *or* or *nor,* the verb agrees with the nearer part.

Either the painter or the carpenter knows the cost.

The cabinets or the bookcases are too costly.

When one part of the subject is singular and the other is plural, the sentence will be awkward unless you put the plural part second.

Awkward   Neither the owners nor the builder agrees.

Improved   Neither the builder nor the owners agree.

21e   *Everyone* and other indefinite pronouns

Indefinite pronouns do not refer to specific persons or things. They include *anybody, anyone, each, everybody, everyone, neither, no one, one,* and *somebody.* Most are singular in meaning and take singular verbs.

Something smells.   Neither is right.

Four indefinite pronouns are always plural in meaning: *both, few, many, several.*

Both are correct.   Several were invited.

Six indefinite pronouns may be either singular or plural in meaning: *all, any, more, most, none, some.* The verb with one of these pronouns depends on what the pronoun refers to:

All of the money is reserved for emergencies.

All of the funds are reserved for emergencies.

21f   *Team* and other collective nouns

A **collective noun** such as *team* or *family* names a group of persons or things. A collective noun takes a singular verb when the group acts as a unit.

The team has won five of the last six meets.

But when the group's members act separately, use a plural verb.

The old team have gone to various colleges.

If such a sentence seems awkward, reword it: *The members of the old team have gone to various colleges.*

21g *Who, which,* and *that*

When used as subjects, *who, which,* and *that* refer to another word in the sentence. The verb agrees with this other word.

Mayor Garber ought to listen to the people who work for her.

Bardini is the only aide who has her ear.

Bardini is one of the aides who work unpaid. [Of the aides who work un-paid, Bardini is one.]

Bardini is the only one of the aides who knows the community. [Of the aides, only one, Bardini, knows the community.]

21h *News* and other singular nouns ending in *-s*

Singular nouns° ending in *-s* include *athletics, economics, mathematics, measles, mumps, news, physics, politics,* and *statistics.* They take singular verbs.

After so long a wait, the news has to be good.

Statistics is required of psychology majors.

Politics requires compromise.

These words take plural verbs when they describe individual items rather than bodies of activity or knowledge.

The statistics prove him wrong.
The mayor's politics make compromise difficult.

21i Verb preceding subject

Is voting a right or a privilege?

Are a right and a privilege the same thing?

There are differences between them.

Here are some possible solutions.

21j *Is, are,* and other linking verbs

Make a linking verb° such as *is* or *are* agree with its subject, usually the first element in the sentence, not with other words referring to the subject.

°Defined in "Grammar Terms," page 340.

The child's sole support is her court-appointed guardians.

Her court-appointed guardians are the child's sole support.

Exercise   Agreement of subject and verb

Rewrite the following paragraphs to change the underlined words from plural to singular. (You will sometimes need to add *a* or *the* for the singular, as in the example.) Then change verbs as necessary so that they agree with their new subjects. Answers to sentences 1–6 appear at the end of the book.

Example:
Siberian tigers are an endangered subspecies.
The Siberian tiger is an endangered subspecies.

1 Siberian tigers are the largest living cats in the world, much bigger than their relative the Bengal tiger. 2 They grow to a length of nine to twelve feet, including their tails, and to a height of about three and a half feet. 3 They can weigh over six hundred pounds. 4 These carnivorous hunters live in northern China and Korea as well as in Siberia. 5 During the long winter of this Arctic climate, the yellowish striped coats get a little lighter in order to blend with the snow-covered landscape. 6 The coats also grow quite thick because the tigers have to withstand temperatures as low as −50°F.

7 Siberian tigers sometimes have to travel great distances to find food. 8 They need about twenty pounds of food a day because of their size and the cold climate, but when they have fresh food they may eat as much as a hundred pounds at one time. 9 They hunt mainly deer, boars, and even bears, plus smaller prey such as fish and rabbits. 10 They pounce on their prey and grab them by the back of the neck. 11 Animals that are not killed immediately are thrown to the ground and suffocated with a bite to the throat. 12 Then the tigers feast.

21j

PRONOUNS

22 Pronoun Forms

A noun° or pronoun° changes form to show the reader how it functions in a sentence. These forms—called cases—are **subjective** (such as *I, she, they, man*), **objective** (such as *me, her, them, man*), and **possessive** (such as *my, her, their, man's*). A list of the case forms appears on pages 340–41.

22a Compound subjects and objects: *she and I* vs. *her and me*

Subjects° and objects° consisting of two or more nouns and pronouns have the same case forms as they would if one pronoun stood alone.

compound subject
She and Ming discussed the proposal.

compound object
The proposal disappointed her and him.

To test for the correct form, try one pronoun alone in the sentence. The case form that sounds correct is probably correct for all parts of the compound.

The prize went to [he, him] and [I, me].
The prize went to him. The prize went to me. [Objective.]
The prize went to him and me.

Note Avoid using the pronoun *myself* in place of the personal pronoun *I* or *me*: *Max and I* [not *myself*] *studied for the test. Everyone went except me* [not *myself*]. For more on the *-self* pronouns, see pages 335–36.

22b Subject complements: *it was she*

Both a subject and a subject complement° appear in the same form—the subjective case.

subject
complement
The one who cares most is she.

If this construction sounds stilted to you, use the more natural order: *She is the one who cares most.*

22c *Who* vs. *whom*

The choice between *who* and *whom* depends on the use of the word.

Questions

At the beginning of a question, use *who* for a subject and *whom* for an object.

subject ↘
object ↙
Who wrote the policy? Whom does it affect?

Test for the correct form by answering the question with the form of *he* or *she* that sounds correct. Then use the same form in the question.

[Who, Whom] does one ask?
One asks her. [Objective.]
Whom does one ask?

Subordinate clauses

A subordinate clause contains a subject and a predicate but begins with a subordinating word. In a subordinate clause, use *who* or *whoever* for a subject, *whom* or *whomever* for an object.

subject ↘
Give old clothes to whoever needs them.

object ↙
I don't know whom the mayor appointed.

Test for the correct form by rewriting the subordinate clause as a sentence. Replace *who* or *whom* with the form of *he* or *she* that sounds correct. Then use the same form in the original subordinate clause.

Few people know [who, whom] they should ask.
They should ask her. [Objective.]
Few people know whom they should ask.

Note Don't let expressions such as *I think* and *she says* confuse you when they come between the subject *who* and its verb.

subject ↘
He is the one who I think is best qualified.

22d Other constructions

We or *us* with a noun

The choice of *we* or *us* before a noun depends on the use of the noun.

object of
preposition ↘
Freezing weather is welcomed by us skaters.

subject ↘
We skaters welcome freezing weather.

Pronoun in an appositive

An **appositive** is a word or word group that renames a noun or pronoun. Within an appositive the form of a pronoun depends on the function of the word the appositive renames.

object of verb
The class elected two representatives, DeShawn and me.

subject
Two representatives, DeShawn and I, were elected.

Pronoun after *than* or *as*

After *than* or *as* in a comparison, the form of a pronoun indicates what words may have been omitted. A subjective pronoun is the subject of the omitted verb:

subject
Some critics like Glass more than she [does].

An objective pronoun is the object of the omitted verb:

object
Some critics like Glass more than [they like] her.

22d

Subject and object of an infinitive

An **infinitive** is the plain form° of the verb plus *to* (*to swim*). Both its object and its subject are in the objective form, as shown in the following examples:

subject of
infinitive
The school asked him to speak.

object of
infinitive
Students chose to invite him.

Form before a gerund

A **gerund** is the *-ing* form of a verb used as a noun (*a runner's breathing*). Generally, use the possessive form of a pronoun or noun immediately before a gerund.

The coach disapproved of their lifting weights.

The coach's disapproving was a surprise.

Exercise   Pronoun forms

Revise all inappropriate case forms in the following paragraph. If a sentence is correct as given, mark the number preceding it. Answers to sentences 1–6 appear at the end of the book.

°Defined in "Grammar Terms," page 340.

Example:

"Between she and him," the interviewer said, "I think he is the better choice."

"Between her and him," the interviewer said, "I think he is the better choice."

1 Written four thousand years ago, *The Epic of Gilgamesh* tells the story of Gilgamesh and his friendship with Enkidu. 2 Gilgamesh was a bored king who his people thought was too harsh. 3 Then he met Enkidu, a wild man whom had lived with the animals in the mountains. 4 Immediately, him and Gilgamesh wrestled to see whom was more powerful. 5 After hours of struggle, Enkidu admitted that Gilgamesh was stronger than him. 6 Now the friends needed adventures worthy of them, the two strongest men on earth. 7 Gilgamesh said, "Between you and I, mighty deeds will be accomplished, and our fame will be everlasting." 8 Among their acts, Enkidu and him defeated a giant bull, Humbaba, cut down the bull's cedar forests, and brought back the logs to Gilgamesh's treeless land. 9 Their heroism won them great praise from the people. 10 When Enkidu died, Gilgamesh mourned his death, realizing that no one had been a better friend than him. 11 When Gilgamesh himself died many years later, his people raised a monument praising Enkidu and he for their friendship and their mighty deeds of courage.

23 Agreement of Pronoun and Antecedent

The word a pronoun refers to is its **antecedent**.

Successful students complete their homework.
antecedent   pronoun

For clarity, a pronoun should agree with its antecedent in person° (first, second, third), number° (singular, plural), and gender° (masculine, feminine, neuter).

23a Antecedents with *and*

The dean and my adviser have offered their help.

Note When *each* or *every* precedes the compound antecedent, the pronoun is singular.

°Defined in "Grammar Terms," page 340.

Every girl and woman took her seat.

23b Antecedents with *or* or *nor*

When parts of an antecedent are joined by *or* or *nor,* the pronoun agrees with the nearer part.

Tenants or owners must present their grievances.

Either the tenant or the owner will have her way.

When one subject is plural and the other singular, put the plural subject second to avoid awkwardness.

Neither the owner nor the tenants have made their case.

23c *Everyone, person,* and other indefinite words

Indefinite words do not refer to any specific person or thing. They include indefinite pronouns° (such as *anyone, everybody, everything, none, no one, somebody*) and generic nouns° (such as *person, individual, child, student*).

Most indefinite pronouns and all generic nouns are singular in meaning. When they serve as antecedents, they take singular nouns:

Each of the animal shelters has its population of homeless pets.
indefinite pronoun

Every worker in our shelter cares for his or her favorite animal.
generic noun

Four indefinite pronouns are plural in meaning: *both, few, many, several.* As antecedents, they take plural pronouns:

Many of the animals show affection for their caretakers.

Six indefinite pronouns may be singular or plural in meaning: *all, any, more, most, none, some.* As antecedents, they take singular pronouns if they refer to singular words, plural pronouns if they refer to plural words:

Most of the shelter's equipment was donated by its original owner. [*Most* refers to *equipment.*]

Most of the veterinarians donate their time. [*Most* refers to *veterinarians.*]

°Defined in "Grammar Terms," page 340.

None may be singular even when referring to a plural word, especially to emphasize the meaning "not one": *None* [*Not one*] *of the shelters has increased its capacity.*

Most agreement problems arise with the singular indefinite words. We often use these words to mean something like "many" or "all" rather than "one" and then refer to them with plural pronouns, as in *Everyone has their own locker* or *A person can padlock their locker.* Often, too, we mean indefinite words to include more than one gender and thus resort to *they* instead of the **generic *he***—the masculine pronoun referring to more than just males, as in *Everyone deserves his privacy.*

Although some experts accept *they, them,* and *their* with singular indefinite words, most do not, and many teachers and employers regard the plural as incorrect. To be safe, work for agreement between singular indefinite words and the pronouns that refer to them. You have several options:

- **Change the indefinite word to a plural, and use a plural pronoun to match.**

  Faulty   Each athlete is entitled to his own locker.

  Revised All athletes are entitled to their own lockers. [*Is* changes to *are,* and *locker* changes to *lockers.*]

- **Rewrite the sentence to omit the pronoun.**

  Revised Each athlete is entitled to a locker.

- **Use *he or she* (*him or her, his or her*) to refer to the indefinite word.**

  Revised Each athlete is entitled to his or her own locker.

He or she can be awkward, so avoid using it more than once in several sentences. Also avoid the combination *he/she,* which many readers do not accept.

23d *Team* and other collective nouns

A **collective noun** has singular form and names a group of persons or things: *army, audience, family, group, team.* Use a singular pronoun with a collective noun when referring to the group as a unit:

The committee voted to disband itself.

When referring to the individual members of the group, use a plural pronoun.

The old team have gone their separate ways.

23d

If the preceding sentence sounds awkward, you can reword it: *The members of the old team have gone their separate ways.*

Exercise   Agreement of pronoun and antecedent

Revise the following sentences so that pronouns and their antecedents agree in person and number. Try to avoid the generic *he* (see the previous page). If you change the subject of a sentence, be sure to change the verb as necessary for agreement. Mark the number preceding any sentence that is correct as given. Possible answers to sentences 1–4 appear at the end of the book.

Example:
Each child should have the opportunity pursue their interests.

Each child should have the opportunity to pursue his or her interests. *Or:* All children should have the opportunity to pursue their interests.

1 Despite their extensive research and experience, neither child psychologists nor parents have yet figured out how children become who they are. 2 Of course, the family has a tremendous influence on the development of a child in their midst. 3 Each member of the immediate family exerts their own unique pull on the child. 4 Other relatives, teachers, and friends can also affect the child's view of the world and of themselves. 5 The workings of genetics also strongly influence the child, but it may never be fully understood. 6 The psychology community cannot agree in its views of whether nurture or nature is more important in a child's development. 7 Another debated issue is whether the child's emotional development or their intellectual development is more central. 8 Just about everyone has their strong opinion on these issues, often backed up by evidence. 9 Neither the popular press nor scholarly journals devote much of their space to the wholeness of the child.

24   Reference of Pronoun to Antecedent

If a pronoun° does not refer clearly to the word it substitutes for (its **antecedent**), readers will have difficulty grasping the pronoun's meaning.

24a Single antecedent

When either of two nouns can be a pronoun's antecedent, the reference will not be clear.

°Defined in "Grammar Terms," page 340.

Confusing   Emily Dickinson is sometimes compared with Jane Austen, but she led a more reclusive life.

Revise such a sentence in one of two ways:

■ **Replace the pronoun with the appropriate noun.**

Clear   Emily Dickinson is sometimes compared with Jane Austen, but Dickinson led a more reclusive life.

■ **Avoid repetition by rewriting the sentence.** If you use the pronoun, make sure it has only one possible antecedent.

Clear   Despite occasional comparison of their lives, Emily Dickinson was more reclusive than Jane Austen.

Clear   Though sometimes compared with her, Emily Dickinson was more reclusive than Jane Austen.

24b Close antecedent

A clause° beginning *who, which,* or *that* should generally fall immediately after the word it refers to.

Confusing   Jody found a lamp in the attic that her aunt had used.

Clear   In the attic Jody found a lamp that her aunt had used.

24c Specific antecedent

A pronoun should refer to a specific noun° or other pronoun. Readers can only guess at the meaning of a pronoun when its antecedent is not stated outright.

Vague *this, that, which,* or *it*

This, that, which, or *it* should refer to a specific noun, not to a whole word group expressing an idea or situation.

Confusing   The British knew little of the American countryside, and they had no experience with the colonists' guerrilla tactics. This gave the colonists an advantage.

Clear   The British knew little of the American countryside, and they had no experience with the colonists' guerrilla tactics. This ignorance and inexperience gave the colonists an advantage.

°Defined in "Grammar Terms," page 340.

Implied nouns

A pronoun cannot refer clearly to a noun that is merely implied by some other word or phrase, such as *news* in *newspaper* or *happiness* in *happy*.

Confusing	In Cohen's report she made claims that led to a lawsuit.
Clear	In her report Cohen made claims that led to a lawsuit.
Confusing	Her reports on psychological development generally go unnoticed outside it.
Clear	Her reports on psychological development generally go unnoticed outside the field.

Indefinite *it, they,* or *you*

It and *they* should have definite antecedents.

Confusing	In the average television drama they present a false picture of life.
Clear	The average television drama presents a false picture of life.

You should clearly mean "you, the reader," and the context must support such a meaning.

Inappropriate	In the fourteenth century you had to struggle to survive.
Revised	In the fourteenth century one [or a person or people] had to struggle to survive.

24d Consistency in pronouns

Within a sentence or a group of related sentences, pronouns should be consistent. You may shift pronouns unconsciously when you start with *one* and soon find it too stiff.

Inconsistent pronouns	One will find when reading that your concentration improves with practice, so that you comprehend more in less time.
Revised	You will find when reading that your concentration improves with practice, so that you comprehend more in less time.

Inconsistent pronouns also occur when singular shifts to plural: *Everyone closed his or her* [not *their*] *book.* See pages 113–14.

24d

Exercise **Pronoun reference**

Revise the following paragraph as needed so that pronouns are consistent and refer to specific, appropriate antecedents. Possible answers to sentences 1–4 appear at the end of the book.

Example:

In Yellowstone National Park they have bison, pronghorn antelope, and bears.

<u>Bison, pronghorn antelope, and bears</u> <u>live</u> in Yellowstone National Park.

1 "Life begins at forty" is a cliché many people live by, and this may or may not be true. 2 Whether one agrees or not with the cliché, you can cite many examples of people whose public lives began at forty. 3 For instance, when she was forty, Pearl Buck's novel *The Good Earth* won the Pulitzer Prize. 4 Kenneth Kanuda, past president of Zambia, was elected to it in 1964, when he was forty. 5 Catherine I became Empress of Russia at age forty, more feared than loved by them. 6 Paul Revere at forty made his famous ride to warn American revolutionary leaders that the British were going to arrest them, which gave the colonists time to prepare for battle. 7 Forty-year-old Nancy Astor joined the British House of Commons in 1919 as its first female member, though they did not welcome her. 8 In 610 CE, Muhammad, age forty, began to have visions that became the foundation of the Muslim faith and still inspire millions of people to become one.

MODIFIERS

25 Adjectives and Adverbs

Adjectives modify nouns° (*good child*) and pronouns° (*special someone*). **Adverbs** modify verbs° (*see well*), adjectives (*very happy*), other adverbs (*not very*), and whole word groups (*Otherwise, the room was empty*). The only way to tell if a modifier should be an adjective or an adverb is to determine its function in the sentence.

°Defined in "Grammar Terms," page 340.

25a Adjective vs. adverb

Use only adverbs, not adjectives, to modify verbs, adverbs, or other adjectives.

Not They took each other serious. They related good.

But They took each other seriously. They related well.

25b Adjective with linking verb: *felt bad*

A **linking verb** such as *seem, become, feel, look,* and forms of *be* connects the subject and a word that describes the subject. If the word after a verb modifies the subject, the verb is linking and the word should be an adjective. If the word after the verb describes the verb, it should be an adverb.

Two word pairs are especially tricky. One is *bad* and *badly*:

The weather grew bad.
linking adjective
verb

She felt bad.
linking adjective
verb

Flowers grow badly in such soil.
verb adverb

The other word pair is *good* and *well. Good* serves only as an adjective. *Well* may serve as an adverb with a host of meanings or as an adjective meaning only "fit" or "healthy."

Decker trained well.
verb adverb

She felt well.
linking adjective
verb

Her health was good.
linking adjective
verb

25c Comparison of adjectives and adverbs

Comparison° allows adjectives and adverbs to show degrees of quality or amount by changing form: *red, redder, reddest; awful, more awful, most awful; quickly, less quickly, least quickly.* A dictionary will list the *-er* and *-est* endings if they can be used. Otherwise, use *more* and *most* or *less* and *least.*

Some modifiers are irregular, changing their spelling for comparison: for example, *good, better, best; many, more, most; badly, worse, worst.*

°Defined in "Grammar Terms," page 340.

Comparisons of two or more than two

Use the *-er* form, *more,* or *less* when comparing two items. Use the *-est* form, *most,* or *least* when comparing three or more items.

> Of the two tests, the litmus is <u>better</u>.
> Of all six tests, the litmus is <u>best</u>.

Double comparisons

A double comparison combines the *-er* or *-est* ending with the word *more* or *most.* It is redundant.

> Chang was the <u>wisest</u> [not <u>most wisest</u>] person in town.
> He was <u>smarter</u> [not <u>more smarter</u>] than anyone else.

Complete comparisons

A comparison should be complete.

- **The comparison should state a relation fully enough to ensure clarity.**

Unclear	Car makers worry about their industry more than environmentalists.
Clear	Car makers worry about their industry more than environmentalists <u>do</u>.
Clear	Car makers worry about their industry more than <u>they worry about</u> environmentalists.

- **The items being compared should in fact be comparable.**

Illogical	The cost of a hybrid car can be greater than a gasoline-powered car. [Illogically compares a cost and a car.]
Revised	The cost of a hybrid car can be greater than <u>the cost of</u> [or <u>that of</u>] a gasoline-powered car.

25d Double negatives

In a **double negative** two negative words cancel each other out. Some double negatives are intentional, as *She was <u>not unhappy</u>* indicates with understatement that she was indeed happy. But most double negatives say the opposite of what is intended: *Nadine did <u>not feel nothing</u>* asserts that Nadine felt other than nothing, or something.

Faulty	The IRS <u>cannot hardly</u> audit all tax returns. <u>None</u> of its audits <u>never</u> touch many cheaters.
Revised	The IRS <u>cannot</u> audit all tax returns. Its audits <u>never</u> touch many cheaters.

25e Present and past participles as adjectives ESL

Both present participles° and past participles° may serve as adjectives: *a burning house* (present), *a burned house* (past). As in the examples, the two participles usually differ in the time they indicate.

But some present and past participles—those derived from verbs expressing feeling—can have altogether different meanings. The present participle refers to something that causes the feeling: *That was a frightening storm.* The past participle refers to something that experiences the feeling: *They quieted the frightened horses.* Similar pairs include the following:

annoying/annoyed	pleasing/pleased
boring/bored	satisfying/satisfied
confusing/confused	surprising/surprised
exciting/excited	tiring/tired
exhausting/exhausted	troubling/troubled
interesting/interested	worrying/worried

25f Articles: *a, an, the* ESL

Articles° usually trouble native English speakers only in the choice of *a* versus *an*: *a* for words beginning with consonant sounds (*a bridge*), *an* for words beginning with vowel sounds, including a silent *h* (*an apple, an hour*).

For nonnative speakers, *a, an,* and *the* can be difficult because many other languages use such words quite differently or not at all. In English, their uses depend on their context and the kinds of nouns they precede.

Singular count nouns

A **count noun** names something countable and can form a plural: *glass/glasses, mountain/mountains, woman/women, child/children.*

- *A* or *an* precedes a singular count noun when your reader does not already know its identity, usually because you have not mentioned it before.

  A scientist in our chemistry department developed a process to strengthen metals. [*Scientist* and *process* are being introduced for the first time.]

- *The* precedes a singular count noun that has a specific identity for your reader, usually because (1) you have mentioned it before, (2) you identify it immediately before or after you state it, (3) it is

°Defined in "Grammar Terms," page 340.

unique (the only one in existence), or (4) it refers to an institution or facility that is shared by the community.

A scientist in our chemistry department developed a process to strengthen metals. The scientist patented the process. [*Scientist* and *process* were identified before.]

The most productive laboratory is the research center in the chemistry department. [*Most productive* identifies *laboratory*. *In the chemistry department* identifies *research center*. And *chemistry department* is a shared facility.]

The sun rises in the east. [*Sun* and *east* are unique.]

Many men and women aspire to the presidency. [*Presidency* is a shared institution.]

Plural count nouns

A or *an* never precedes a plural noun. *The* does not precede a plural noun that names a general category. *The* does precede a plural noun that names specific representatives of a category.

Men and women are different. [*Men* and *women* name general categories.]
The women joined a team. [*Women* refers to specific people.]

Noncount nouns

A **noncount noun** names something that is not usually considered countable in English, and so it does not form a plural. Examples include the following:

Abstractions: confidence, democracy, education, equality, evidence, health, information, intelligence, knowledge, luxury, peace, pollution, research, success, supervision, truth, wealth, work

Emotions: anger, courage, happiness, hate, love, respect, satisfaction

Food and drink: bread, flour, meat, milk, salt, water, wine

Natural events and substances: air, blood, dirt, gasoline, gold, hair, heat, ice, oil, oxygen, rain, smoke, wood

Groups: clergy, clothing, equipment, furniture, garbage, jewelry, junk, legislation, mail, military, money, police

Fields of study: architecture, accounting, biology, business, chemistry, engineering, literature, management, psychology, science

A or *an* never precedes a noncount noun. *The* does precede a noncount noun that names specific representatives of a general category.

25f

Vegetation suffers from drought. [*Vegetation* names a general category.]

The vegetation in the park withered or died. [*Vegetation* refers to specific plants.]

Note Many nouns are sometimes count nouns and sometimes noncount nouns.

The library has a room for readers. [*Room* is a count noun meaning "walled area."]

The library has room for reading. [*Room* is a noncount noun meaning "space."]

Proper nouns

A **proper noun** names a particular person, place, or thing and begins with a capital letter: *February, Joe Allen. A* or *an* never precedes a proper noun. *The* does occasionally, as with oceans (*the Pacific*), regions (*the Middle East*), rivers (*the Snake*), some countries (*the United States*), and some universities (*the University of Texas*).

Sarah Garcia lives in Boulder and attends the University of Colorado.

25f

Exercise   **Adjectives and adverbs**

Revise the following paragraph to correct errors in the use of adjectives and adverbs. Answers to sentences 1–5 appear at the end of the book.

Example:
Google Maps can warn about traffic moving slow.
Google Maps can warn about traffic moving slowly.

1 Americans often argue about which professional sport is better: basketball, football, or baseball. 2 Basketball fans contend that their sport offers more action because the players are constant running and shooting. 3 Because it is played indoors in relative small arenas, basketball allows fans to be more closer to the action than the other sports. 4 Football fanatics say they don't hardly stop yelling once the game begins. 5 They cheer when their team executes a complicated play good. 6 They roar more louder when the defense stops the opponents. 7 They yell loudest when a receiver catches a pass for a touchdown. 8 In contrast, the supporters of baseball believe that it is the better sport. 9 It combines the one-on-one duel of pitcher and batter struggling valiant with the tight teamwork of double and triple plays. 10 Because the game is played slow and careful, fans can analyze and discuss the manager's strategy.

26 Misplaced and Dangling Modifiers

For clarity, modifiers generally must fall close to the words they modify.

26a Misplaced modifiers

A **misplaced modifier** falls in the wrong place in a sentence. It may be awkward, confusing, or even unintentionally funny.

Clear placement

Confusing   He served steak to the men on paper plates.

Revised   He served the men steak on paper plates.

Confusing   Many dogs are killed by autos and trucks roaming unleashed.

Revised   Many dogs roaming unleashed are killed by autos and trucks.

Only and other limiting modifiers

Limiting modifiers include *almost, even, exactly, hardly, just, merely, nearly, only, scarcely,* and *simply*. They should fall immediately before the word or word group they modify.

Unclear   They only saw each other during meals.

Revised   They saw only each other during meals.

Revised   They saw each other only during meals.

Adverb with sentence elements

Adverbs modify verbs, adjectives, other adverbs, and whole word groups. They can often move around in sentences, but some will be awkward if they interrupt certain sentence elements.

- **A long adverb stops the flow from subject° to verb°:**

                subject   adverb   verb
Awkward   The city, after the hurricane, began massive rebuilding.

                adverb   subject   verb
Revised   After the hurricane, the city began massive rebuilding.

°Defined in "Grammar Terms," page 340.

- A *split infinitive*—an adverb placed between *to* and the verb—annoys many readers:

Awkward   The weather service expected temperatures to not rise.

Revised   The weather service expected temperatures not to rise.

A split infinitive may sometimes be natural and preferable, though it may still bother some readers:

Several US industries expect to more than triple their use of robots.

Order of adjectives ESL

Adjectives modify nouns and pronouns. English follows distinctive rules for arranging two or three adjectives before a noun. (A string of more than three adjectives before a noun is rare.)

Determiner	Opinion	Size or shape	Color	Origin	Material	Noun used as adjective	Noun
many						state	laws
	lovely		green	Thai			birds
a		square			wooden		table
all						business	reports
the			blue		litmus		paper

26b Dangling modifiers

A **dangling modifier** does not sensibly modify anything in its sentence.

Dangling   Passing the building, the vandalism became visible.

Like most dangling modifiers, this one introduces a sentence, contains a verb form (*passing*), and implies but does not name a subject (whoever is passing). Readers assume that this implied subject is the same as the subject of the sentence (*vandalism*). When it is not, the modifier "dangles," unconnected to the rest of the sentence.

Revise dangling modifiers to achieve the emphasis you want.

- **Rewrite the dangling modifier as a complete clause with its own stated subject and verb.** Readers can accept different subjects when they are both stated.

Dangling   Passing the building, the vandalism became visible. ⑦

Revised   As we passed the building, the vandalism became visible.

■ **Change the subject of the sentence to a word the modifier properly describes.**

Dangling   Trying to understand the causes, vandalism has been extensively studied. ⑦

Revised   Trying to understand the causes, researchers have extensively studied vandalism.

Exercise   Misplaced and dangling modifiers

Revise the following paragraph to eliminate any misplaced or dangling modifiers. Possible answers to sentences 1–4 appear at the end of the book.

26b

Example:

Driving north, the vegetation became more sparse.

Driving north, we noticed that the vegetation became more sparse. *Or:* As we drove north, the vegetation became more sparse.

1 In the Central American rain forests, the tungara frogs as evening falls begin their croaking chorus. 2 Male tungara frogs sing "songs" to attract female frogs croaking loudly at night. 3 Hearing the croaking, gatherings of predators such as bullfrogs and bats feast on the frogs. 4 The frogs hope to only mate, but their nightly chorus can result in death instead. 5 The frogs, to save themselves from the attacks of predators, have two responses. 6 First, apparently believing in safety in numbers, the croaking rarely occurs alone for any length of time. 7 Second, the frogs silence several nights a week their group croaking. 8 This silence even though it is only periodic reduces the frogs' chance of eaten by predators. 9 By not croaking alone and not croaking at all on some nights, the frogs' behavior prevents the species from "croaking."

SENTENCE FAULTS

27 Sentence Fragments

A **sentence fragment** is a part of a sentence that is set off as if it were a complete sentence by an initial capital letter and a final period or other punctuation:

Sentence fragment	James studied all weekend. <u>Because he wanted an A on the history exam.</u>
Revised	James studied all weekend <u>because</u> he wanted an A on the history exam.

Although writers occasionally use fragments deliberately and effectively, readers perceive most fragments as serious errors.

ESL Some languages other than English allow the omission of the subject° or the verb.° Except in commands (*Close the door*), English always requires you to state the subject and verb.

27a Tests for fragments

A word group punctuated as a sentence requires two elements: a subject (naming who or what performs the action) and a predicate verb (asserting something about the subject). In addition, the word group cannot be a subordinate clause (beginning with a subordinating word such as *because* or *who*). A complete sentence should pass *all three* of the following tests.

Test 1: Find the predicate verb.

Look for a verb that can serve as the predicate of a sentence. Some fragments lack any verb at all.

Fragment	Millions of sites on the Web.
Revised	Millions of sites <u>make up</u> the Web.

Other sentence fragments contain a verb form, but it is not a predicate verb. Instead, it is often the *-ing* or *to* form (*walking, to walk*):

Fragment	The Web <u>growing</u> with new sites and users every day.
Revised	The Web <u>grows</u> with new sites and users every day.

(See also pp. 93–94 on the use of helping verbs° to prevent sentence fragments.)

Test 2: Find the subject.

The subject of the sentence usually comes before the verb. If there is no subject, the word group is probably a fragment.

Fragment	The Web continues to grow. <u>And shows no sign of slowing down.</u>
Revised	The Web continues to grow. And <u>it</u> shows no sign of slowing down.

Note Commands, in which the subject *you* is understood, are not sentence fragments: [*You*] *Close the door.*

Test 3: Make sure the clause is not subordinate.

A **subordinate clause** begins with either a subordinating conjunction° (such as *because, if, when*) or a relative pronoun° (*who, which, that*). Subordinate clauses serve as parts of sentences, not as whole sentences.

Fragment	The Internet was greatly improved by Web technology. <u>Which allows users to move easily between sites.</u>
Revised	The Internet was greatly improved by Web technology, <u>which</u> allows users to move easily between sites. [The subordinate clause joins a main clause in a complete sentence.]
Revised	The Internet was greatly improved by Web technology. <u>It</u> allows users to move easily between sites. [Substituting *It* for *Which* makes the subordinate clause into a complete sentence.]

Note Questions beginning *who, whom,* or *which* are not sentence fragments: *Who rattled the cage?*

27b Revision of fragments

Correct sentence fragments in one of two ways, depending on the importance of the information in the fragment:

- **Rewrite the fragment as a complete sentence.** The information in the fragment will then have the same importance as that in other complete sentences.

Fragment	Public health improved with the widespread use of vaccines. <u>Which protected children against life-threatening diseases.</u>
Revised	Public health improved with the widespread use of vaccines. <u>They</u> protected children against life-threatening diseases.

°Defined in "Grammar Terms," page 340.

- **Attach the fragment to a main clause.**° The information in the fragment will then be subordinated to that in the main clause.

Fragment   The polio vaccine eradicated the disease from most of the globe. The first vaccine to be used widely.

Revised   The polio vaccine, the first to be used widely, eradicated the disease from most of the globe.

Exercise   Sentence fragments

Revise the following paragraphs to eliminate sentence fragments by combining them with main clauses or rewriting them as complete sentences. Possible answers to the starred items appear at the end of the book.

Example:

A competent and motivated leader. He or she is very important. As a component of any business's success.

A competent and motivated leader is a very important component of any business's success.

27b

*People generally avoid eating mushrooms except those they buy in stores. *But in fact many varieties of mushrooms are edible. *Mushrooms are members of a large group of vegetation called nonflowering plants. *Including algae, mosses, ferns, and coniferous trees. *Even the giant redwoods of California. *Most of the nonflowering plants prefer moist environments. *Such as forest floors, fallen timber, and still water. *Mushrooms, for example. *They prefer moist, shady soil. *Algae grow in water.

Most mushrooms, both edible and inedible, are members of a class called basidium fungi. A term referring to their method of reproduction. The basidia produce spores. Which can develop into mushrooms. This classification including the prized meadow mushroom, cultivated commercially, and the amanitas. The amanita group contains both edible and poisonous species. Another familiar group of mushrooms, the puffballs. They are easily identified by their round shape. Their spores are contained under a thick skin. Which eventually ruptures to release the spores. The famous morels are in still another group. These pitted, spongy mushrooms called sac fungi because the spores develop in sacs.

Anyone interested in mushrooms as food should heed the US Public Health Service warning. Not to eat any wild mushrooms unless their identity and edibility are established without a doubt.

°Defined in "Grammar Terms," page 340.

28 Comma Splices and Fused Sentences

The kernel of a sentence is the main clause° consisting of a subject° and its predicate,° which together express a complete thought that can stand alone. When you combine two main clauses in one sentence, you need to give readers a clear signal that one clause is ending and the other beginning. Two common errors fail to give this signal. In a **comma splice** two main clauses are joined (or spliced) only by a comma, which is usually too weak to signal the link between main clauses.

> Comma splice   The ship was huge, its mast stood eighty feet high.

In a **fused sentence** (or **run-on sentence**) the clauses are not separated at all.

> Fused sentence   The ship was huge its mast stood eighty feet high.

You can repair comma splices and fused sentences with coordination or subordination (pp. 71–72) and at the same time clarify the relations between the clauses.

28a Main clauses without *and, but, or, nor, for, so, yet*

Two main clauses in a sentence are usually separated with a comma and a coordinating conjunction° such as *and* or *but*. These signals tell readers to expect another main clause. When one or both signals are missing, the sentence may be confusing and may require rereading. Revise it in one of the following ways:

- Insert a coordinating conjunction when the ideas in the main clauses are closely related and equally important.

> Comma splice   Some laboratory-grown foods taste good, they are nutritious.
>
> Revised   Some laboratory-grown foods taste good, and they are nutritious.

In a fused sentence insert a comma and a coordinating conjunction.

> Fused sentence   Chemists have made much progress they still have a way to go.
>
> Revised   Chemists have made much progress, but they still have a way to go.

130   °Defined in "Grammar Terms," page 340.

- **Insert a semicolon between clauses if the relation between the ideas is very close and obvious without a conjunction.**

Comma splice Good taste is rare in laboratory-grown vegetables, they are usually bland.

Revised Good taste is rare in laboratory-grown vegetables **;** they are usually bland.

- **Make the clauses into separate sentences when the ideas expressed are only loosely related.**

Comma splice Chemistry has contributed to our understanding of foods, many foods such as wheat and beans can be produced in the laboratory.

Revised Chemistry has contributed to our understanding of foods **.** Many foods such as wheat and beans can be produced in the laboratory.

- **Subordinate one clause to the other when one idea is less important than the other.** Subordination is often more effective than forming separate sentences because it defines the relations between ideas more precisely.

Comma splice The vitamins are adequate, the flavor and color are deficient.

Revised <u>Even though</u> the vitamins are adequate, the flavor and color are deficient.

28b

28b Main clauses related by *however, for example,* and so on

However and *for example* are transitional expressions° that can describe how one main clause relates to another. (See page 350 for additional examples.)

When most transitional expressions relate two main clauses, the clauses must be separated by a period or by a semicolon. The connecting word or phrase is usually set off by a comma or commas.

Comma splice Healthcare costs are higher in the United States than in many other countries, <u>consequently</u> health insurance is also more costly.

Revised Healthcare costs are higher in the United States than in many other countries **.** <u>Consequently</u> **,** health insurance is also more costly.

Revised Healthcare costs are higher in the United States than in many other countries **;** <u>consequently</u> **,** health insurance is also more costly.

°Defined in "Grammar Terms," page 340.

To test whether a word or phrase is a transitional expression, try moving it around in its clause. A transitional expression can move, whereas other connecting words (such as *and* or *because*) cannot.

> Healthcare costs are higher in the United States than in many other countries **;** health insurance **,** consequently **,** is also more costly.

Exercise   Comma splices and fused sentences

Revise each comma splice and fused sentence in the following paragraphs using the technique that seems most appropriate for the meaning. Possible answers to the starred items appear at the end of the book.

Example:

Many people are happy to finish college, however, some miss the campus community.

Many people are happy to finish college **;** however, some miss the campus community.

Many people are happy to finish college **.** However, some miss the campus community.

28b

*What many call the first genocide of modern times occurred during World War I, the Armenians were deported from their homes in Anatolia, Turkey. *The Turkish government assumed that the Armenians were sympathetic to Russia, with whom the Turks were at war. *Many Armenians died because of the hardships of the journey many were massacred. *The death toll was estimated at between 600,000 and 1 million.

Many of the deported Armenians migrated to Russia, in 1918 they established the Republic of Armenia, they continued to be attacked by Turkey, in 1920 they became the Soviet Republic of Armenia rather than surrender to the Turks. Like other Soviet republics, Armenia became independent in 1991, about 3.4 million Armenians live there now.

The Armenians have a long history of conquest by others. As a people, they formed a centralized state in the seventh century BC then they were ruled by the Persian empire until it was conquered by Alexander the Great. Greek and Roman rule followed, internal clan leadership marked by disunity and strife was next. In AD 640 the country was invaded by the Arabs in the eleventh century it was conquered by the Byzantines and then by the Turks, who controlled it until 1920.

PART 5

Punctuation

Essential
Punctuation

This list focuses on the most troublesome punctuation marks and uses, showing correctly punctuated sentences with brief explanations. For the other marks and other uses covered in this part, see "Detailed Contents" inside the back cover.

Comma

- Subways are convenient**,** but they are costly to build.
  Subways are convenient but costly.
  [With *and, but,* etc., only between main clauses. See opposite.]
- Because of their cost**,** new subways are rarely built.
  [With an introductory element. See opposite.]
- Light rail**,** which is less costly**,** is often more feasible.
  Those who favor mass transit often propose light rail.
  [With a nonessential element, not with an essential element. See p. 136.]
- In a few older cities, commuters can choose among subways**,** buses**,** light rail**,** and railroads.
  [Separating items in a series. See p. 138.]

Semicolon

- She chose carpentry**;** she wanted manual work.
  She had a law degree**;** however, she became a carpenter.
  [Between main clauses not joined by *and, but,* etc., and those joined by *however, for example,* etc. See pp. 140–41.]

Colon

- The school has one goal**:** to train businesspeople.
  [With a main clause to introduce information. See p. 143.]

Apostrophe

- Jay Smith**'**s dog saved the life of the Joneses**'** child.
  [Showing possession: -'s for singular nouns; -' alone for plural nouns ending in -*s*. See pp. 144–45.]
- Its [for The dog**'**s] bark warned the family. It**'**s [for It is] an intelligent dog. They**'**re [for They are] happy that their [the Joneses'] child is safe.
  [Not with possessive pronouns, only with contractions. See p. 146.]

Quotation marks

- She asked, **"**Why did you do it**?"**
  Kate Chopin uses irony in **"**The Story of an Hour**."**
  [With direct quotations, with certain titles, and with other punctuation marks. See pp. 148–50.]

29 The Comma

The comma helps to separate sentence elements and to prevent mis-reading. Its main uses (and misuses) appear in this chapter.

29a Comma with *and, but, or, nor, for, so, yet*

Comma between main clauses

Use a comma before *and, but, or, nor, for, so,* and *yet* (the coordinating conjunctions°) when they link main clauses.°

Banks offer many services, but they could do more.

Many banks offer investment advice, and they may help small businesses establish credit.

Note The comma goes before, not after, the coordinating conjunction.

No comma between words, phrases, or subordinate clauses

Generally, do not use a comma before *and, but, or,* and *nor* when they link pairs of words, phrases,° or subordinate clauses°—that is, elements other than main clauses.

Not One bank established special accounts for older depositors, and counseled them on investments.

But One bank established special accounts for older depositors and counseled them on investments.

29b Comma with introductory elements

Use a comma after most elements that begin sentences and are distinct from the main clause.

When a downtown business closes, a small city can suffer.

Fortunately, an entrepreneur has an idea for a new business.

You may omit the comma after a short introductory element if there's no risk that the reader will run the introductory element and main clause together: *By 2020 we may have reduced pollution.*

Note The subject° of a sentence is not an introductory element but a part of the main clause. Thus, do not use a comma to separate the subject and its verb.

°Defined in "Grammar Terms," page 340.

Not	Many people, choose to shop at downtown businesses.
But	Many people choose to shop at downtown businesses.

29c Comma or commas with interrupting and concluding elements

Use a comma or commas to set off information that could be deleted without altering the basic meaning of the sentence.

Note When such optional information falls in the middle of the sentence, be sure to use one comma *before* and one *after* it.

Commas around nonessential elements

A **nonessential** (or **nonrestrictive**) **element** adds information about a word in the sentence but does not limit (or restrict) the word to a particular individual or group. Omitting the underlined element from any sentence below would remove incidental details but would not affect the sentence's basic meaning.

Nonessential modifiers

Hai Nguyen, who emigrated from Vietnam, lives in Denver.

His company, which is ten years old, studies air pollution.

Nguyen's family lives in Baton Rouge and Chicago, even though he lives in Denver.

Nonessential appositives

Appositives are words or word groups that rename nouns.

Hai Nguyen's work, advanced research into air pollution, keeps him in Denver.

His wife, Tina Nguyen, is a doctor in Chicago. [Nguyen has only one wife, so her name merely adds nonessential information about her.]

No commas around essential elements

Do not use commas to set off **essential** (or **restrictive**) **elements**: modifiers and appositives that contain information essential to the meaning of the sentence. Omitting the underlined element from any of the following sentences would alter the meaning substantially, leaving the sentence unclear or too general.

Essential modifiers

People who join recycling programs rarely complain about the extra work.

The programs that succeed are often staffed by volunteers.

Most people recycle because they believe they have a responsibility to the earth.

Essential appositives

The label "Recycle" on products becomes a command.

The activist Susan Bower urges recycling.

The book *Efficient Recycling* provides helpful tips.

Commas around absolute phrases

An **absolute phrase** usually consists of the *-ing* form of a verb plus a subject for the verb. The phrase modifies the whole main clause of the sentence.

Household recycling having succeeded, the city is now extending the program to businesses.

Commas around transitional or parenthetical expressions

A transitional expression° such as *however, for example,* or *of course* forms a link between ideas. It is nonessential and is usually set off with a comma or commas.

Most businesses, consequently, are finding ways to make recycling cost-efficient.

A parenthetical expression° provides supplementary information not essential for meaning. Examples are *fortunately, to be frank,* and *all things considered.* Such an expression may be enclosed in parentheses (see p. 153) or, for more emphasis, in commas.

29c

Recycling, it seems, can be good for the bottom line.

Note Do not add a comma after a coordinating conjunction° (*and, but,* and so on) or a subordinating conjunction° (*although, because,* and so on). To distinguish between these words and transitional or parenthetical expressions, try moving the word or expression around in its clause. Transitional or parenthetical expressions can be moved; coordinating and subordinating conjunctions cannot.

Commas around phrases of contrast

Many recyclers focus just on the environmental benefits, not the inconveniences or costs.

Commas around *yes* and *no*

Almost everyone agrees that, yes, the advantages outweigh the disadvantages.

Commas around words of direct address

Do you agree, readers?

°Defined in "Grammar Terms," page 340.

29d Commas with series

Commas between series items

Use commas to separate the items in lists or series.

The names Belia, Beelzebub, and Lucifer sound ominous.

The comma before the last item in a series (before *and*) is optional, but it is never wrong and it is usually clearer.

No commas around series

Do not use a comma *before* or *after* a series.

Not   The skills of, agriculture, herding, and hunting, sustained the Native Americans.

But   The skills of agriculture, herding, and hunting sustained the Native Americans.

29e Comma with adjectives

Comma between equal adjectives

Use a comma between two or more adjectives° when each one modifies the same word equally. As a test, such adjectives could be joined by *and*.

The book had a worn, cracked binding.

No comma between unequal adjectives

Do not use a comma between adjectives when one forms a unit with the modified word. As a test, the two adjectives could not sensibly be joined by *and*.

The study examined the eye movements of healthy young men.

The researchers watched for one specific movement as the subjects read words on a screen.

29f Commas with dates, addresses, place names, numbers

When they appear within sentences, elements punctuated with commas are also ended with commas.

Dates

July 4, 1776, was the day the Declaration was signed. [Note that commas appear before *and* after the year.]

The United States entered World War II in December 1941. [No comma is needed between a month or season and a year.]

°Defined in "Grammar Terms," page 340.

Addresses and place names

Use the address 806 Ogden Avenue, Swarthmore, Pennsylvania 19081, for all correspondence. [No comma is needed between the state name and zip code.]

Numbers

The new assembly plant cost $7,525,000.

A kilometer is 3,281 feet [*or* 3281 feet].

29g   Commas with quotations

A comma or commas usually separate a quotation from a signal phrase that identifies the source, such as *she said* or *he replied.*

Eleanor Roosevelt said, "You must do the thing you think you cannot do."

"Knowledge is power," wrote Francis Bacon.

"You don't need a weatherman," sings Bob Dylan, "to know which way the wind blows."

Exceptions   Do not use commas with signal phrases in the following situations:

- Use a semicolon or a period after a signal phrase that interrupts a quotation between main clauses. (Main clauses can stand alone as complete sentences.) The use of a semicolon or a period depends on the punctuation of the original:

"That part of my life was over," she wrote; "his words had sealed it shut."

"That part of my life was over," she wrote. "His words had sealed it shut."

- Use a colon when a complete sentence introduces a quotation:

Her statement was clear: "I will not resign."

- Omit commas when a quotation is integrated into your sentence structure, including a quotation introduced by *that:*

James Baldwin insists that "one must never, in one's life, accept . . . injustices as commonplace."

Baldwin thought that the violence of a riot "had been devised as a corrective" to his own violence.

29g

Exercise   The comma

Insert commas as needed in the following paragraphs, and delete any misused commas. If a sentence is correct as given, mark the number preceding it. Answers to sentences 1–5 appear at the end of the book.

Example:

The student center which opened just last year burned down.

The student center, which opened just last year, burned down.

1 Ellis Island New York reopened for business in 1990 but now the customers are tourists not immigrants. 2 This spot which lies in New York Harbor was the first American soil seen, or touched by many of the nation's immigrants. 3 Though other places also served as ports of entry for foreigners none has the symbolic power of, Ellis Island. 4 Between its opening in 1892 and its closing in 1954, over 20 million people about two-thirds of all immigrants were detained there before taking up their new lives in the United States. 5 Ellis Island processed over 2000 newcomers a day when immigration was at its peak between 1900 and 1920.

6 As the end of a long voyage and the introduction to the New World Ellis Island must have left something to be desired. 7 The "huddled masses" as the Statue of Liberty calls them indeed were huddled. 8 New arrivals were herded about kept standing in lines for hours or days yelled at and abused. 9 Assigned numbers they submitted their bodies to the pokings and proddings of the silent nurses and doctors, who were charged with ferreting out the slightest sign, of sickness disability or insanity. 10 That test having been passed, the immigrants faced interrogation by an official through an interpreter. 11 Those, with names deemed inconveniently long or difficult to pronounce, often found themselves permanently labeled with abbreviations, of their names, or with the names, of their hometowns. 12 But, millions survived the examination humiliation and confusion, to take the last short boat ride to New York City. 13 For many of them and especially for their descendants Ellis Island eventually became not a nightmare but the place where a new life began.

30 The Semicolon

The semicolon separates equal and balanced sentence elements, usually main clauses.

30a Semicolon between main clauses not joined by *and, but, or, nor,* etc.

Semicolon between main clauses

Use a semicolon between main clauses° that are not connected by the coordinating conjunction° *and, but, or, nor, for, so,* or *yet.*

°Defined in "Grammar Terms," page 340.

The semicolon signals that one clause is ending and another is beginning.

> Increased taxes are only one way to pay for programs**;** cost cutting also frees up money.

> A new ulcer drug has a mixed reputation**;** doctors find that the drug works but worry about its side effects.

No semicolon between main clauses and subordinate elements

Do not use a semicolon between a main clause and a subordinate element, such as a subordinate clause° or a phrase.°

> Not   According to African authorities; Pygmies today number only about 35,000.

> But   According to African authorities**,** Pygmies today number only about 35,000.

> Not   Anthropologists have campaigned; for the protection of the Pygmies' habitat.

> But   Anthropologists have campaigned for the protection of the Pygmies' habitat.

30b Semicolon with *however, for example,* and so on

Use a semicolon between main clauses° that are related by transitional expressions,° such as *however, after all, for example,* and *therefore.*

> Blue jeans are fashionable all over the world**;** however, the American originators still wear more jeans than anyone else.

A transitional expression may move around within its clause, so the semicolon will not always come just before the expression. The transitional expression itself is usually set off with a comma or commas.

> Blue jeans are fashionable all over the world**;** the American originators**,** however**,** still wear more jeans than anyone else.

30c Semicolons with series

Semicolons between series items

Use semicolons (rather than commas) to separate items in a series when the items contain commas.

> The custody case involved Amy Dalton, the child**;** Ellen and Mark Dalton, the parents**;** and Ruth and Hal Blum, the grandparents.

°Defined in "Grammar Terms," page 340.

No semicolon before a series

Do not use a semicolon to introduce a series. (Use a colon or a dash instead.)

Not   Teachers have heard all sorts of reasons why students do poorly; psychological problems, family illness, too much work, too little time.

But   Teachers have heard all sorts of reasons why students do poorly: psychological problems, family illness, too much work, too little time.

Exercise   **The semicolon**

Insert semicolons in the following paragraph wherever they are needed. Also eliminate any misused or needless semicolons, substituting other punctuation as appropriate. Answers to starred sentences appear at the end of the book.

Example:

The moviegoers were silent as the lights came up, they seemed stunned by the ending.

The moviegoers were silent as the lights came up; they seemed stunned by the ending.

*The set, sounds, and actors in the movie captured the essence of horror films. *The set was ideal; dark, deserted streets, trees dipping their branches over the sidewalks, mist hugging the ground and creeping up to meet the trees, looming shadows of unlighted, turreted houses. *The sounds, too, were appropriate, especially terrifying was the hard, hollow sound of footsteps echoing throughout the film. But the best feature of the movie was its actors; all of them tall, pale, and thin to the point of emaciation. With one exception, they were dressed uniformly in gray and had gray hair. The exception was an actress who dressed only in black; as if to set off her pale yellow, nearly white, long hair; the only color in the film. The glinting black eyes of another actor stole almost every scene, indeed, they were the source of the film's mischief.

31   The Colon

The colon is mainly a mark of introduction, but it has a few other conventional uses as well.

31a Colon for introduction

Colon at the end of a main clause

The colon ends a main clause°—a word group that can stand alone as a sentence—and introduces various additions:

> *Soul food* has a deceptively simple definition**:** the ethnic cooking of African Americans. [Introduces an explanation.]

> At least three soul food dishes are familiar to most Americans**:** fried chicken, barbecued spareribs, and sweet potatoes. [Introduces a series.]

> Soul food has one disadvantage**:** fat. [Introduces an appositive.°]

> One soul food chef has a solution**:** "Instead of using ham hocks to flavor beans, I use smoked turkey wings. The soulful, smoky taste remains, but without all the fat of pork." [Introduces a quotation.]

No colon inside a main clause

Do not use a colon inside a main clause, especially after *such as* or a verb.

> Not The best-known soul food dish <u>is</u>: fried chicken. Many Americans have not tasted delicacies <u>such as</u>: chitlins and black-eyed peas.

> But The best-known soul food dish is fried chicken. Many Americans have not tasted delicacies <u>such as</u> chitlins and black-eyed peas.

31b Colon with salutation of business letter, title and subtitle, and divisions of time

Salutation of a business letter
Dear Ms. Burak**:**

Title and subtitle
*Anna Freud***:** *Her Life and Work*

Time
12**:**26   6**:**00

Exercise   Colons and semicolons

In the following paragraphs, insert colons or semicolons as needed and delete or replace them where they are misused. If a sentence is correct as given, mark the number preceding it. Answers to sentences 1–4 appear at the end of the book.

> *Example:*
> Alex has three goals in the coming year; getting in shape, finishing college, and finding a job.

°Defined in "Grammar Terms," page 340.

Alex has three goals in the coming year**:** getting in shape, finishing college, and finding a job.

1 Sunlight is made up of three kinds of radiation: visible rays; infrared rays, which we cannot see; and ultraviolet rays, which are also invisible. 2 Infrared rays are the longest; measuring 700 nanometers and longer; while ultraviolet rays are the shortest; measuring 400 nanometers and shorter. 3 Especially in the ultraviolet range; sunlight is harmful to the eyes. 4 Ultraviolet rays can damage the retina: furthermore, they can cause cataracts on the lens.

5 The lens protects the eye by: absorbing much of the ultraviolet radiation and thus protecting the retina. 6 Protecting the retina, however, the lens becomes a victim; growing cloudy and blocking vision. 7 The best way to protect your eyes is: to wear hats that shade the face and sunglasses that screen out ultraviolet rays. 8 Many sunglass lenses have been designed as ultraviolet screens; many others are extremely ineffective. 9 Sunglass lenses should screen out ultraviolet rays and be dark enough so that people can't see your eyes through them, otherwise, the lenses will not protect your eyes, and you will be at risk for cataracts later in life. 10 People who spend much time outside in the sun; owe it to themselves to buy and wear sunglasses that shield their eyes.

32 The Apostrophe

The apostrophe (') appears as part of a word to indicate possession, the omission of one or more letters, or (in a few cases) plural number.

32a Apostrophe with possessives

The **possessive** form of a word indicates that it owns or is the source of another word: *the dog's fur, everyone's hope.* For nouns° and indefinite pronouns,° such as *everyone,* the possessive form always includes an apostrophe and often an *-s.* (Only the possessives *yours, his, hers, its, ours, theirs,* and *whose* do not use apostrophes.)

Note The apostrophe or apostrophe-plus-*s* is an *addition.* Before this addition, always spell the name of the owner or owners without dropping or adding letters.

Singular words: Add -*'s.*

Some of the earth**'**s forests are regenerating.

Everyone**'**s fitness can be improved through daily exercise.

°Defined in "Grammar Terms," page 340.

The *-'s* ending for singular words usually pertains to singular words ending in *-s*.

> Sandra Cisneros*'*s work is highly regarded.
>
> The business*'*s customers sued the owners.

However, some writers add only the apostrophe to singular words ending in *-s*, especially when the additional *s* would make the word difficult to pronounce (*Moses'*) or when the name sounds like a plural (*Rivers'*).

Plural words ending in *-s*: Add *-'* only.

> Workers*'* incomes have fallen slightly over the past year.
>
> Many students take several years*'* leave after high school.
>
> The Murphys*'* son lives at home.

Plural words not ending in *-s*: Add *-'s*.

> Children*'*s educations are at stake
>
> We need to attract the media*'*s attention.

Compound words: Add *-'s* only to the last word.

> The brother-in-law*'*s business failed.
>
> Taxes are always somebody else*'*s fault.

Two or more owners: Add *-'s* depending on possession.

> Zimbale*'*s and Mason*'*s comedy techniques are similar. [Each comedian has his own technique.]
>
> The children recovered despite their mother and father*'*s neglect. [The mother and father were jointly neglectful.]

32b Misuses of the apostrophe

No apostrophe with plural nouns

The plurals of nouns° are generally formed by adding *-s* or *-es*: *boys, families, Joneses.* Don't add an apostrophe to form the plural:

> Not   The Jones' controlled the firm's until 2011.
>
> But   The Joneses controlled the firms until 2011.

No apostrophe with singular verbs

Verbs° ending in *-s never* take an apostrophe:

> Not   The subway break's down less often now.
>
> But   The subway breaks down less often now.

°Defined in "Grammar Terms," page 340.

32b

No apostrophe with possessive personal or relative pronouns

His, hers, its, ours, yours, and *theirs*—all without apostrophes—are possessive forms of the personal pronouns° *he, she, it, we, you,* and *they.* Likewise, *whose*—without an apostrophe—is the possessive of the relative pronoun° *who.*

Not	Who's house is it? The house is her's. It's roof leaks.
But	Whose house is it? The house is hers. Its roof leaks.

Don't confuse possessive pronouns with contractions. See the examples below.

32c Apostrophe with contractions

Standard contractions

A **contraction** replaces one or more letters, numbers, or words with an apostrophe, as in the following examples:

it is	it's	cannot	can't
they are	they're	does not	doesn't
you are	you're	were not	weren't
who is	who's	class of 2019	class of '19

Contractions vs. possessive pronouns

Don't confuse contractions with possessive pronouns:

Contractions	Possessive pronouns
It's a book.	Its cover is green.
They're coming.	Their car broke down.
You're right.	Your idea is good.
Who's coming?	Whose party is it?

32d Apostrophe with plural abbreviations, dates, and words or characters named as words

You'll sometimes see apostrophes used to form the plurals of abbreviations (*BA's*), dates (*1900's*), and words or characters used as words (*but's*). However, current style guides recommend against the apostrophe in these cases.

BAs   PhDs   1990s   2000s

The sentence has too many *buts.*
Two *3s* end the zip code.

Note Italicize or underline a word or character that is named as a word (see p. 169), but not the added -*s.*

°Defined in "Grammar Terms," page 340.

Exercise **The apostrophe**

Revise the following paragraph to correct mistakes in the use of apostrophes or any confusion between contractions and possessive pronouns. If a sentence is correct as given, mark the number preceding it. Answers to sentences 1–4 appear at the end of the book.

Example:

Many developing nation's are improving they're citizens lives.

Many developing nations are improving their citizens' lives.

1 People who's online experiences include blogging, Web cams, and social-networking sites are often used to seeing the details of other peoples private lives. 2 Many are also comfortable sharing they're own opinions, photographs, and videos with family, friend's, and even stranger's. 3 However, they need to realize that employers and even the government can see they're information, too. 4 Employers commonly search for applicants' names on social-networking Web sites such as *Twitter* and *Facebook*. 5 Many companies monitor their employees outbound e-mail. 6 People can take steps to protect their personal information by adjusting the privacy settings on their social-networking pages. 7 They can avoid posting photos of themselves that they wouldnt want an employer to see. 8 They can avoid sending personal e-mail while their at work. 9 Its the individuals responsibility to keep certain information private.

33 Quotation Marks

Quotation marks—either double (" ") or single (' ')—mainly enclose direct quotations from speech and from writing.

This chapter treats the main uses of quotation marks. Additional issues with quotations are discussed elsewhere in this book:

- **Punctuating *she said* and other signal phrases with quotations.** See page 139.
- **Using brackets and the ellipsis mark to indicate changes in quotations.** See pages 154–56.
- **Quoting sources versus paraphrasing or summarizing them.** See pages 205–07.
- **Integrating quotations into your text.** See pages 207–10.
- **Avoiding plagiarism with quotations.** See pages 215–17.

- **Formatting long prose quotations and poetry quotations.** See pages 265 (MLA style), 295 (APA style), and 315 (Chicago style).

Note Always use quotation marks in pairs, one at the beginning of a quotation and one at the end.

33a Quotation marks with direct quotations

Double quotation marks

A **direct quotation** reports exactly what someone said or wrote.

"Life," said the psychoanalyst Karen Horney, "remains a very efficient therapist."

Note Do not use quotation marks with a direct quotation that you set off from your text, as in the exercise on page 150. And do not use them with an **indirect quotation**, which reports what someone said or wrote but not in the exact words of the original: *Karen Horney remarked that life is a good therapist.*

Single quotation marks

Use single quotation marks to enclose a quotation within a quotation.

"In formulating any philosophy," Woody Allen writes, "the first consideration must always be: What can we know? Descartes hinted at the problem when he wrote, 'My mind can never know my body, although it has become quite friendly with my leg.'"

Dialog

When quoting a conversation, use double quotation marks and begin a new paragraph for each speaker.

"What shall I call you? Your name?" Andrews whispered rapidly, as with a high squeak the latch of the door rose.

"Elizabeth," she said. "Elizabeth."

—Graham Greene, *The Man Within*

33b Quotation marks for titles of works

Do not use quotation marks for the titles of your own papers. Within your text, however, use quotation marks to enclose the titles of works that are published or released within larger works. Use underlining or italics for all other titles (see pp. 168–69).

Short story	Short poem
"The Gift of the Magi"	"Her Kind"

Article in a periodical	**Unpublished speech**
"Does 'Scaring' Work?"	"Horses and Healing"
Page or work on a Web site	**Episode of a television or radio program**
"Reader's Page" (on the site *Friends of Prufrock*)	"The Mexican Connection" (on *60 Minutes*)
Essay	**Subdivision of a book**
"Joey: A 'Mechanical Boy'"	"The Mast Head" (Chapter 35 of *Moby-Dick*)
Song	
"Satisfaction"	

Note APA and CSE styles do not use quotation marks for titles within source citations. (See pp. 280 and 320.)

33c Quotation marks with words used in a special sense

On movie sets movable "wild walls" make a one-walled room seem four-walled on film.

Avoid using quotation marks to excuse slang or to express irony—that is, to indicate that you are using a word with a different or even opposite meaning than usual.

Not Americans "justified" their treatment of the Indians.

But Americans attempted to justify their treatment of the Indians.

Note Use italics or underlining to highlight words you are defining. (See p. 169.)

33d Quotation marks with other punctuation

Commas and periods: Inside quotation marks

Jonathan Swift wrote a famous satire, "A Modest Proposal," in 1729.

"Swift's 'A Modest Proposal,'" wrote one critic, "is so outrageous that it cannot be believed."

Exception When a source citation in your text immediately follows a quotation, place any comma or period *after* the citation:

One critic calls the essay "outrageous" (Olms 26).

Colons and semicolons: Outside quotation marks

Some years ago the slogan in elementary education was "learning by playing"; now educators stress basic skills.

33d

We all know the meaning of "basic skills": reading, writing, and arithmetic.

Dashes, question marks, and exclamation points: Inside quotation marks only if part of the quotation

When a dash, exclamation point, or question mark is part of the quotation, place it *inside* quotation marks. Don't use any other punctuation, such as a period or comma.

"But must you—" Marcia hesitated, afraid of the answer.

"Go away!" I yelled.

Did you say, "Who is she?" [When both your sentence and the quotation would end in a question mark or exclamation point, use only the mark in the quotation.]

When a dash, question mark, or exclamation point applies only to the larger sentence, not to the quotation, place it *outside* quotation marks—again, with no other punctuation.

The question Betty Friedan posed in 1963—"Who knows what women can be?"—encouraged others to seek answers.

Who said, "Now cracks a noble heart"?

33d

Exercise Quotation marks

Insert quotation marks in the following paragraph. If a sentence is correct as given, mark the number preceding it. Answers to sentences 1–5 appear at the end of the book.

Example:
Adele released her first single, Hometown Glory, in 2007.
Adele released her first single, "Hometown Glory," in 2007.

1 In a history class we talked about a passage from Abraham Lincoln's *Gettysburg Address*, delivered on November 19, 1863:

2 Four score and seven years ago our fathers brought forth on this continent, a new nation, conceived in Liberty, and dedicated to the proposition that all men are created equal. 3 Now we are engaged in a great civil war, testing whether that nation, or any nation so conceived and so dedicated, can long endure.

4 What was Lincoln referring to in the first sentence? the teacher asked. 5 Perhaps we should define *score* first. 6 Explaining that a score is twenty years, she said that Lincoln was referring to the document in which he colonies had declared independence from England eighty-seven years earlier, in 1776.

7 One student commented, Lincoln's decision to end slavery is implied in that first sentence. 8 The President was calling on the authority of the Founding Fathers.

9 Lincoln gave the speech at the dedication of the National Cemetery in Gettysburg, Pennsylvania, which was the site of a very bloody Civil War battle, another student added.

10 A third student noted that in the second sentence Lincoln was posing the central question of the war: whether a nation founded on equality can long endure.

34 End Punctuation

End a sentence with one of three punctuation marks: a period, a question mark, or an exclamation point.

34a Period for most sentences and some abbreviations

Statement
The airline went bankrupt.

Mild command
Think of the possibilities.

Indirect question°
The article asks how we can improve math education.
It asks what cost we are willing to pay.

Abbreviations
Use periods with abbreviations that end in small letters. Otherwise, omit periods from abbreviations.

Dr.	Mr., Mrs.	e.g.	Feb.	ft.
St.	Ms.	i.e.	p.	a.m., p.m.
PhD	BC, AD	USA	IBM	JFK
BA	AM, PM	US	USMC	AIDS

Note When a sentence ends in an abbreviation with a period, don't add a second period: *My first class is at 8 a.m.*

34b Question mark for direct questions°

What is the result?
What is the difference between those proposals?

°Defined in "Grammar Terms," page 340.

34c Exclamation point for strong statements and commands

No**!** We must not lose this election**!**
Stop the car**!**

Note Use exclamation points sparingly to avoid seeming overly dramatic.

Exercise   End punctuation

Insert appropriate end punctuation (periods, question marks, or exclamation points) where needed in the following paragraph. Answers to starred lines appear at the end of the book.

Example:

Noticing my luggage, the bus driver asked where I was from?
Noticing my luggage, the bus driver asked where I was from**.**

*When visitors first arrive in Hawaii, they often encounter an unex-
*pected language barrier Standard English is the language of business and
*government, but many of the people speak Pidgin English Instead of an
*excited "Aloha" the visitors may be greeted with an excited Pidgin
*"Howzit" or asked if they know "how fo' find one good hotel" Many
Hawaiians question whether Pidgin will hold children back because it prevents communication with *haoles*, or Caucasians, who run many businesses Yet many others feel that Pidgin is a last defense of ethnic diversity
on the islands To those who want to make standard English the official
language of the state, these Hawaiians may respond, "Just 'cause I speak
Pidgin no mean I dumb" They may ask, "Why you no listen" or, in standard English, "Why don't you listen"

35 Other Marks

The other marks of punctuation are the dash, parentheses, the ellipsis mark, brackets, and the slash.

35a Dash or dashes: Shifts and interruptions

The dash (—) punctuates sentences, while the hyphen (-) punctuates words. Form a dash using two hyphens (--), with no extra space before, after, or between the hyphens. Or use the character called an em-dash on your word processor.

Note Be sure to use a pair of dashes when a shift or interruption falls in the middle of a sentence.

Shift in tone or thought

The novel—if one can call it that—appeared in 2004.

Nonessential element

The qualities Monet painted—sunlight, shadows, deep colors—typified the rivers and gardens he used as subjects. [Commas may also set off nonessential elements. See p. 136.]

Introductory series

Shortness of breath, skin discoloration, persistent indigestion—all these may signify cancer.

Concluding series or explanation

The patient undergoes a battery of tests—imaging, blood work, and perhaps even biopsy. [A colon may also set off a concluding series. See p. 143.]

35b Parentheses: Nonessential elements

Parentheses always come in pairs, one before and one after the punctuated material.

Parenthetical expressions

Parentheses de-emphasize explanatory or supplemental words or phrases. (Commas emphasize these expressions more and dashes still more.)

The population of Philadelphia (now about 1.5 million) has declined since 1950.

Don't put a comma before an opening parenthesis. After a parenthetical expression, place any punctuation *outside* the closing parenthesis.

Not The population of Philadelphia compares with that of Phoenix, (about 1.5 million.)

But The population of Philadelphia compares with that of Phoenix (about 1.5 million).

If a complete sentence falls within parentheses, place the period *inside* the closing parenthesis.

The population of Philadelphia has been dropping. (See p. 77 for population data since 1950.)

Labels for lists within text

Outside the Middle East, the countries with the largest oil reserves are (1) Venezuela (297 billion barrels), (2) Canada (197 billion barrels), and (3) Russia (116 billion barrels).

Do not use parentheses for such labels when you set a list off from your text.

35c Ellipsis mark: Omissions from quotations

The ellipsis mark, consisting of periods separated by space (. . .), generally indicates an omission from a quotation. The following examples quote from or refer to the passage below about environmentalism:

Original quotation

"At the heart of the environmentalist world view is the conviction that human physical and spiritual health depends on sustaining the planet in a relatively unaltered state. Earth is our home in the full, genetic sense, where humanity and its ancestors existed for all the millions of years of their evolution. Natural ecosystems—forests, coral reefs, marine blue waters—maintain the world exactly as we would wish it to be maintained. When we debate the global environment and extinguish the variety of life, we are dismantling a support system that is too complex to understand, let alone replace, in the foreseeable future."
—Edward O. Wilson, "Is Humanity Suicidal?"

1. Omission of the middle of a sentence

Wilson observes, "Natural ecosystems . . . maintain the world exactly as we would wish it to be maintained."

2. Omission of the end of a sentence, without source citation

Wilson writes, "Earth is our home. . . ." [The sentence period, closed up to the last word, precedes the ellipsis mark.]

3. Omission of the end of a sentence, with source citation

Wilson writes, "Earth is our home . . ." (27). [The sentence period follows the source citation.]

4. Omission of parts of two or more sentences

Wilson writes, "At the heart of the environmentalist world view is the conviction that human physical and spiritual health depends on sustaining the planet . . . where humanity and its ancestors existed for all the millions of years of their evolution."

5. Omission of one or more sentences

As Wilson puts it, "At the heart of the environmentalist world view is the conviction that human physical and spiritual health depends on sustaining the planet in a relatively unaltered state. . . . When we debase the global environment and extinguish the variety of life, we are dismantling a support system that is too complex to understand, let alone replace, in the foreseeable future."

6. Omission from the middle of a sentence through the end of another sentence

"Earth is our home. . . . When we debase the global environment and extinguish the variety of life, we are dismantling a support system that is too complex to understand, let alone replace, in the foreseeable future."

7. Omission of the beginning of a sentence, leaving a complete sentence

a. Bracketed capital letter

"[H]uman physical and spiritual health," Wilson writes, "depends on sustaining the planet in a relatively unaltered state." [No ellipsis mark is needed because the brackets around the *H* indicate that the letter was not capitalized originally and thus that the beginning of the sentence has been omitted.]

b. Small letter

According to Wilson, "human physical and spiritual health depends on sustaining the planet in a relatively unaltered state." [No ellipsis mark is needed because the small *h* indicates that the beginning of the sentence has been omitted.]

35c

c. Capital letter from the original

One reviewer comments, ". . . Wilson argues eloquently for the environmentalist world view" (Hami 28). [An ellipsis mark *is* needed because the quoted part of the sentence begins with a capital letter and it's otherwise not clear that the beginning of the original sentence has been omitted.]

8. Use of a word or phrase

Wilson describes the earth as "our home." [No ellipsis mark needed.]

Note these features of the examples:

- Use an ellipsis mark when it is not otherwise clear that you have left out material from the source, as when you omit one or more sentences (examples 5 and 6) or when the words you quote form a complete sentence that is different in the original (examples 1–4 and 7c).

- **You don't need an ellipsis mark when it is obvious that you have omitted something,** such as when a bracketed capital letter or a small letter indicates omission (examples 7a and 7b) or when a phrase clearly comes from a larger sentence (example 8).
- **Place an ellipsis mark after the sentence period** *except* **when a parenthetical source citation follows the quotation,** as in example 3. Then the sentence period falls after the citation.

If your quotation omits one or more lines of poetry or paragraphs of prose, show the omission with an entire line of ellipsis marks across the full width of the quotation.

35d Brackets: Changes in quotations

Though they have specialized uses in mathematical equations, brackets mainly indicate that you have altered a quotation to fit it into your sentence.

Jackson praised the report, saying that "[t]he study's findings give researchers new insights into [Alzheimer's] disease."

35e Slash: Options and breaks in poetry lines

35e

Option

Some teachers oppose pass / fail courses.

Break in poetry lines that run into your text

Many readers have sensed a reluctant turn away from death in Frost's lines "The woods are lovely, dark and deep, **/** But I have promises to keep."

Exercise   Punctuation

The following paragraphs are unpunctuated except for periods at the ends of sentences. Insert commas, semicolons, colons, apostrophes, quotation marks, dashes, or parentheses where they are appropriate. When different marks would be appropriate in the same place, be able to defend the choice you make. Possible answers to sentences 1–7 appear at the end of the book.

Example:

As an advertisement once put it The best way to start a day is with a good cup of coffee.

As an advertisement once put it **,** **"**The best way to start a day is with a good cup of coffee.**"**

1 Brewed coffee is the most widely consumed beverage in the world.
2 Its believed that coffee cultivation and trade began on the Arabian

Peninsula in the fifteenth century. 3 By the middle or late sixteenth century travelers had introduced the beverage to the Europeans who at first resisted it because of its strong flavor and effect as a mild stimulant. 4 The French Italians and other Europeans incorporated coffee into their diets by the mid-seventeenth century the English however preferred tea which they were then importing from India. 5 Only after the Boston Tea Party 1773 did Americans begin drinking coffee in large quantities. 6 Now though the United States is one of the top coffee-consuming countries. 7 More than 150000000 Americans drink at least one cup of coffee each day.

8 Produced from the fruit of an evergreen tree coffee is grown primarily in Latin America southern Asia and Africa. 9 Coffee trees require a hot climate high humidity rich soil with good drainage and partial shade consequently they thrive on the east or west slopes of tropical volcanic mountains where the soil is laced with potash and drains easily. 10 The coffee beans actually seeds grow inside bright red berries. 11 The berries are picked by hand and the beans are extracted by machine leaving a pulpy fruit residue that can be used for fertilizer. 12 The beans are usually roasted in ovens a chemical process that releases the beans essential oil caffeol which gives coffee its distinctive aroma. 13 Over a hundred different varieties of beans are produced in the world each with a different flavor attributable to three factors the species of plant the soil where the variety was grown and the climate of the region.

35

PART **6**

Spelling and Mechanics

Essential

This list covers the main conventions of spelling and mechanics. For a detailed guide to this part, see "Detailed Contents" inside the back cover.

Spelling

- Proofread for correct spelling. Don't rely on your spelling checker. (See opposite.)

- Follow spelling rules for *ie* vs. *ei*, attaching endings to words, and forming plurals. (See opposite.)

- Use the hyphen to form compound words and to divide words at the ends of lines. (See p. 163.)

Capital letters

- Use capital letters appropriately for proper nouns and adjectives and for the titles of works and persons. (See pp. 165–67.)

Italics or underlining

- Use italics or underlining primarily for the titles of works published separately from other works. Ensure that italics or underlining in source citations conforms to your discipline's or instructor's requirements. (See pp. 168–69.)

Abbreviations

- Use abbreviations appropriately for the discipline or field you are writing in. (See pp. 170–71.)

Numbers

- Express numbers in numerals or words appropriately for the discipline or field you are writing in. (See pp. 171–72.)

36 Spelling and the Hyphen

Spelling, including using the hyphen, is a skill you can acquire by paying attention to words and by developing three habits:

- **Carefully proofread your writing.**
- **Cultivate a healthy suspicion of your spellings.**
- **Check a dictionary every time you doubt a spelling.**

36a Spelling checkers

A spelling checker can help you find and track spelling errors in your papers. But its usefulness is limited, mainly because it can't spot the confusion of words with similar spellings, such as *their/they're/there*. A grammar/style checker may flag such words, but only the ones listed in its dictionary, and you still must select the correct spelling. Proofread your papers to catch spelling errors.

See page 16 for more on spelling checkers.

36b Spelling rules

We often misspell syllables rather than whole words. The following rules focus on troublesome syllables.

ie and *ei*

Follow the familiar jingle: *i* before *e* except after *c* or when pronounced "ay" as in *neighbor* and *weigh*.

i before *e*	believe	thief
e before *i*	receive	ceiling
ei pronounced "ay"	freight	vein

Exceptions Remember common exceptions with this sentence: *The weird foreigner neither seizes leisure nor forfeits height.*

Silent final *e*

Drop a silent *e* when adding an ending that begins with a vowel. Keep the *e* if the ending begins with a consonant.

advise + able = advisable   care + ful = careful

Exceptions Keep the final *e* before a vowel to prevent confusion or mispronunciation: *dyeing, changeable*. Drop the *e* before a consonant when another vowel comes before the *e*: *argument, truly*.

Final *y*

When adding to a word ending in *y*, change *y* to *i* when it follows a consonant. Keep the *y* when it follows a vowel, precedes *ing*, or ends a proper name.

beauty, beauties	day, days
worry, worried	study, studying
supply, supplier	Minsky, Minskys

Consonants

When adding an ending to a one-syllable word that ends in a consonant, double the consonant if it follows a single vowel. Otherwise, don't double the consonant.

slap, slapping	pair, paired

For words of more than one syllable, double the final consonant when it follows a single vowel and ends a stressed syllable once the new ending is added. Otherwise, don't double the consonant.

submit, submitted	despair, despairing
refer, referred	refer, reference

Plurals

Most nouns form plurals by adding *s* to the singular form. Nouns ending in *s, sh, ch,* or *x* add *es* to the singular.

boy, boys	kiss, kisses
table, tables	lurch, lurches
Murphy, Murphys	tax, taxes

Nouns ending in a vowel plus *o* add *s*. Nouns ending in a consonant plus *o* add *es*.

ratio, ratios	hero, heroes

Form the plural of a compound noun by adding *s* to the main word in the compound. The main word may not fall at the end.

passersby	breakthroughs
fathers-in-law	city-states

Some English nouns that come from other languages form the plural according to their original language.

analysis, analyses   medium, media
crisis, crises   phenomenon, phenomena
criterion, criteria   piano, pianos

ESL Noncount nouns do not form plurals, either regularly (with an added *s*) or irregularly. Examples of noncount nouns include *equipment, intelligence,* and *wealth.* See page 122.

American vs. British or Canadian spellings **ESL**

American and British or Canadian spellings differ in ways such as the following:

American	British or Canadian
color, humor	colour, humour
theater, center	theatre, centre
canceled, traveled	cancelled, travelled
judgment	judgement
realize, analyze	realise, analyse
defense, offense	defence, offence

36c The hyphen

Use the hyphen to form compound words and to divide words at the ends of lines.

Compound words

Compound words may be written as two words (*decision makers*), as a single word (*breakthrough*), or as a hyphenated word (*cross-reference*). Check a dictionary for the spelling of a compound word. Except as explained below, any compound not listed in the dictionary should be written as two words.

Sometimes a compound word comes from combining two or more words into a single adjective.° When such a compound adjective precedes a noun, a hyphen forms the words clearly into a unit.

> She is a well-known actor.
> Some Spanish-speaking students work as translators.

When a compound adjective follows the noun, the hyphen is unnecessary.

> The actor is well known.
> Many students are Spanish speaking.

The hyphen is also unnecessary in a compound modifier containing an *-ly* adverb, even before the noun: *clearly defined terms.*

°Defined in "Grammar Terms," page 340.

36c

Fractions and compound numbers

Hyphens join the parts of fractions: *three-fourths, one-half.* And the whole numbers *twenty-one* to *ninety-nine* are always hyphenated.

Prefixes and suffixes

Do not use hyphens with prefixes except as follows:

- With the prefixes *self-, all-,* and *ex-*: *self-control, all-inclusive, ex-student.*
- With a prefix before a capitalized word: *un-American.*
- With a capital letter before a word: *T-shirt.*
- To prevent misreading: *de-emphasize, re-create a story.*

The only suffix that regularly requires a hyphen is *-elect*, as in *president-elect*.

Word division at the end of a line

You can avoid short lines in your documents by setting your word processor to divide words automatically. To divide words manually, follow these guidelines:

- **Divide words only between syllables** —for instance, *win-dows,* not *wi-ndows.* Check a dictionary for correct syllable breaks.
- **Never divide a one-syllable word.**
- **Leave at least two letters on the first line and three on the second line.** If a word cannot be divided to follow this rule (for instance, *a-bus-er*), don't divide it.
- **Do not add a hyphen when breaking an electronic address** because readers may perceive any added hyphens as part of the address. The documentation styles differ in where they allow breaks in URLs. For example, MLA style allows a break after punctuation marks, while APA style allows a break before most punctuation marks.

36c

Exercise   Spelling

In the following paragraph, select the correct spellings from the choices in brackets. Refer as needed to the preceding rules or a dictionary. Answers to sentences 1–5 appear at the end of the book.

Example:

The boat [passed, past] so fast that our sailboat rocked violently in [its, it's] wake.

The boat <u>passed</u> so fast that our sailboat rocked violently in <u>its</u> wake.

1 Science [affects, effects] many [important, importent] aspects of our lives, though many people have a [pore, poor] understanding of the [role, roll] of scientific breakthroughs in [their, they're] health. 2 Many people [beleive, believe] that [docters, doctors], more than science, are [responsable, responsible] for [improvements, improvments] in health care. 3 But scientists in the [labratory, laboratory] have made crucial steps in the search for [knowlege, knowledge] about health and [medecine, medicine]. 4 For example, one scientist [who's, whose] discoveries have [affected, effected] many people is Ulf Von Euler. 5 In the 1950s Von Euler's discovery of certain hormones [lead, led] to the invention of the birth control pill. 6 Von Euler's work was used by John Rock, who [developed, developped] the first birth control pill and influenced family [planing, planning]. 7 Von Euler also discovered the [principal, principle] neurotransmitter that controls the heartbeat. 8 Another scientist, Hans Selye, showed what [affect, effect] stress can have on the body. 9 His findings have [lead, led] to methods of [baring, bearing] stress. 10 It's important not to [lose, loose] [site, sight] of these discoveries.

37 Capital Letters

As a rule, capitalize a word only when a dictionary or conventional use says you must. Consult one of the style guides listed on page 219 for special uses of capitals in the social, natural, and applied sciences.

37a First word of a sentence

No one expected the outcome.

37b Proper nouns° and proper adjectives°

Specific persons and things

Stephen King   Boulder Dam

Specific places and geographical regions

New York City   the Northeast, the South

But: northeast of the city, going south, northern

Days of the week, months, holidays

Monday   Yom Kippur
May   Christmas

But: winter, spring, summer, fall

°Defined in "Grammar Terms," page 340.

Historical events, documents, periods, movements

Vietnam War	Renaissance
Constitution	Romantic Movement

Government offices, departments, and institutions

Polk Municipal Court	House of Representatives
El Camino Hospital	Department of Defense

But: the court, the department, the hospital

Academic institutions and departments

University of Kansas	Department of Nursing
Santa Monica College	Haven High School

But: the university, college course, high school diploma

Organizations, associations, and their members

B'nai B'rith	Democratic Party, Democrats
Rotary Club	League of Women Voters
Atlanta Falcons	Chicago Symphony Orchestra

Races, nationalities, and their languages

Native American	Germans
African American	Swahili
Caucasian	Italian

But: blacks, whites

Religions, their followers, and terms for the sacred

Christianity, Christians	God
Judaism, Orthodox Jew	the Bible (*but* biblical)
Islam, Muslims	the Koran, the Qur'an

Common nouns as parts of proper nouns

Uncle Dan	Lake Superior
Professor Allen	Pacific Ocean
Main Street	Ford Motor Company

But: my uncle, the professor, the ocean, the company

37c Titles and subtitles of works

Capitalize all the words in a title and subtitle *except* articles (*a, an, the*), *to* in infinitives,° coordinating conjunctions° (*and, but,* etc.), and prepositions° (*with, between,* etc.). Capitalize even these words

---

°Defined in "Grammar Terms," page 340.

when they are the first or last word in the title or when they fall after a colon or semicolon.

"Once More to the Lake"	*Management: A New Theory*
Learning from Las Vegas	"The Truth about AIDS"
"Knowing Whom to Ask"	*An End to Live For*

Note   The preceding guidelines reflect MLA style for English and some other humanities. Other disciplines' style guides have different rules for capitals within source citations. See pages 280 (APA style) and 320 (CSE style).

37d Titles of persons

Title before name	Professor Jane Covington
Title after name	Jane Covington, a professor

37e Electronic communication

Online messages written in all-capital letters or with no capitals are difficult to read, and those in all-capitals are often considered rude. Use capital letters according to the rules in 37a–37d in all your online communication.

Exercise   Capital letters

Revise the following paragraph to correct errors in capitalization, consulting a dictionary as needed. If a sentence is correct as given, mark the number preceding it. Answers to sentences 1–5 appear at the end of the book.

37e

Example:

The first book on the reading list is zora neale hurston's *their eyes were watching god.*

The first book on the reading list is Zora Neale Hurston's *Their Eyes Were Watching God.*

1 San Antonio, texas, is a thriving city in the southwest that has always offered much to tourists interested in the roots of spanish settlement in the new world. 2 Most visitors stop at the Alamo, one of five Catholic Missions built by Priests to convert native americans and to maintain spain's claims in the area. 3 The Alamo is famous for being the site of an 1836 battle that helped to create the republic of Texas. 4 San Antonio has grown tremendously in recent years. 5 The Hemisfair plaza and the San Antonio river link tourist and convention facilities. 6 Restaurants, Hotels,

and shops line the River. 7 the haunting melodies of "Una paloma blanca" and "malagueña" lure passing tourists into Casa rio and other mexican restaurants. 8 The university of Texas at San Antonio has expanded, and a Medical Center lies in the Northwest part of the city. 9 A marine attraction on the west side of San Antonio entertains grandparents, fathers and mothers, and children with the antics of dolphins and seals. 10 The City has attracted high-tech industry, creating a corridor between san antonio and austin.

38 Italics or Underlining

Italic type and underlining indicate the same thing: the word or words are being distinguished or emphasized. Always use one or the other consistently throughout a document in both text and source citations.

Text
Growing older is one of several themes that Joan Didion explores in *Blue Nights*.

Source citation (MLA style)
Didion, Joan. *Blue Nights*. Vintage, 2011.

38a Titles of works

Do not italicize or underline the title of your own paper unless it contains an element (such as a book title) that requires highlighting.

Within your text, italicize or underline the titles of works that are published, released, or produced separately from other works. Use quotation marks for all other titles (see pp. 148–49).

Book
War and Peace

Web site
Friends of Prufrock
YouTube

Computer software
Google Chrome

Long musical work
The Beatles' *Revolver*
But: Symphony in C

Work of visual art
Michelangelo's *David*

Long poem
Paradise Lost

Play	Movie
Hamlet	*Psycho*

Periodical	Pamphlet
Philadelphia Inquirer	*The Truth about Alcoholism*

Television or radio program	Published speech
Game of *Thrones*	Lincoln's *Gettysburg Address*

Exceptions Legal documents, the Bible, and parts of them are generally not italicized or underlined.

We studied the Book of Revelation in the Bible.

38b Ships, aircraft, spacecraft, trains

Challenger	*Orient Express*	*Queen Mary 2*
Apollo XI	*Montrealer*	*Spirit of St. Louis*

38c Foreign words and phrases

The scientific name for the brown trout is *Salmo trutta*. [The Latin names for plants and animals are always highlighted.]

The Latin *De gustibus non est disputandum* translates roughly as "There's no accounting for taste."

38d Words or characters named as words

Italicize or underline words or characters (letters or numbers) that are referred to as themselves rather than used for their meanings, including terms you are defining.

Some children pronounce *th*, as in *thought*, with an *f* sound.

The word *syzygy* refers to a straight line formed by three celestial bodies, as in the alignment of the earth, sun, and moon.

38e Alternatives in electronic communication

Some forms of electronic communication do not allow highlighting for the purposes described in this chapter. If you can't use italics or underlining to distinguish book titles and other elements, type an underscore before and after the element: *Measurements coincide with those in _Joule's Handbook_*. You can also emphasize words with asterisks before and after: *I *will not* be able to attend*.

Don't use all-capital letters for emphasis; they shout. (See also p. 167.)

38e

39 Abbreviations

The following guidelines on abbreviations pertain to the text of a nontechnical document. For any special requirements of the discipline you are writing in, consult one of the style guides listed on page 219. In all disciplines, writers increasingly omit periods from abbreviations that end in capital letters. (See p. 151.)

If a name or term (such as *operating room*) appears often in a piece of writing, then its abbreviation (*OR*) can cut down on extra words. Spell out the full term at its first appearance, give the abbreviation in parentheses, and use the abbreviation thereafter.

39a Familiar abbreviations

Titles before names	Dr., Mr., Mrs., Ms., Rev., Gen.
Titles after names	MD, DDS, DVM, PhD, Sr., Jr.
Institutions	LSU, UCLA, TCU, NASA
Organizations	CIA, FBI, YMCA, AFL-CIO
Corporations	IBM, CBS, ITT, GM
People	JFK, LBJ, FDR
Countries	USA, UK
Specific numbers	no. 36 *or* No. 36
Specific amounts	$7.41, $1 million
Specific times	11:26 AM, 8:04 a.m., 2:00 PM, 8:05 p.m.
Specific dates	44 BC, AD 1492, 44 BCE, 1492 CE

Note The abbreviations BC ("before Christ"), BCE ("before the common era"), and CE ("common era") always follow the date. In contrast, AD (*anno domini*, "in the year of the Lord") always precedes the date.

39b Latin abbreviations

Generally, use the common Latin abbreviations (without italics or underlining) only in source citations and comments in parentheses.

i.e.	*id est:* that is		et al.	*et alii:* and others
cf.	*confer:* compare		etc.	*et cetera:* and so forth
e.g.	*exempli gratia:* for example		NB	*nota bene:* note well

He said he would be gone a fortnight (i.e., two weeks).
Bloom et al., editors, *Anthology of Light Verse*

39c Words usually spelled out

Generally spell out certain kinds of words in the text of academic, general, and business writing. (In technical writing, however, abbreviate units of measurement.)

Units of measurement
Mount Everest is 29,028 feet high.

Geographical names
Lincoln was born in Illinois.

Names of days, months, and holidays
The truce was signed on Tuesday, April 16, and was ratified by Christmas.

Names of people
Robert Frost wrote accessible poems.

Courses of instruction
The writer teaches psychology and composition.

And
The new rules affect New York City and environs. [Use the ampersand, &, only in the names of business firms: *Lee & Sons*.]

40 Numbers

This chapter addresses the use of numbers (numerals versus words) in the text of a nontechnical document. Usage does vary, so consult one of the style guides listed on page 219 for the requirements of the discipline you are writing in.

40a Numerals, not words

Numbers requiring three or more words		Round numbers over a million	
366	36,500	26 million	2.45 billion

Addresses
355 Heckler Avenue
Washington, DC 20036

Exact amounts of money
$3.5 million $4.50

Days and years
June 18, 1985   AD 12
456 BC   12 CE

The time of day
9:00 AM   3:45 PM

Decimals, percentages, and fractions
22.5   3½
48% (*or* 48 percent)

Scores and statistics
a ratio of 8 to 1   21 to 7
a mean of 26

Pages, chapters, volumes, acts, scenes, lines
Chapter 9, page 123
Hamlet, act 5, scene 3

Note Two numbers in a row can be confusing. Rewrite to separate the numbers:

Confusing Out of 530, 101 children caught the virus.
Clear Out of 530 <u>children</u>, 101 caught the virus.

40b Words, not numerals

Numbers of one or two words
<u>sixty</u> days, <u>forty-two</u> laps, <u>one hundred</u> people

In business and technical writing, use words only for numbers under 11 (*ten reasons,* <u>*four laps*</u>).

Beginnings of sentences
<u>Seventy-five</u> riders entered the race.

40b

If a number beginning a sentence requires more than two words to spell out, reword the sentence so that the number falls later.

Faulty <u>103</u> visitors returned.
Awkward <u>One hundred three</u> visitors returned.
Revised Of the visitors, <u>103</u> returned.

PART 7

Research and Documentation

Research and Documentation

This list covers the main considerations in using and documenting sources. For a detailed guide to this part, see "Detailed Contents" inside the back cover.

Research strategy

- Formulate a question about your subject that can guide your research. (See opposite.)
- Set goals for your sources: library vs. Internet, primary vs. secondary, and so on. (See opposite.)

Tracking sources

- Prepare a working, annotated bibliography to locate and assess possible sources. (See p. 180.)
- Use files, printouts, photocopies, and notes to keep track of promising sources. (See p. 181.)

Finding sources

- Begin your search for sources with your library's Web site. (See p. 182.)
- Develop search terms that describe your subject effectively. (See p. 183.)
- Consult appropriate sources to answer your research question. (See pp. 185–92.)

Evaluating and synthesizing sources

- Evaluate both print and online sources for their relevance and reliability. (See p. 193.)
- Synthesize sources to find their relationships and to support your own ideas. (See p. 203.)

Integrating sources

- Summarize, paraphrase, or quote sources depending on the significance of the sources' ideas or wording. (See p. 205.)
- Work source material smoothly and informatively into your own text. (See p. 207.)
- Show clear boundaries where your borrowing of source material begins and ends. (See p. 211.)

Avoiding plagiarism

- Do not plagiarize, either deliberately or carelessly, by presenting the words or ideas of others as your own. (See p. 212.)

Documenting sources

- Using the style guide appropriate for your discipline, document your sources and format your paper. (See p. 219 for a list of style guides and Chapters 48 for MLA style, 49 for APA style, 50 for Chicago style, and 51 for CSE style.)

41 Developing a Research Strategy

Research writing gives you a chance to work like a detective solving a case. The mystery is the answer to a question you care about. The search for the answer leads you to consider what others think about your subject, to build on that information, and ultimately to become an expert in your own right.

41a Subject, question, and thesis

Seek a research subject that you care about and want to know more about. Starting with such an interest and with your own views will motivate you and will make you a participant in a dialog when you begin examining sources.

Asking a question or questions about your subject opens avenues of inquiry. In asking questions, you can consider what you already know about the subject, explore what you don't know, and begin to develop your own perspective. (See below for suggestions on using your own knowledge.)

Try to narrow your research question so that you can answer it in the time and space you have available. The question *How does human activity affect the environment?* is very broad, encompassing issues as diverse as pollution, climate change, population growth, land use, and biodiversity. In contrast, the question *How can buying environmentally friendly products help the environment?* or *How, if at all, should carbon emissions be taxed?* is much narrower. Each question also requires more than a simple yes-or-no answer, so that answering it, even tentatively, demands thought about pros and cons, causes and effects.

As you read and write, your question will probably evolve to reflect your increasing knowledge of the subject. Eventually its answer will become the thesis of your paper, the main idea that all the paper's evidence supports. (See also p. 3.)

41b Goals for sources

Before you start looking for sources, consider what you already know about your subject and where you are likely to find information on it.

Your own knowledge

Discovering what you already know about your topic will guide you in discovering what you don't know and thus need to research.

Take some time to write down everything you know about the subject: facts you have learned, opinions you have heard or read elsewhere, and of course your own opinions.

When you've explored your thoughts, make a list of questions for which you don't have answers, whether factual (*How much do Americans spend on environmentally friendly products?*) or more open-ended (*Are green products worth the higher prices?*). These questions will give you clues about the sources you need to look for first.

Kinds of sources

For many research projects, you'll want to consult a mix of sources, as described in this section. You may start by seeking the outlines of your subject—the range and depth of opinions about it—in reference works and articles in popular periodicals or through a search of the Web. Then, as you refine your views and your research question, you'll move on to more specialized sources, such as scholarly books and periodicals and your own interviews or surveys. (See pp. 185–92 for more on each kind of source.)

Sources through the library or the open Web

The print and electronic sources available at your library or through its Web site—mainly reference works, books, and articles in periodicals—have two big advantages over most of what you'll find on the open Web: library sources are cataloged and indexed for easy retrieval; and they are generally reliable, having been screened first by their publishers and then by the library's staff. In contrast, the retrieval systems of the open Web are more difficult to use effectively, and the sources themselves tend to be less reliable because most do not pass through any screening before being posted. (There are many exceptions, such as online scholarly journals and reference works. But these sources are generally available through your library's Web site as well.)

Most instructors expect research writers to consult library sources. But they'll accept sources from the open Web, too, if you have used them judiciously. Even with its disadvantages, the Internet can be a valuable resource for primary sources, current information, and a diversity of views. For guidelines on evaluating both library and open-Web sources, see pages 193–203.

Primary and secondary sources

Use **primary sources** when they are required by the assignment or are appropriate for your subject. Primary sources are documents and objects that were created during the period you are studying. They consist of firsthand or original accounts, such as works of literature, historical documents (letters, speeches, and so on), eyewitness reports (including articles by journalists who are on location), reports on experiments or surveys conducted by the writer, and sources you originate (interviews, experiments, observations, or correspondence).

Many assignments will allow you to use **secondary sources**, which report and analyze information drawn from other sources, often primary ones. Examples include a reporter's summary of a controversial issue, a historian's account of a battle, a critic's reading of a poem, and a psychologist's evaluation of several studies. (Sometimes a secondary source may actually be your primary source, as when you analyze a historian's account or respond to a critic's interpretation.) In themselves, secondary sources may contain helpful summaries and interpretations that direct, support, and extend your own thinking. However, most research-writing assignments require your own ideas to go beyond those in such sources.

Scholarly and popular sources

The scholarship of acknowledged experts is essential for depth, authority, and specificity. Most instructors expect students to emphasize scholarly sources in their research. But the general-interest views and information of popular sources can provide everyday examples, anecdotes, and stories that can help you apply scholarly approaches to your subject, and they can provide context for very recent topics.

Use the following guidelines to determine whether a source is scholarly or popular.

- **Check the title.** Is it technical, or does it use a general vocabulary?
- **Check the publisher.** Is it a scholarly journal (such as *Cultural Geographies*) or a publisher of scholarly books (such as Harvard University Press), or is it a popular magazine (such as *Consumer Reports or Time*) or a publisher of popular books (such as Little, Brown)? For more on the distinction between scholarly and popular sources, see pages 186 and 195.
- **Check the length of periodical articles.** Scholarly articles are generally much longer than magazine and newspaper articles.
- **Check the author.** Search the Web for the author. Is he or she an expert on the topic?
- **Check the URL.** A Web site's URL, or electronic address, includes an abbreviation that can tell you something about the origin of

41b

the source: for example, scholarly sources usually end in *edu*, *org*, or *gov*, while popular sources usually end in *com*. (See pp. 195 and 200–03 for more on types of online sources.)

■ **Check for sources.** Scholarly authors cite their sources formally in notes or a bibliography.

Older and newer sources

Check the publication date. For most subjects a combination of older, established sources (such as books) and current sources (such as newspaper articles, interviews, or Web sites) will provide both background and up-to-date information. Only historical subjects or very current subjects require an emphasis on one extreme or another.

Impartial and biased sources

Seek a range of viewpoints. Sources that attempt to be impartial can offer an overview of your subject and trustworthy facts. Sources with clear biases can give you a range of views about a subject and enrich your understanding of it. Of course, to discover bias, you may have to read the source carefully (see pp. 193–203); but you can infer quite a bit just from a bibliographical listing.

■ **Check the author.** Do a Web search to find out more about the author. Is he or she a respected researcher (thus more likely to be objective) or a leading proponent of a certain view (less likely to be objective)?

■ **Check the title.** It may reveal something about point of view. (Consider these contrasting titles: "Go for the Green" versus "Green Consumerism and the Struggle for Northern Maine.")

Sources with helpful features

Depending on your topic and how far along your research is, you may want to look for sources with features such as illustrations (which can clarify important concepts), bibliographies (which can direct you to other sources), and indexes (which can help you develop keywords for electronic searches; see pp. 183–85).

41b

42 Tracking Sources

Accurate records are essential for tracking where sources come from and for citing them in your writing. As you search, compile the publication information for sources in a working bibliography, and make notes about a source's usefulness in an annotated bibliography. As you discover sources that look promising, keep track of them by saving them to files, making printouts or photocopies, or taking notes on useful information.

42a Working bibliography

A **working bibliography** is a list of potential sources with their publication information. The following lists tell you what to record. For source samples that show where you can find the required information, see pages 238–39, 240, 242, 244–45 and 254 (MLA style) and pages 286–87 and 291 (APA style).

For a print or electronic books

Library call number
Name(s) of author(s), editor(s), translator(s), and other contributors
Title and subtitle
Publication data: (1) place of publication; (2) publisher's name; (3) date of publication; (4) title of any database or Web site used to reach the book; (5) publisher of any Web site used to find the book
Other important data, such as edition or volume number
Format (print, Web, Kindle file, etc.)
DOI, permalink, or complete URL (see the note on the next page)

For periodical articles

Name(s) of author(s)
Title and subtitle of article
Title of periodical
Publication data: (1) volume number and issue number (if any) in which the article appears; (2) date of issue; (3) page numbers on which article appears
Title of any database used to reach the source
DOI, permalink, or complete URL (see the note on the next page)

For Web material and other electronic sources

Name(s) of author(s) and other contributors
Title and subtitle of source

Title of Web site
Publication data: publisher and date of publication
Any publication data for the source in another medium (print, film, etc.)
Format of online source (Web site or page, podcast, e-mail, etc.)
Date you consulted the source
Title of any database used to reach the source
Complete URL, DOI, or permalink (see the note below)

For other sources

Name(s) of author(s) or creator(s) and other contributors
Title of the work
Title of any larger work of which the source is a part (television series, album, etc.)
Publication or production data: (1) publisher's or producer's name; (2) date of publication, release, or production; (3) identifying numbers (if any)
Format or medium (live performance, lecture, DVD, map, TV episode, etc.)

Note Documentation styles generally require DOIs (Digital Object Identifiers) or URLs for citations of electronic sources. Always record the DOI (if one is available) and the complete URL so that you'll have whatever is needed for your final citation of a source. For more on DOIs and URLs, see pages 231 (MLA style), 281 (Chicago style), 306 (APA style), and 322 (CSE style).

42b Annotated bibliography

Creating annotations for the sources in your working bibliography converts the list into a tool for assessing sources. The annotations can help you discover gaps that may remain in your sources and can help you decide which sources to pursue in depth. As you discover and evaluate each possible source, record not only its publication information but also the following:

- **What you know about the content of the source.** Periodical databases and book catalogs generally include abstracts, or summaries, of sources that can help with this part of the annotation.
- **How you think the source may be helpful in your research.** Does it offer expert opinion, statistics, an important example, or a range of views? Does it place your subject in a historical, social, or economic context?
- **Your assessment of the source.** Consider how reliable the source is and how it might fit into your research. (See pp. 193–204 for more on evaluating and synthesizing sources.)

42b

The following example shows a summary, a list of potentially useful features, and an assessment:

Gore, Al. *Our Choice: A Plan to Solve the Climate Crisis*. Rodale, 2009.

Publication information for source

A sequel to Gore's *An Inconvenient Truth* that emphasizes solutions to global warming. Expands on the argument that global warming is a serious threat, with recent examples of natural disasters. Proposes ways that governments, businesses, and individuals can reduce or reverse the risks of global warming. Includes helpful summaries of scientific studies, short essays on various subjects, and dozens of images, tables, charts, and graphs.

Summary of source from working bibliography

Ideas on use of source

Compelling overview of possible solutions, with lots of data that seem thorough and convincing. But the book is aimed at a general audience and doesn't have formal source citations. Can use it for broad concepts, but for data I'll have to track down Gore's scholarly sources.

Assessment of source

As you become more familiar with your sources, you can use your initial annotated bibliography to record your evaluation of them and more detailed thoughts on how they fit into your research.

42c Files, printouts, photocopies, and notes

The following tips can help you keep track of potentially useful sources as you locate them in the library, in databases, and on the Web. For each type of source, consult the lists on pages 179–80 for the publication information to record on each photocopy, printout, or file so that you can track and cite the source.

42c

- **Save or print out database sources.** As you locate database articles that look useful, save an electronic version (often a PDF file). If you are unable to save a copy, consider printing the article. Include any pages that give publication information, such as journal name, publication date, volume number, author's name, database name, and DOI.
- **Save or print out Web and other online sources.** Save potentially useful online material to a file or print it, making sure to include the information for electronic sources in the list on pages 179–80. For Web content, include the URL and/or the DOI so that you can find the source again.

- **Photocopy or take notes on print sources.** When you find a possible print source, such as a book, enter the key publication information into your working bibliography, or scan or photocopy the title page and the copyright page. For an article, scan or photocopy the periodical's table of contents. As you assess the usefulness of any print source, scan or photocopy the pages that relate to your topic, or take handwritten or typed notes.

Note Whatever method you use to track and record source information, you'll need to take care not to plagiarize by confusing the words and ideas of sources with your own words and ideas. See pages 212–18 on avoiding plagiarism.

43 Finding Sources

Your library and a computer connected to the Internet give you access to an almost infinite range of sources. The challenge is to find appropriate and worthy sources for your needs. This chapter shows you how.

Note As you look for sources, avoid the temptation to seek a "silver bullet"—that is, to locate two or three perfect sources that already say everything you want to say about your subject. Instead, read and synthesize many sources so that you develop your own ideas. For more on synthesis, see pages 203–04.

43a Your library's Web site

As you conduct academic research, your library's Web site will be your gateway to ideas and information. Always start with your library's Web site, not with a public search engine such as *Google*.

Advantages of a library search

The library site will lead you to vast resources that aren't available on the open Web. More important, every resource has been checked by editors and librarians to ensure its value. Although *Google* and other search engines can help you get a quick sense of how your project is talked about, they are not geared toward academic research, and many of their sources will be unreliable for academic research. In the end, a library search will be more efficient and more effective than an open-Web search.

Resources available through your library

Your library's Web site may offer the following tools for finding sources.

- **The library catalog:** Searchable from the library's Web site, the catalog is a database that lists all the resources the library owns or subscribes to. At some libraries, the catalog finds books, e-books, and the titles of periodicals within online databases. At other libraries, the catalog functions as a centralized search engine that covers all the library's holdings and subscriptions and locates articles in databases.
- **Online databases:** Searchable from the library's Web site, databases include articles from journals, magazines, and newspapers as well as reference works, primary sources, and more. Your library's Web site will likely list databases alphabetically and by discipline. As you use a database, be aware of what it does and does not offer, and check other databases if the one you are using does not have relevant sources on your topic. (For more on databases, see pp. 186–88.)
- **Research guides:** Many libraries provide guides that direct users to resources on particular subjects, such as twentieth-century English literature, social psychology, or human genetics.
- *Google Scholar*: Your library may provide a link to *Google Scholar*, a search engine for scholarly books and articles. It is particularly useful for subjects that range across disciplines. *Google Scholar* can connect to your library's holdings if you set it to do so under Scholar Preferences, but it may list books and articles that are not available to you. Your library is still the best resource for material that is easily available to you, so begin there.

43b

43b Electronic searches

A search that is too broad can miss helpful sources while returning hundreds of irrelevant ones. A search that is too narrow can exclude important sources. Take time early in your research to develop search terms that describe your subject effectively.

Types of search terms

Know the difference between keywords and subject headings:

- **Keywords** are the terms you type when you begin a search. In a library catalog or a database, a keyword looks for that word (or words) in titles, authors, and subject headings and sometimes within lists of keywords supplied by the author or in user tags added by readers. On the open Web, a keyword search looks for your terms anywhere in the record. As a researcher, your challenge is to find keywords that others have used to describe your subject.

- **Subject headings** (also called *subject terms*) tell you what a source is about. They are assigned to books and articles by people who have categorized the sources, so they can be more efficient than keywords at finding relevant sources. To find subject headings, use and refine your keywords until you find a promising source. On the source record, check the list of subject headings to see how the source is categorized (see p. 188 for an example). Then use the terms that best describe your subject in your searches.

Refinement of searches

Databases, catalogs, and search engines provide systems that you can use to refine your search terms for your purposes. The basic operations appear below, but resources do differ. You can learn a search engine's system by consulting its Advanced Search page.

- **Use *AND* or + to narrow the search by including only sources that use all the given words.** The keywords *green AND products* request only the sources that contain both words.

- **Use *NOT* or – ("minus") to narrow the search by excluding irrelevant words.** *Green AND products NOT guide* excludes sources that use the word *guide*.

- **Use *OR* to broaden the search by giving alternative keywords.** *Green AND products OR goods* allows for sources that use a synonym for *products*.

- **Use quotation marks and parentheses to form search phrases.** For instance, *"green products"* requests the exact phrase, not the separate words.

- **Use wild cards to permit different versions of the same word.** In *consum**, for instance, the wild card * indicates that sources may include *consume, consumer, consumerism,* and *consumption* as well as *consumptive, consumedly,* and *consummate*. If a wild card opens up your search too much, you may be better off using *OR: consumption OR consumerism*. (Some systems use ?, :, or + for a wild card instead of *.)

43b

- **Be sure to spell your keywords correctly.** Some search tools will look for close matches or approximations, but correct spelling gives you the best chance of finding relevant sources.

43c Reference works

Reference works, often available through your library and on the open Web, include encyclopedias, dictionaries, digests, bibliographies, indexes, handbooks, atlases, and almanacs. Your research *must* go beyond these sources, but they can help you decide whether your subject really interests you, can help you develop your keywords for electronic searches, and can direct you to more detailed sources. Preliminary research in reference works can also help you develop keywords for electronic searches and can direct you to more detailed sources on your topic.

Note The Web-based encyclopedia *Wikipedia* (*wikipedia.org*) is one of the largest reference sites on the Internet. Like any encyclopedia, *Wikipedia* can provide background information for research on a topic. But unlike other encyclopedias, *Wikipedia* is a **wiki**, a kind of Web site that can be contributed to or edited by anyone. Ask your instructor whether *Wikipedia* is an acceptable source before you use it. If you do use it, you must carefully evaluate any information you find, following the guidelines on pages 194–201.

43d Books

Your library's catalog is searchable via the library's Web site. Unless you seek a specific author or title, you'll want to search for books by using keywords or subject headings. In a keyword search, you start with your own search terms. In a subject-heading search, you use the headings on the records of promising sources to locate similar sources.

Using the tips above and on the preceding page, experiment with your own search terms until you locate a source that seems relevant to your subject. The book's detailed record will show Library of Congress subject headings that you can use to find similar books.

43e

43e Periodicals

Periodicals include newspapers, academic journals, and magazines, either printed or online. Newspapers are useful for detailed accounts of past and current events. Journals and magazines can be harder to distinguish, but their differences are important (see the next page). Most college instructors expect students' research to rely more on journals than on magazines.

Journals	Magazines
Examples	
American Anthropologist, Journal of Black Studies, Journal of Chemical Education	*The New Yorker, Time, Rolling Stone, People*
Availability	
Mainly college and university libraries, either on library shelves or in online databases	Public libraries, newsstands, bookstores, the open Web, and online databases
Purpose	
Advance knowledge in a particular field	Express opinion, inform, or entertain
Authors	
Specialists in the field	May or may not be specialists in their subjects
Readers	
Often specialists in the field	Members of the general public or a subgroup with a particular interest
Source citations	
Source citations always included	Source citations rarely included
Length of articles	
Usually long, ten pages or more	Usually short, fewer than ten pages
Frequency of publication	
Quarterly or less often	Weekly, biweekly, or monthly
Pagination of issues	
May be paged separately (like a magazine) or may be paged sequentially throughout an annual volume, so that issue number 3 (the third issue of the year) could open on page 373	Paged separately, each beginning on page 1

43e

Periodical databases

Periodical databases index the articles in journals, magazines, and newspapers. Often these databases include abstracts, or summaries, of the articles, and they may offer the full text of the articles as well. Your library subscribes to many databases, and you can search most of them through the library's Web site. They vary widely in what they index. To decide which ones to use, consider what you're looking for:

- **Does your research subject span more than one discipline?** If so, start with a broad database such as EBSCOhost's *Academic Search Complete, ProQuest Research Library,* or *JSTOR.* A broad database covers many subjects and disciplines but does not index the full range of periodicals in each subject. If your library offers a centralized search engine that searches across multiple databases, you can start there.
- **Does your research subject focus on a single discipline?** If so, start with a discipline-specific database such as *Historical Abstracts, MLA International Bibliography, Biological Abstracts,* or *Education Search Complete.* A specific database covers few subjects but includes most of the available periodicals in each subject. If you don't know the name of an appropriate database, the library's Web site probably lists possibilities by discipline.
- **Do you need primary sources?** Some specialized databases collect primary sources—for instance, historical newspapers, literary works not available in print, diaries, letters, music recordings, album liner notes. To determine whether you have access to such materials through your library, consult the list of databases on your library's Web site and read the descriptions to find out what each offers.
- **Which databases most likely include the kinds of resources you need?** The Web sites of most libraries provide lists of databases organized alphabetically and by discipline. Some libraries also provide research guides, which list potentially helpful databases for your search terms. To determine each database's focus, check the description of the database or the list of indexed resources. The description will also tell you the time period the database covers, so you'll know whether you also need to consult older print indexes at the library.

43e

Database searches

The screen shot on the next page shows partial results from a search of EBSCOhost's *Academic Search Complete.* For each source, the record lists title, author(s), publication information, and subject headings that can help you refine your search terms (see p. 184). Clicking on the titles leads to a more detailed record for each article, including an abstract (a summary) that can tell you whether you want to pursue the article further. An abstract is not the article, however, and should not be used or cited as if it were.

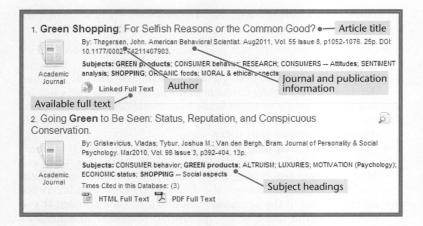

1. **Green Shopping**: For Selfish Reasons or the Common Good? ●— Article title

By: Thøgersen, John. American Behavioral Scientist. Aug2011, Vol. 55 Issue 8, p1052-1076. 25p. DOI: 10.1177/0002764211407903.

Academic Journal

Subjects: GREEN products; CONSUMER behavior; RESEARCH; CONSUMERS -- Attitudes; SENTIMENT analysis; SHOPPING; ORGANIC foods; MORAL & ethical aspects

Journal and publication information

Author

Linked Full Text

Available full text

2. Going **Green** to Be Seen: Status, Reputation, and Conspicuous Conservation.

Academic Journal

By: Griskevicius, Vladas; Tybur, Joshua M.; Van den Bergh, Bram. Journal of Personality & Social Psychology. Mar2010, Vol. 98 Issue 3, p392-404. 13p.

Subjects: CONSUMER behavior; **GREEN products**; ALTRUISM; LUXURIES; MOTIVATION (Psychology); ECONOMIC status; SHOPPING -- Social aspects

Times Cited in this Database: (3)

Subject headings

HTML Full Text   PDF Full Text

Note Many databases allow you to limit your search to so-called peer-reviewed or refereed journals—that is, scholarly journals whose articles have been reviewed before publication by experts in the field and then revised by the author. Limiting your search to peer-reviewed journals can help you navigate huge databases that might otherwise return scores of unusable articles.

43f The Web

As an academic researcher, you enter the Web in two ways: through your library's Web site and through public search engines such as *Bing* and *Google*. The library entrance, discussed in the preceding sections, is your main path to the books and articles that, for most subjects, should make up most of your sources. The open Web, discussed here, can lead to a wealth of information, but it also has disadvantages that limit its usefulness for academic research:

43f

- **The Web is a wide-open network.** Anyone with the right tools can place information on the Internet, and even a carefully conceived search can turn up sources with widely varying reliability: journal articles, government documents, scholarly data, term papers written by high school students, sales pitches masked as objective reports, wild theories. You must be especially diligent about evaluating open-Web sources (see pp. 194–203).
- **The Web changes constantly.** No search engine can keep up with the Web's daily additions and deletions, and a source you find today may be updated or gone tomorrow. You should not put

off consulting an online source that you think you may want to use.

- **The Web is not all-inclusive.** Most books and many periodicals are available only via the library, not directly via the Web.

To find sources on the Web, you use a search engine that catalogs Web sites in a series of directories and conducts keyword searches. For a good range of sources, try out more than a single search engine, perhaps as many as four or five, because no search engine can catalog the entire Web. Also expect to use trial and error to minimize the irrelevant hits and maximize the relevant ones. For example, a student researching consumption of environmentally friendly products first used the keywords *green consumption* and turned up 3.4 million items. Revising his terms to *"green consumption" "environmental issues,"* he cut the results to 2400 items. Finally, he added *site:.org* to the end of his keywords, limiting the results to nonprofit organizations, and got just 387 items.

43g Social media

Online sources that you reach through social media can put you directly in touch with experts and with others whose ideas and information may inform your research. Like Web sites, these social media are unfiltered, so you must always evaluate them carefully. (See pp. 201–03.)

- **E-mail** allows you to communicate with others who may be interested in your subject, such as a teacher at your school or an expert in another state.
- **Social-networking sites** are increasingly being used by organizations, businesses, individuals, and even scholars to communicate with others.
- **Blogs** are Web sites on which an author or authors post time-stamped comments, generally centering on a common theme, in a format that allows readers to respond.
- **Discussion lists** (or listservs) use e-mail to connect subscribers who are interested in a common subject. Many have a scholarly or technical purpose.
- **Newsgroups and Web forums** allow users to discuss particular subjects by posting messages to threaded conversations.

43g

Note If your paper includes social-media correspondence that is not already public—for instance, an e-mail or a discussion-group posting—ask the author for permission to use it.

43h Government publications

Government publications provide a vast array of data, reports, policy statements, public records, and other historical and contemporary information. For US government publications, consult the Government Publishing Office at *www.gpo.gov*. Also helpful is *www.usa.gov*, a portal to a range of government documents and information.

Many federal, state, and local government agencies post important publications—legislation, reports, press releases—on their own Web sites. You can find lists of sites for various federal agencies by using the keywords *United States federal government* with a search engine. Use the name of a state, city, or town with *government* for state and local information.

43i Visuals, audio, and video

Visuals, audio, and video can be used as both primary and secondary sources in academic writing. A painting, an advertisement, or a video of a speech might be the subject of a paper and thus a primary source. A podcast of a radio interview or a college lecture might serve as a secondary source. Because many Web sources for multimedia are unfiltered—they can be posted by anyone—you must always evaluate them as carefully as you would any source on the open Web.

- **Visuals** such as charts, graphs, and photographs can be found in print or online. Online sources for visuals include public databases such as *American Memory* (Library of Congress); public directories such as *Art Project* by *Google*; and databases available through your library.
- **Audio files** such as podcasts, Webcasts, and CDs record radio programs, interviews, speeches, and music. They are available on the Web and through your library. Online sources of audio include *American Memory* and the podcasts at *podcastdirectory.com*.
- **Video files** capture performances, speeches and public presentations, news events, and other activities. They are available on the Web and on DVD or Blu-ray disc from your library. Online sources of video include *American Memory*; *YouTube* and the *Internet Archive*, which include commercials, historical footage, current events, and much more; and search engines such as *Google*.

Caution You must cite every visual, audio, and video source fully in your paper, just as you cite text sources, with author, title, and publication information.

43j Your own sources

Academic writing will often require you to conduct primary research for information of your own.

Personal interviews

An interview with an expert can be especially helpful for a research project because it allows you to ask questions precisely geared to your topic. You can conduct an interview in person, over the telephone, or online. A personal interview is preferable if you can arrange it, because you can see the person's expressions and gestures as well as hear his or her tone.

Here are a few guidelines for interviews:

- **Prepare a list of open-ended questions to ask**—perhaps ten or twelve for a one-hour interview. Do some research on these questions before the interview to discover background on the issues and your subject's published views on the issues.
- **Pay attention to your subject's answers** so that you can ask appropriate follow-up questions. Take care in interpreting answers, especially if you are online and thus can't depend on facial expressions, gestures, and tone of voice to convey the subject's attitudes.
- **Keep thorough notes.** Take notes during an in-person or telephone interview, or record the interview if your subject agrees. For online interviews, save the discussion in a file of its own.
- **Verify quotations.** Before you quote your subject in your paper, check with him or her to ensure that the quotations are accurate.
- **Send a thank-you note immediately after the interview.** Promise your subject a copy of your finished paper, and send the paper promptly.

Surveys

Asking questions of a defined group of people can provide information about respondents' attitudes, behavior, backgrounds, and expectations. Use the following tips to plan and conduct a survey:

- **Decide what you want to find out.** The questions you ask should be dictated by your purpose. Formulating a **hypothesis** about your subject—a generalization that can be tested—will help you refine your purpose.
- **Define your population.** Think about the kinds of people your hypothesis is about—for instance, college men or preschool children. Plan to sample this population so that your findings will be representative.

43j

- **Write your questions.** Surveys may contain closed questions that direct the respondent's answers (checklists and multiple-choice, true/false, or yes/no questions) or open-ended questions that allow brief, descriptive answers. Avoid loaded questions that reveal your own biases or make assumptions about subjects' answers.
- **Test your questions.** Use a few respondents with whom you can discuss the answers. Eliminate or recast questions that respondents find unclear, discomforting, or unanswerable.
- **Tally the results.** Count the actual numbers of answers, including any nonanswers.
- **Seek patterns in the raw data.** Such patterns may confirm or contradict your hypothesis. Revise the hypothesis or conduct additional research if necessary.

Observation

Observation can be an effective way to gather fresh information on your subject. You may observe in a controlled setting—for instance, watching children at play in a child-development lab. Or you may observe in a more open setting—for instance, watching the interactions among students at a cafeteria on your campus. Use these guidelines for planning and gathering information through observation:

- **Be sure that what you want to learn *can* be observed.** You can observe people's choices and interactions, but you would need an interview or a survey to discover people's attitudes or opinions.
- **Allow ample time.** Observation requires several sessions of several hours in order to be reliable.
- **Record your impressions.** Throughout the observation sessions, take careful notes on paper, a computer, or a mobile device. Always record the date, time, and location for each session.
- **Be aware of your own bias.** Such awareness will help you avoid the common pitfall of seeing only what you expect or want to see.

43j

44 Evaluating and Synthesizing Sources

Research writing is much more than finding sources and reporting their contents. The challenge and interest come from selecting appropriate sources and then interacting with them through critical reading. To read critically, you analyze a text, identifying its main ideas, evidence, bias, and other relevant elements; you evaluate its usefulness and quality; and you synthesize its ideas and information with other texts and with your own ideas.

44a Evaluation of sources

Not all the sources you find will prove worthwhile: some may be irrelevant to your project, and others may be unreliable. Gauging the relevance and reliability of sources is the essential task of evaluating them.

Note In evaluating sources you need to consider how they come to you. The sources you find through the library, both print and online, have been previewed for you by their publishers and by the library's staff. They still require your critical reading, but you can have some confidence in the information they contain. With online sources, however, you can't assume similar previewing, so your critical reading must be especially rigorous.

Library sources

To evaluate sources you find through the library, look at dates, titles, summaries, introductions, headings, author biographies, bibliographies, and any source citations. Try to answer the following questions about each source.

Relevance

- **Does the source devote some attention to your subject?** Check whether the source focuses on your subject or covers it marginally, and compare the source's coverage to that in other sources.
- **Is the source appropriately specialized for your needs?** Check the source's treatment of a topic you know something about, to ensure that it is neither too superficial nor too technical.
- **Is the source up to date enough for your subject?** Check the publication date. If your subject is current, your sources should be, too.

Reliability

- **Where does the source come from?** It matters whether you found the source through your library or directly on the Internet. (If on the Internet, see below and pp. 200–03.) Check whether a library source is popular or scholarly. Scholarly sources, such as refereed journals and university press books, are generally deeper and more reliable.
- **Is the author an expert in the field?** The authors of scholarly publications tend to be experts. To verify expertise, check an author's credentials in a biography (if the source includes one), in a biographical reference, or by searching the author's name on the Web.
- **What is the bias of the source?** Every author has a point of view that influences the selection and interpretation of evidence. How do the author's ideas relate to those in other sources? What areas does the author emphasize, ignore, or dismiss? When you're aware of sources' biases, you can acknowledge and attempt to balance them.
- **Is the source fair, reasonable, and well written?** Does it provide sound reasoning and a fair picture of opposing views? Is the tone calm and objective? Is the source logically organized and error-free?
- **Are the claims well supported, even if you don't agree with the author?** Does the author provide accurate, relevant, representative, and adequate evidence to back up his or her claims? Does the author cite sources, and if so are they reliable?

See pages 196–97 for an example of how a student applied these criteria to two library sources.

Web sites

The same critical reading that serves you with library sources will help you evaluate Web sites. You would not use a popular magazine such as *People* in academic research—unless, say, you were considering it as a primary source in a paper analyzing popular culture. Similarly, you would not use a celebrity's Web site, a fan site, or a gossip site as a source unless you were placing it in a larger academic context.

Even Web sites that seem worthy pose challenges for evaluation because they have not undergone prior screening by editors and librarians. On your own, you must distinguish scholarship from corporate promotion, valid data from invented statistics, well-founded opinion from clever propaganda.

To evaluate a Web site, add the following questions to those on the previous two pages.

- **What type of site are you viewing**—for example, is it scholarly, informational, or commercial?
- **Who is the author or publisher?** How credible is the person or group responsible for the site?
- **What is the purpose of the site?** What does the site's author or publisher intend to achieve? Are there ads on the site, signaling that the site is trying to make money from its content?
- **What is the bias of the site?** Does the site advocate for one side or another of a particular issue?
- **What does context tell you?** What do you already know about the site's subject that can inform your evaluation? What kinds of support or other information do the site's links provide?
- **What does presentation tell you?** Is the site's design well thought out and effective? Is the writing clear and error-free?
- **How worthwhile is the content?** Are the site's claims well supported by evidence? Is the evidence from reliable sources?

The following discussion elaborates on each of these questions. Pages 198–99 illustrate how a student applied the questions to two Web sites.

Note To evaluate a Web document, you'll often need to refer to the site's home page to discover the author or publisher, date of publication, and other relevant information. The page you're reading may include a link to the home page. If it doesn't, you can find it by editing the URL in the Address or Location field of your browser.

Determine the type of site.

When you search the Web, you're likely to encounter various types of sites:

- **Scholarly sites:** These sites have a knowledge-building interest, and they are likely to be reliable. They may include research reports with supporting data and extensive documentation of scholarly sources. For such sites originating in the United States, the URLs generally end in *edu* (originating from an educational institution), *org* (a nonprofit organization), or *gov* (a government department or agency). Sites originating in other countries will usually end with a country code such as *uk* (United Kingdom) or *kr* (South Korea).
- **Informational sites:** Individuals, schools, nonprofit organizations, corporations, and government bodies all produce sites intended

44a

(text continues on p. 200)

Evaluating library sources

Below are a student's evaluations of the two library sources on the facing page. The student was researching consumption of environmentally friendly products.

Makower	Jackson
Origin	
Interview with Joel Makower published in *Vegetarian Times*, a popular magazine.	Article by Tim Jackson published in the *Journal of Industrial Ecology*, a scholarly journal sponsored by two universities: MIT and Yale.
Author	
Gives Makower's credentials at the beginning of the interview: the author of a book on green products and of a monthly newsletter on green businesses.	Includes a biography at the end of the article that describes Jackson as a professor at the University of Surrey (UK) and lists his professional activities related to the environment.
Bias	
Describes and promotes green products. Concludes with an endorsement of a for-profit Web site that tracks and sells green products.	Gives multiple views of green consumerism. Argues that environmental solutions will involve green products and less consumption but differently than proposed by others.
Reasonableness and writing	
Presents Makower's data and perspective on distinguishing good from bad green products, using conversational writing in an informal presentation.	Presents and cites opposing views objectively, using formal academic writing.
Source citations	
Lacks citations for claims and data.	Lists scholarly and government sources in dozens of citations.
Assessment	
Unreliable for academic research: The article comes from a non-scholarly source, takes a one-sided approach to consumption, and depends on statistics credited only to Makower.	**Reliable for academic research:** The article comes from a scholarly journal, discusses many views and concedes some, and includes evidence from and citations of reliable sources.

44a

Unreliable source for academic research: An interview with Joel Makower, published in *Vegetarian Times*

Reliable source for academic research: An article by Tim Jackson, published in the *Journal of Industrial Ecology*

44a

Evaluating Web sites

Opposite are screen shots from two Web sites that a student consulted for a paper on green consumerism. The evaluation answers the questions on page 195.

Wikipedia

Center for Climate and Energy Solutions

Author and publisher

Author of the page is not given. Web site is *Wikipedia*, the online encyclopedia to which anyone can contribute anonymously.

Author is an expert on energy and public policy. Publisher is the Center for Climate and Energy Solutions, a nonprofit group.

Purpose and bias

Informational page with no stated or obvious bias.

Informational site with the stated purpose of promoting policy on energy and climate change. Report expresses bias toward sustainable electricity production.

Context

An encyclopedia site publishing general information on a wide variety of topics.

Nonprofit organization's site dedicated to publishing current research on energy and climate issues.

Presentation

Clean, professional-looking page with mostly error-free writing.

Clean, professionally designed site with error-free writing.

Content

Article gives basic information about energy use with links to other pages but not to extensive citations of scholarly research.

Report is current (date below the author's name), it describes scenarios for meeting future electricity needs, and it cites scholarly sources.

Assessment

Unreliable for academic research: The page has no listed author and few scholarly citations. A *Wikipedia* page is suitable for background information but not as evidence in an academic paper.

Reliable for academic research: The report has a bias toward sustainable electricity production, but the publisher is reputable and the author is an expert and cites scholarly sources.

44a

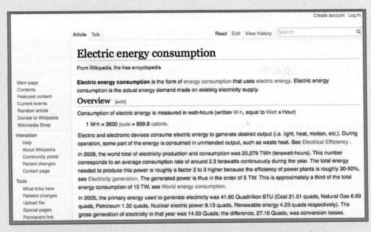

Unreliable source for academic research: A page on the Web site
Wikipedia
Courtesy of Wikipedia.org. http://en.wikipedia.org/wiki/Electric_energy_consumption.

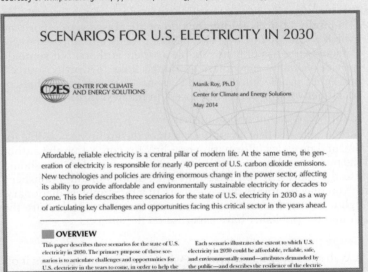

Reliable source for academic research: A report published on the Web site
Center for Climate and Energy Solutions

44a

(continued from p. 195)

to centralize information on particular subjects. The sites' URLs may end in *edu, org, gov,* or *com* (originating from a commercial organization). Such sites generally do not have the knowledge-building focus of scholarly sites and may omit supporting data and documentation, but they can provide useful information and often include links to scholarly sources.

- **Advocacy sites:** Many sites present the views of individuals or organizations that promote certain policies or actions. Their URLs usually end in *org,* but they may end in *edu* or *com.* Most advocacy sites have a strong bias. Some include serious, well-documented research to support their positions, but others select or distort evidence.

- **Commercial sites:** Corporations and other businesses maintain Web sites to explain or promote themselves or to sell goods and services. URLs of commercial sites usually end in *com*; however, some end in *biz,* and those of businesses based outside the United States often end in the country code. Although business sites intend to further the publishers' profit-making purposes, they can include reliable data.

- **Personal sites:** Sites maintained by individuals range from diaries of a family's travels to opinions on political issues to reports on evolving scholarship. The sites' URLs usually end in *com* or *edu.* Personal sites are only as reliable as their authors, but some do provide valuable eyewitness accounts, links to worthy sources, and other usable information. Personal sites are often blogs or social-networking pages, discussed on the next three pages.

Identify the author and publisher.

A reputable site lists its authors, names the group responsible for the site, and provides information or a link for contacting the author and the publisher. If none of this information is provided, you should not use the source. If you have only the author's or the publisher's name, you may be able to discover more in a biographical dictionary, through a keyword search, or in your other sources. Make sure the author and the publisher have expertise on the subject.

44a

Gauge purpose and bias.

A Web site's purpose determines what ideas and information it offers. Inferring that purpose tells you how to interpret what you see on the site. If a site is intended to sell a product or advocate a particular position, it may emphasize favorable ideas and information while ignoring or even distorting unfavorable information or opposing views.

In contrast, if a site is intended to build knowledge—for instance, a scholarly project or journal—it will likely acknowledge diverse views and evidence.

Determining the purpose and bias of a site often requires looking beyond the first page. To start, read critically what the site says about itself, usually on a page labeled "About." Be suspicious of any site that doesn't provide information about itself and its goals.

Consider context.

Look outside the site itself. What do you already know about the site's subject and the prevailing views of it? Where does this site seem to fit into that picture? What can you learn from this site that you don't already know? Do the links on the site support its credibility?

Look at presentation.

Considering both the look of a site and the way it's written can illuminate its intentions and reliability. Do the site's elements all support its purpose, or is the site cluttered with irrelevant material and graphics? Is the text clearly written and focused on the purpose, or is it difficult to understand? Does the site seem carefully constructed and well maintained, or is it sloppy? How intrusive are any pop-up advertisements?

Analyze content.

With information about a site's author, purpose, and context, you're in a position to evaluate its content. Are the ideas and information current, or are they dated? Are they slanted and, if so, in what direction? Are the views and data authoritative, or do you need to balance them—or even reject them? Are claims made on the site supported by evidence drawn from reliable sources?

Other online sources

Social media and multimedia require the same critical scrutiny as Web sites do. Social media—including e-mail, blogs, *Twitter*, discussion groups, wikis, and *Facebook* pages—can be sources of reliable data and opinions, but they can also contain misleading data and skewed opinions. Multimedia—visuals, audio, and video—can provide valuable support for your ideas, but they can also mislead or distort. For example, a *YouTube* search using "I have a dream" brings up videos of Martin Luther King, Jr., delivering his famous speech as well as videos of people speaking hatefully about King and the speech.

To evaluate social media and multimedia, ask the following questions.

44a

- **Who is the author or creator?** How credible is that person? You may be able to learn about the background of an author or creator with a keyword search of the Web or in a biographical dictionary. You can also get a sense of the interests and biases of an author or creator by tracking down his or her other work. If you can't identify the author or creator at all, you can't use the source.
- **What is the author's or creator's purpose?** What can you tell about *why* the author/creator is publishing the work? Look for cues in the work—claims, use (or lack) of evidence, and treatment of opposing views—to figure out how to position the source among your other sources.
- **What does the context reveal?** What do others' responses to the work indicate about the source's balance and reliability? On a blog or *Facebook* page, for example, look at the comments others have posted. Try to understand negative comments: sometimes online anonymity encourages angry responses to reasonable postings.

THE **BLOG** | Featuring fresh takes and real-time analysis from HuffPost's signature lineup of contributors

American Anthropological Association
World's largest organization of individuals interested in anthropology

Author is a university professor and represents a professional academic organization.

Title reveals purpose and bias.

Green Consumerism Is No Solution

Posted: 06/14/2013 4:50 pm

Like 399 people like this. Be the first of your friends.

Posting has been shared and commented on.

| 128 | 61 | 5 | 7 | 4 |

f Share Tweet 8+1 Email Comment

GET GREEN NEWSLETTERS:
Enter email   SUBSCRIBE

Written by Richard Wilk

Presentation is clear and error-free. Content is current and links to supporting data.

Greenwashing is not just for corporations anymore -- it has gone personal. Instead of feeling guilty about the huge gaps between wealthy and poor, the ways consumerism causes global warming, or how our daily pleasures cause rainforest destruction and despoil the sea, we can drink a few cups of fair-trade coffee, eat a rainforest crunch bar and

44a

- **How worthwhile is the content?** Are the claims made by the author/creator supported by evidence from reliable sources? Verify any sources with your own research: are they reputable? If not or if there is no supporting information, you shouldn't use the source.
- **How does the source compare with other sources?** Do the claims seem accurate and fair given what you've seen in sources you know to be reliable? Always consider social-media and multimedia sources in comparison to other sources so that you can distinguish singular, untested views from more mainstream views that have been subject to verification.

44b Synthesis of sources

Evaluating sources moves you into the most significant part of research writing: making connections among sources and your own ideas. This **synthesis** is an essential step in reading sources critically, and it continues through the drafting and revision of a research paper. As you make connections among sources, you shape your own perspective on your subject, and you move toward writing a paper that builds new knowledge.

Respond to sources.

Write down what your sources lead you to think. Do you agree or disagree with the author? Why do you agree or disagree? What new information and approaches to your subject does the source open for you? Is there anything in the source that you need to research further before you can understand it? Does the source prompt questions that you should keep in mind while reading other sources?

Connect sources.

When you notice a link between sources, write about it. Does one source help you understand another—perhaps commenting on it or supplying additional information? Do two sources differ in what they think is important about your subject? Do two sources interpret facts differently or make different arguments? Do two or more sources support an idea of your own or a view of your topic that you've read about?

Heed your own insights.

Apart from ideas prompted by your sources, you are sure to come up with your own thoughts about your subject—a question you haven't seen anyone else ask, a point of confusion that suddenly becomes clear, a view of the subject that others have not taken. These

44b

insights may happen any time, so be sure to record them when they occur to you.

Draw your own conclusions.

As your research proceeds, the responses, connections, and insights you form through your synthesis of sources will lead you to answer your starting research question with a statement of your thesis (see p. 175). They will also lead you to the main ideas supporting your thesis, which will form the main sections of your paper. Be sure to write them down as they occur to you.

Use sources to support your conclusions.

Effective synthesis requires careful handling of evidence from sources so that it fits smoothly into your sentences and yet is clearly distinct from your own ideas. When drafting your paper, make sure that each paragraph focuses on an idea of your own, with the support for the idea coming from your sources. Generally, open each paragraph with your idea, provide evidence from a source or sources with appropriate citations, and close with an interpretation of the evidence. (For an example of such a paragraph, see p. 4.)

45 Integrating Sources into Your Text

Integrating source material into your sentences is a key skill in showing how you have synthesized others' ideas and information with your own. Evidence drawn from sources should *back up* your conclusions, not *be* your conclusions: you don't want to let your evidence overwhelm your own point of view. To keep your ideas in the forefront, you do more than merely present borrowed material; you introduce and interpret it as well.

Integrating sources into your text may involve several conventions discussed elsewhere in this book:

- **Using commas to punctuate signal phrases** (p. 139).
- **Placing other punctuation marks with quotation marks** (pp. 149–50).
- **Using brackets and the ellipsis mark to indicate changes in quotations** (pp. 154–56).
- **Formatting long prose quotations and poetry quotations** (MLA, p. 265; APA, p. 295; and Chicago, p. 315).

45a Summary, paraphrase, and direct quotation

As you take notes from sources or work source material into your draft, you can summarize, paraphrase, quote, or combine methods. The choice should depend on why you are using a source.

Caution **Summaries, paraphrases, and quotations all require source citations. A summary or paraphrase without a source citation or a quotation without quotation marks is plagiarism.** (See pp. 212–18 for more on plagiarism.)

Summary

When you **summarize**, you condense an extended idea or argument into a sentence or more in your own words. (See pp. 35–36 for tips.) Summary is most useful when you want to record the gist of an author's idea without the background or supporting evidence. Here, for example, is a passage from a scholarly essay about consumption and its impact on the environment.

Original quotation

Such intuition is even making its way, albeit slowly, into scholarly circles, where recognition is mounting that ever-increasing pressures on ecosystems, life-supporting environmental services, and critical natural cycles are driven not only by the sheer number of resource users and the inefficiencies of their resource use, but also by the patterns of resource use themselves. In global environmental policymaking arenas, it is becoming more and more difficult to ignore the fact that overdeveloped countries must restrain their consumption if they expect underdeveloped countries to embrace a more sustainable trajectory. And while global population growth still remains a huge issue in many regions around the world—both rich and poor—per-capita growth in consumption is, for many resources, expanding eight to twelve times faster than population growth.

—Thomas Princen, Michael Maniates, and Ken Conca,
Confronting Consumption, p. 4

Summary

Overconsumption may be a more significant cause of environmental problems than increasing population is.

Paraphrase

When you **paraphrase**, you follow the author's original presentation much more closely than in a summary, but you still restate it in your own words. Paraphrase is most useful when you want to reconstruct an author's line of reasoning but don't feel the original words merit direct quotation. Here is a paraphrase of the quotation from *Confronting Consumption*.

Paraphrase

Scholars are coming to believe that consumption is partly to blame for changes in ecosystems, reduction of essential natural resources, and changes in natural cycles. Policy makers increasingly see that developing nations will not adopt practices that reduce pollution and waste unless wealthy nations consume less. Rising population around the world does cause significant stress on the environment, but consumption is increasing even more rapidly than population.

Follow these guidelines when paraphrasing:

- **Read the material until you understand it.**
- **Restate the main ideas in your own words and sentence structures.** Use phrases if complete sentences seem cumbersome.
- **Be careful not to distort the author's meaning.**
- **Be careful not to plagiarize the source.** Use your own words and sentence structures, and always record a citation in your notes. Especially if your source is difficult or complex, you may be tempted to change just a few words or to modify the sentence structure just a bit. But that is plagiarism, not paraphrase.

For examples of poor and revised paraphrases, see pages 216–17.

ESL If English is not your first language, you may have difficulty paraphrasing the ideas in sources because synonyms don't occur to you or you don't see how to restructure sentences. Before attempting a paraphrase, read the original passage several times. Then, instead of "translating" line by line, try to state the gist of the passage without looking at it. Check your effort against the original to be sure you have captured the source author's meaning and emphasis without using his or her words and sentence structures. If you need a synonym for a word, look it up in a dictionary.

Direct quotation

45a

Whether to quote a source instead of paraphrasing or summarizing it depends on the kind of source and on how important its exact words are. Quote extensively from primary sources that you are analyzing, such as historical documents or literary works. Quote selectively from secondary sources, such as other writers' views of primary sources. Summarize or paraphrase from secondary sources unless the material passes *both* of these bulleted tests:

- **The author's original satisfies one of these requirements:**
  The language is unusually vivid, bold, or inventive.
  The quotation cannot be paraphrased without distortion or loss of meaning.

You take issue with the words themselves.
The quotation emphasizes the view of an important expert.
The quotation is a graph, diagram, or table.

■ **The quotation is as short as possible:**
It includes only material relevant to your point.
It is edited to eliminate examples and other unneeded material.

When taking a quotation from a source, copy the material *carefully*. Take down the author's exact wording, spelling, capitalization, and punctuation. Proofread every direct quotation *at least twice*, and be sure you have supplied big quotation marks so that later you won't confuse the direct quotation with a paraphrase or summary. And always cite the source of the quotation in your draft.

45b Introduction and interpretation of source material

Note Most examples on the following pages use the documentation style of the Modern Language Association (MLA) and also present-tense° verbs that are typical of much writing in the humanities. For specific variations in the academic disciplines, see pages 210–11.

Introduction

Work all quotations, paraphrases, and summaries smoothly into your own sentences, adding words as necessary to mesh structures.

Awkward   One editor disagrees with this view and "a good reporter does not fail to separate opinions from facts" (Lyman 52).

Revised   One editor disagrees with this view, <u>maintaining that</u> "a good reporter does not fail to separate opinions from facts" (Lyman 52).

To mesh your own and your source's words, you may sometimes need to make a substitution or addition to the quotation, signaling your change with brackets:

Words added

"The tabloids [of England] are a journalistic case study in bad reporting," claims Lyman (52).

Verb form changed

A bad reporter, Lyman implies, is one who "[fails] to separate opinions from facts" (52). [The bracketed verb replaces *fail* in the original.]

Capitalization changed

"[T]o separate opinions from facts" is a goal of good reporting (Lyman 52). [In the original, *to* is not capitalized.]

°Defined in "Grammar Terms," page 340.

45b

Noun supplied for pronoun

The reliability of a news organization "depends on [reporters'] trustworthiness," says Lyman (52). [The bracketed noun replaces *their* in the original.]

Interpretation

Even when it does not conflict with your own sentence structure, source material will be ineffective if you merely dump it in readers' laps without explaining how you intend it to be understood. In the following passage, we must figure out for ourselves that the writer's sentence and the quotation state opposite points of view.

Dumped Many news editors and reporters maintain that it is impossible to keep personal opinions from influencing the selection and presentation of facts. "True, news reporters, like everyone else, form impressions of what they see and hear. However, a good reporter does not fail to separate opinions from facts" (Lyman 52).

Revised Many news editors and reporters maintain that it is impossible to keep personal opinions from influencing the selection and presentation of facts. Yet not all authorities agree with this view. One editor grants that "news reporters, like everyone else, form impressions of what they see and hear." But, he insists, "a good reporter does not fail to separate opinions from facts" (Lyman 52).

Signal phrases

In the preceding revised passage, the words *One editor grants* and *he insists* are **signal phrases**: they tell readers who the source is and what to expect in the quotations. Signal phrases usually contain (1) the source author's name (or a substitute for it, such as *One editor* and *he*) and (2) a verb that indicates the source author's attitude or approach to what he or she says, as *grants* implies concession and *insists* implies argument.

Following are some verbs to use in signal phrases. For the appropriate tense of such verbs (present, as here, or past or present perfect) see pages 210–11.

45b

Author is neutral		Author infers or suggests	
comments	points out	analyzes	finds
describes	records	asks	predicts
explains	relates	assesses	proposes
illustrates	reports	believes	reveals
mentions	says	concludes	shows
notes	sees	considers	speculates
observes	thinks		suggests
	writes		supposes

Author	Author	Author	derides
argues	agrees	is uneasy or	laments
claims	accepts	disparaging	warns
contends	admits	belittles	
defends	agrees	bemoans	
disagrees	concedes	complains	
holds	concurs	condemns	
insists	grants	deplores	
maintains		deprecates	

Note that some signal verbs, such as *describes* and *assesses*, cannot be followed by *that*.

Vary your signal phrases to suit your interpretation of source material and also to keep readers' interest. A signal phrase may precede, interrupt, or follow the borrowed material:

Signal phrase precedes

Lyman insists that "a good reporter does not fail to separate opinions from facts" (52).

Signal phrase interrupts

"However," Lyman insists, "a good reporter does not fail to separate opinions from facts" (52).

Signal phrase follows

"[A] good reporter does not fail to separate opinions from facts," Lyman insists (52).

Background information

You can add information to source material to integrate it into your text and inform readers why you are using it. Often, you may want to provide the author's name in the text:

Author named

Harold Lyman grants that "news reporters, like everyone else, form impressions of what they see and hear." But, Lyman insists, "a good reporter does not fail to separate opinions from facts" (52).

45b

If the source title adds information about the author or the context of the borrowed material, you can provide the title in the text:

Title given

Harold Lyman, in his book *The Conscience of the Journalist*, grants that "news reporters, like everyone else, form impressions of what they see and hear." But, Lyman insists, "a good reporter does not fail to separate opinions from facts" (52).

Finally, if the source author's background and experience reinforce or clarify the borrowed material, you can provide those credentials in the text:

Credentials given

Harold Lyman, a newspaper editor for more than forty years, grants that "news reporters, like everyone else, form impressions of what they see and hear." But, Lyman insists, "a good reporter does not fail to separate opinions from facts" (52).

You need not name the author, title, or credentials in your text when you are simply establishing facts or weaving together facts and opinions from varied sources to support a larger point. In the following passage, the information is more important than the source, so the author's name is confined to a parenthetical acknowledgment:

To end the abuses of the British, many colonists were urging three actions: forming a united front, seceding from Britain, and taking control of their own international trade and diplomacy (Wills 325–36).

Discipline styles for interpreting sources

The preceding guidelines for interpreting source material apply generally across academic disciplines, but there are differences in verb tenses and documentation style.

English and some other humanities

Writers in English, foreign languages, and related disciplines use MLA style for documenting sources (see Chapter 48) and generally use the present tense° of verbs in signal phrases. (See the list of signal-phrase verbs on pp. 208–09.) In discussing sources other than works of literature, the present perfect tense° is also sometimes appropriate:

Lyman insists... [present].
Lyman has insisted... [present perfect].

In discussing works of literature, use only the present tense to describe both the work of the author and the action in the work:

Kate Chopin builds irony into every turn of "The Story of an Hour." For example, Mrs. Mallard, the central character, finds joy in the death of her husband, whom she loves, because she anticipates "the long procession of years that would belong to her absolutely" (23).

Avoid shifting tenses in writing about literature. You can, for instance, shorten quotations to avoid their past-tense° verbs.

45b

°Defined in "Grammar Terms," page 340.

Shift   Her freedom <u>elevates</u> her, so that "she <u>carried</u> herself unwittingly like a goddess of victory" (24).

No shift   Her freedom <u>elevates</u> her, so that she <u>walks</u> "unwittingly like a goddess of victory" (24).

History and other humanities

Writers in history, art history, philosophy, and related disciplines generally use the present tense or present perfect tense of verbs in signal phrases. (See the list of possible verbs on pp. 208–09.)

Lincoln persisted, as Haworth <u>has noted</u>, in "feeling that events controlled him."[3]

What Miller <u>calls</u> Lincoln's "severe self-doubt"[6] undermined his effectiveness on at least two occasions.

The raised numbers after the quotations are part of the Chicago documentation style, used in history and other disciplines and discussed in Chapter 50.

Social and natural sciences

Writers in the sciences generally use a verb's present tense just for reporting the results of a study (*The data suggest* . . .). Otherwise, they use a verb's past tense or present perfect tense in a signal phrase, as when introducing an explanation, interpretation, or other commentary. (Thus, when you are writing for the sciences, generally convert the list of signal-phrase verbs on pp. 208–09 from the present to the past or present perfect tense.)

In an exhaustive survey of the literature published between 1990 and 2010, Walker (2014) <u>found</u> "no proof, merely a weak correlation, linking place of residence and rate of illness" (p. 121).

Lin (2013) <u>has suggested</u> that preschooling may significantly affect children's academic performance through high school (p. 251).

These passages conform to the documentation style of the American Psychological Association (APA), discussed in Chapter 49. APA style or the similar CSE style (Chapter 51) is used in sociology, education, nursing, biology, and many other sciences.

45c

45c Clear boundaries for source material

Position source citations in your text to accomplish two goals: (1) make it clear exactly where your borrowing of source material begins and ends; (2) keep the citations as unobtrusive as possible. You can accomplish both goals by placing an in-text citation at the end of the sentence element containing the borrowed material. This sentence element may be a phrase or a clause, and it may begin, interrupt, or conclude the sentence. The following examples are in MLA style.

The inflation rate might climb as high as 30% (Kim 164), an increase that could threaten the small nation's stability.

The inflation rate, which might climb as high as 30% (Kim 164), could threaten the small nation's stability.

The small nation's stability could be threatened by its inflation rate, which, one source predicts, might climb as high as 30% (Kim 164).

In the last example the addition of *one source predicts* clarifies that Kim is responsible only for the inflation-rate prediction, not for the statement about stability.

When your paraphrase or summary of a source runs longer than a sentence, clarify the boundaries by using the author's name in the first sentence and placing the parenthetical citation at the end of the last sentence.

Juliette Kim studied the effects of acutely high inflation in several South American and African countries since World War II. She discovered that a major change in government accompanied or followed the inflationary period in 56% of cases (22-23).

46 Avoiding Plagiarism

The knowledge building that is the focus of academic writing rests on the honesty of all participants, including students, in using and crediting sources. This standard of honesty derives from the idea that the work of an author is his or her intellectual property: if you use that work, you must acknowledge the author's ownership. At the same time, source acknowledgments tell readers what your own writing is based on, adding to your integrity as a researcher and creating the trust that knowledge building requires.

Plagiarism (from a Latin word for "kidnapper") is the presentation of someone else's work as your own. Whether deliberate or careless, plagiarism is a serious offense. It breaks trust, and it undermines or even destroys your credibility as a researcher and writer. In most colleges, a code of academic honesty calls for severe consequences for plagiarism: a reduced or failing grade, suspension from school, or expulsion. The way to avoid plagiarism is to acknowledge your sources: keep track of the ones you consult for each paper you write, and document them within the paper and in a list of works cited.

ESL The concepts of originality, intellectual property, and plagiarism are not universal. In some other cultures, for instance, students may be encouraged to copy the words of scholars without acknowledging the sources, in order to demonstrate their mastery of or respect for the scholars' work. In the United States, however, using an author's work without a source citation is a serious offense, whether it is careless or intentional. If you have questions about the guidelines in this chapter, ask your instructor for advice.

46a Deliberate and careless plagiarism

Instructors usually distinguish between deliberate plagiarism, which is cheating, and careless plagiarism, which often stems from a writer's inexperience with managing sources.

Deliberate plagiarism

Deliberate plagiarism is intentional: the writer chooses to cheat by turning in someone else's work as his or her own. Students who deliberately plagiarize deprive themselves of an education in honest research. When their cheating is detected, the students often face stiff penalties, including expulsion.

Following are examples of deliberate plagiarism:

Copying a phrase, a sentence, or a longer passage from a source and passing it off as your own by not adding quotation marks and a source citation.

Summarizing or paraphrasing someone else's ideas without acknowledging the source in a citation.

Handing in as your own work a paper you have copied off the Web, had a friend write, or accepted from another student.

Handing in as your own work a paper you have purchased from a paperwriting service. **Paying for research or a paper does not make it your work.**

Careless plagiarism

Careless plagiarism is unintentional: grappling with complicated information and ideas in sources, the writer neglects to put quotation marks around a source's exact words or neglects to include a source

46a

citation for a quotation, paraphrase, or summary. Most instructors and schools do not permit careless plagiarism, but they treat it less harshly than deliberate plagiarism—at least the first time it occurs.

Here are examples of careless plagiarism:

Reading sources without taking notes on them and then not distinguishing what you recently learned from what you already knew.

Copying and pasting material from a source into your document without placing quotation marks around the other writer's work.

Forgetting to add a source citation for a paraphrase. Even though a paraphrase casts another person's idea in your own words, you still need to cite the source of the idea.

Omitting a source citation for another's idea because you are unaware of the need to acknowledge the idea.

Checklist for avoiding plagiarism

Know your source.

Are you using

- your own experience,
- common knowledge, or
- someone else's material?

You must acknowledge someone else's material.

Quote carefully.

- Check that every quotation exactly matches its source.
- Insert quotation marks around every quotation that you run into your text. (A quotation set off from the text does not need quotation marks. See pp. 265, 295, and 315.)
- Indicate any omission from a quotation with an ellipsis mark and any addition with brackets.
- Acknowledge the source of every quotation.

Paraphrase and summarize carefully.

- Use your own words and sentence structures for every paraphrase and summary. If you have used the author's words, add quotation marks around them.
- Acknowledge the source of the idea(s) in every paraphrase or summary.

Cite sources responsibly.

- Acknowledge every use of borrowed material in each place you use it.
- Include all your sources in your list of works cited. See Chapters 48–51 for citing sources in common documentation styles.

46a

Plagiarism and the Internet

The Internet has made it easier to plagiarize than ever before: with just a few clicks, you can copy and paste passages or whole documents into your own files. If you do so without quoting and acknowledging your source, you plagiarize.

The Internet has also made plagiarism easier to detect. Instructors can use search engines to find specific phrases or sentences anywhere on the Web, including among scholarly publications, all kinds of Web sites, and term-paper collections. They can search term-paper sites as easily as students can, looking for similarities with papers they've received. They can also use detection software—such as *Turnitin, PlagiServe,* and *Glatt Plagiarism Services*—which compares students' work with other work anywhere on the Internet, seeking matches as short as a few words.

Some instructors suggest that their students use plagiarism-detection programs to verify that their own work does not include careless plagiarism, at least not from the Internet.

46b What *not* to acknowledge

Your independent material

You are not required to acknowledge your own observations, thoughts, compilations of facts, or experimental results, expressed in your own words and format.

Common knowledge

You need not acknowledge **common knowledge**: the standard information of a field of study as well as folk literature and common-sense observations.

If you do not know a subject well enough to determine whether a piece of information is common knowledge, make a record of the source. As you read more about the subject, the information may come up repeatedly without acknowledgment, in which case it is probably common knowledge. But if you are still in doubt when you finish your research, always acknowledge the source.

46c

46c What *must* be acknowledged

You must always acknowledge other people's independent material—that is, any facts or ideas that are not common knowledge or your own. The source may be anything, including a book, an article, a movie, an interview, a comic strip, a Web page, a map, a tweet, or an opinion expressed on the radio. You must acknowledge summaries or paraphrases of ideas or facts as well as quotations of the language and format in which ideas or facts appear: wording, sentence structures, arrangement, and special graphics (such as a diagram). You must acknowledge another's material no matter how you use it, how much of it you use, or how often you use it.

Note See pages 206–07 on integrating quotations into your own text without plagiarism. And see pages 218–20 on acknowledging sources.

Copied language: Quotation marks and a source citation

The following example baldly plagiarizes the original quotation from Jessica Mitford's *Kind and Usual Punishment*, page 9. Without quotation marks or a source citation, the example matches Mitford's wording (underlined) and closely parallels her sentence structure:

Original quotation	"The character and mentality of the keepers may be of more importance in understanding prisons than the character and mentality of the kept."
Plagiarism	But the character of prison officials (the keepers) is of more importance in understanding prisons than the character of prisoners (the kept).

To avoid plagiarism, the writer has two options: (1) paraphrase and cite the source (see the examples on the next page) or (2) use Mitford's actual words *in quotation marks* and *with a source citation* (here, in MLA style):

Revision (quotation)	According to Mitford, a critic of the penal system, "The character and mentality of the keepers may be of more importance in understanding prisons than the character and mentality of the kept" (9).

Even with a source citation and with a different sentence structure, the following example is still plagiarism because it uses some of Mitford's words (underlined) without quotation marks:

46c

Plagiarism	According to Mitford, a critic of the penal system, the psychology of the kept may say less about prisons than the psychology of the keepers (9).
Revision (quotation)	According to Mitford, a critic of the penal system, the psychology of "the kept" may say less about prisons than the psychology of "the keepers" (9).

Paraphrase or summary: Your own words and a source citation

The following example changes Mitford's sentence structure, but it still uses her words (underlined) without quotation marks and without a source citation:

| Plagiarism | <u>In understanding prisons</u>, we should know more about the <u>character and mentality of the keepers</u> than <u>of the kept</u>. |

To avoid plagiarism, the writer can use quotation marks and cite the source (facing page) or *use his or her own words* and still *cite the source* (because the idea is Mitford's, not the writer's):

| Revision (paraphrase) | Mitford holds that we may be able to learn more about prisons from the psychology of the prison officials than from that of the prisoners (9). |
| Revision (paraphrase) | We may understand prisons better if we focus on the personalities and attitudes of the prison workers rather than those of the inmates (Mitford 9). |

In the next example, the writer cites Mitford and does not use her words but still plagiarizes her sentence structure:

| Plagiarism | Mitford, a critic of the penal system, maintains that <u>the psychology of prison officials may be more informative about prisons than the psychology of prisoners</u> (9). |
| Revision (paraphrase) | Mitford, a critic of the penal system, maintains that we may be able to learn less from the psychology of prisoners than from the psychology of prison officials (9). |

46d Online sources

You should acknowledge online sources as you would any other source: whenever you use someone else's independent material in any form. But online sources may present additional challenges as well:

- **Record complete publication information each time you consult an online source.** Online sources may change from one day to the next or even disappear entirely. See pages 179–80 for the information to record. If you do not have the proper information, you *may not* use the source.
- **Immediately put quotation marks around any text that you copy and paste into your document.** If you don't add quotation marks right away, you risk forgetting which words belong to the source and which are yours. If you don't know whose words you are using, recheck the source or *do not* use them.
- **Acknowledge linked sites.** If you use not only a Web site but also one or more of its linked sites, you must acknowledge the linked sites as well. One person's using a second person's work does not release you from the responsibility to cite the second work.
- **Seek the author's permission before using an e-mail message or private online posting.** Obtaining permission advises the author that

46d

his or her ideas are about to be distributed more widely and lets the author verify that you have not misrepresented the ideas.

If you want to use material in something you publish online, such as your own Web site, seek permission from the copyright holder in addition to citing the source. Generally, you can find information about copyright holders and permissions on the copyright page of a print publication (following the title page) and on a page labeled something like "Terms of Use" on a Web site. If you don't see an explicit release for student use, assume you must seek permission.

47 Documenting Sources

Every time you borrow the words, facts, or ideas of others, you must **document** the source—that is, supply a reference (or document) telling readers that you borrowed the material and where you borrowed it from.

Editors and instructors in most academic disciplines require special documentation formats (or styles) in their scholarly journals and in students' papers. All the styles share two features:

- **Citations in the text signal that material is borrowed and refer readers to detailed information about the sources.** The following text citation is in MLA documentation style:

  Veterans are more likely to complete college degrees if they have not only professional support but also a community of peers (Dao A16).

- **Detailed source information, either in footnotes or at the end of the paper, tells how to locate the sources.** The following source listing, also in MLA style, provides detailed publication information for the source summarized above.

  Dao, James. "Getting Them Through: Helping Veterans Graduate." *The New York Times,* 5 Feb. 2013, pp. A16+.

47a Discipline styles for documentation

Aside from the similarities of citations in the text and detailed source information, the disciplines' documentation styles vary markedly in citation form, arrangement of source information, and other particulars. Each discipline's style reflects the needs of its practitioners for certain kinds of information presented in certain ways. For instance, the currency of a source is important in the social and natural sciences, where studies build on and correct each other; thus in-text citations in these disciplines usually include a source's date of publication. In the humanities, however, currency is less important, so in-text citations do not include the date of publication.

The documentation formats of the disciplines are described in style guides, including those in the following list. This book presents four styles whose guides are starred in the list: MLA, used in English and some other humanities; APA, used in the social sciences; Chicago, used in history and some other humanities; and CSE, used in the natural and applied sciences. If you are unsure of which guide or documentation style you should use, ask your instructor.

Humanities

*The Chicago Manual of Style. 16th ed. 2010. (See pp. 303–15.)

*A Manual for Writers of Research Papers, Theses, and Dissertations. By Kate L. Turabian. 8th ed. Rev. Wayne C. Booth, Gregory G. Colomb, Joseph M. Williams, and the University of Chicago Press Editorial Staff. 2013. (See pp. 303–15.)

*MLA Handbook. 8th ed. 2016. (See pp. 220–65.)

Social sciences

American Political Science Association. *Style Manual for Political Science.* 2006. *www.apsanet.org/Portals/54/APSA%20Files/publications/APSAStyleManual 2006.pdf.*

*Publication Manual of the American Psychological Association. 6th ed. 2010. (See pp. 277–95.)

American Sociological Association. *ASA Style Guide.* 5th ed. 2014.

Linguistic Society of America. "Unified Style Sheet." 2007. *www.linguistic society.org/sites/default/files/style-sheet_0.pdf.*

A Uniform System of Citation (law). 20th ed. 2015.

Sciences and mathematics

American Chemical Society. *ACS Style Guide: A Manual for Authors and Editors.* 3rd ed. 2006.

American Medical Association Manual of Style. 10th ed. 2007.

**Council of Science Editors. *Scientific Style and Format: The CSE Manual for Authors, Editors, and Publishers.* 8th ed. 2014. (See pp. 318–25.)

47a

If no style is specified, use the guide from the preceding list that's most appropriate for the discipline in which you're writing. Do follow one system for citing sources—and one system only—so that you provide all the necessary information in a consistent format.

47b Bibliography software

Bibliography software can help you format your source citations in the style of your choice, and some programs can help you keep track of sources as you research. Your library may offer one or more bibliography programs, such as *RefWorks* or *Endnote*, or you can find free options on the Web, such as *Zotero*, *Bibme*, and *EasyBib*.

The programs vary in what they can do. Some simply prompt you for needed information (author's name, book title, and so on) and then format the information into a bibliography following the format of your documentation style. Others go beyond formatting to help you organize your sources, export citations from databases, and insert in-text citations as you write.

As helpful as bibliography programs can be, they don't always work the way they're advertised, and they can't substitute for your own care and attention in giving your sources accurate and complete acknowledgment. Always ask your instructors if you may use such software for your papers, and always review the citations compiled by any software to ensure that they meet your instructors' requirements.

48 MLA Documentation and Format

English, foreign languages, and some other humanities use the documentation style of the Modern Language Association, described in the *MLA Handbook* (8th ed., 2016).

In MLA style, you twice acknowledge the sources of borrowed material:

- **In your text, a brief citation adjacent to the borrowed material directs readers to a complete list of all the works you cite.** The citation consists of the author's last name and usually the page number in the source where the borrowed material appears. If the author's name is not mentioned in your sentence, it appears in parentheses with the page number:

In-text citation

Among African cities, says one observer, in Johannesburg "a spirit of optimism glows" (Gaddis 155).

■ **At the end of your paper, the list of works cited includes complete bibliographical information for every source.**

Works-cited entry

Gaddis, Anicee. "Johannesburg." *Transculturalism: How the World Is Coming Together*, edited by Claude Grunitzky, True Agency, 2008, pp. 154-57.

48a MLA in-text citations

Writing in-text citations

In-text citations of sources must include just enough information for the reader to locate both of the following:

■ The *source* in your list of works cited.
■ The *place* in the source where the borrowed material appears.

For any kind of source, you can usually meet both these requirements by providing the author's last name and (if the source uses them) the page numbers where the material appears. The reader can find the source in your list of works cited and find the borrowed material in the source itself.

The box on the next page directs you to all the models of in-text citations.

1. Author not named in your text

When you have not already named the author in your sentence, provide the author's last name and the page number(s), with no punctuation between them, in parentheses.

One researcher concludes that "women impose a distinctive construction on moral problems, seeing moral dilemmas in terms of conflicting responsibilities" (Gilligan 105-06).

2. Author named in your text

When you have already given the author's name with the material you're citing, give just the page number(s) in parentheses.

Carol Gilligan concludes that "women impose a distinctive construction on moral problems, seeing moral dilemmas in terms of conflicting responsibilities" (105-06).

MLA
48a

MLA in-text citations

1. Author not named in your text *221*
2. Author named in your text *221*
3. Work with two authors *222*
4. Work with more than two authors *222*
5. Work by an author of two or more cited works *222*
6. Anonymous work *223*
7. Work with a corporate author *223*
8. Electronic or other nonprint source *223*
   a. Work with a named author and stable page numbers *224*
   b. Work with a named author and no page numbers *224*
   c. Work with a named author on an e-reader or other device *224*
   d. Work with a named author and numbered paragraphs or sections *224*
   e. Work with no named author *224*
   f. Audio or video *224*
9. One-page work or entire work *225*
10. Work with no page or other reference numbers *225*
11. Multivolume work *225*
12. Source referred to by another source (indirect source) *225*
13. Literary work *226*
14. The Bible *227*
15. Two or more works in the same citation *227*

3. Work with two authors

If the source has two authors, give both of their last names in the text or in the citation. Separate the names with and:

As Frieden and Sagalyn observe, "The poor and the minorities were the leading victims of highway and renewal programs" (29).

According to one study, "The poor and the minorities were the leading victims of highway and renewal programs" (Frieden and Sagalyn 29).

MLA 48a

4. Work with more than two authors

If the source has more than two authors, give only the first author's name followed by et al. (the abbreviation for the Latin *et alii,* "and others").

Increased competition means that employees of public relations firms may find their loyalty stretched in more than one direction (Wilcox et al. 417).

5. Work by an author of two or more cited works

If your list of works cited includes two or more works by the same author, then your citation must tell the reader which of the author's works you are referring to. Give the title either in the text or in a parenthetical citation. In a parenthetical citation, omit any *A*, *An*, or *The* and shorten the title if it is longer than a noun preceded by its modifiers, if any. For instance, *Time's Arrow, Time's Cycle* shortens to *Time's Arrow*. In the following example, *Arts* is short for Gardner's full title, *The Arts and Human Development*.

At about age seven, children begin to use appropriate gestures with their stories (Gardner, *Arts* 144-45).

If the title does not start with a noun or a noun preceded by modifiers, shorten the title to the first word (again excluding *A*, *An*, or *The*): for instance, shorten *As the Eye Moves* to *As*.

6. Anonymous work

For a work with no named author or editor (whether an individual or an organization), use a full or shortened version of the title, as explained with the previous model. In your list of works cited, you alphabetize an anonymous work by the first word of the title excluding *A*, *An*, or *The* (see p. 235), and the first word of a shortened title will be the same.

"The Right to Die" notes that a death-row inmate may demand execution to achieve a fleeting notoriety (16).

One article notes that a death-row inmate may demand his own execution to achieve a fleeting notoriety ("Right" 16).

7. Work with a corporate author

Some works list as author a government body, association, committee, company, or other group. Cite such a work by the organization's name except when it and the publisher are the same. When the organization and publisher have the same name, omit the author and cite the work by the title (see model 6 above).

A 2016 report by the Nevada Department of Education provides evidence of an increase in graduation rates (12).

8. Electronic or other nonprint source

Electronic or other nonprint sources vary widely, including articles in databases, e-books, Web pages, *Facebook* posts, films or videos, and tweets. If possible, cite such a source as you would any other source, giving author and page number; but often these elements and others are lacking. The following models give a range of possibilities.

MLA 48a

a. Work with a named author and stable page numbers

Brannon observes that students respond readily to some poets (53).

b. Work with a named author and no page numbers

Smith reports that almost 20% of commercial banks have been audited in recent years.

If you give the author's name in your text, you will not need a parenthetical citation, but you must list the source in your works cited.

If the author's name does not appear in your text, give it in a parenthetical citation:

Clean cars are defined as vehicles with low pollution emissions and high fuel economy (Hagedorn).

c. Work with a named author on an e-reader or other device

Writing about post-Saddam Iraq, the journalist George Packer describes the tense relationship that existed between Kurdistan and the rest of the country (ch. 1).

Because page numbers are not always the same on Kindles, iPads, and other e-readers and tablets, give the chapter number, not the device's page numbers.

d. Work with a named author and numbered paragraphs or sections

Twins reared apart report similar feelings (Palfrey, pars. 6-7).

If the work gives numbered paragraphs or sections, use the abbreviation par., pars., sec., or secs. to tell readers that you are citing one or more paragraphs or sections rather than page numbers.

e. Work with no named author

Many decades after its release, *Citizen Kane* is still remarkable for its rich black-and-white photography.

When your works-cited entry lists the work under its title, cite the work by title in your text, as explained in model 6. This example, a film, gives the title in the text, so it omits a parenthetical citation (see model 9).

f. Audio or video

In an episode of *Master of None*, the characters recognize how little they know about the lives of their fathers in their native countries of India and China ("Parents" 14:02-27).

You may view or listen to a video or audio source on a device that displays the time span of the recording you are citing. Give the start and stop times of your source in hours (if any), minutes, and seconds, separated by colons. The numbers in the example cite 14 minutes, 2 to 27 seconds.

9. One-page work or entire work

When you cite a work that's a single page long or cite an entire work—for instance, a one-page article, a tweet, a Web site, a book, or a film—you may omit any page or other reference number. If the work you cite has an author, try to give the name in the text. If the work does not have an author, give the title.

Boyd deals with the need to acknowledge and come to terms with our fear of nuclear technology.

10. Work with no page or other reference numbers

When the work you cite, print or nonprint, has no page or other reference numbers, give the author's name, if available, in your text or in a parenthetical citation. (If no author is listed, give the title.)

In the children's classic picture book *The Very Busy Spider,* hard work and patience are rewarded when the spider catches a fly in her web (Carle).

11. Multivolume work

If you consulted only one volume of a multivolume work, your list of works cited will say so (see model 20 on p. 247), and you can treat the volume as you would any book.

If you consulted more than one volume of a multivolume work, give the appropriate volume before the page number (here volume 5):

After issuing the Emancipation Proclamation, Lincoln said, "What I did, I did after very full deliberations, and under a very heavy and solemn sense of responsibility" (5: 438).

12. Source referred to by another source (indirect source)

When you want to use a quotation that is already in quotation marks—indicating that the author you are reading is quoting someone else—try to find the original source and quote directly from it. If you can't find the original source, then your citation must indicate that your quotation of it is indirect.

George Davino maintains that "even small children have vivid ideas about nuclear energy" (qtd. in Boyd 22).

The list of works cited then includes only Boyd (the work consulted), not Davino.

13. Literary work

Novels, plays, and poems are often available in many editions, so your instructor may ask you to provide information that will help readers find the passage you cite no matter what edition they consult.

a. Novel

Toward the end of James's novel, Maggie suddenly feels "the thick breath of the definite—which was the intimate, the immediate, the familiar, as she hadn't had them for so long" (535; pt. 6, ch. 41).

Give the page number first, followed by a semicolon and then information on the appropriate part or chapter of the work.

b. Poem not divided into parts

In Shakespeare's Sonnet 73 the speaker identifies with the trees of late autumn, "Bare ruined choirs, where late the sweet birds sang" (line 4). "In me," Shakespeare writes, "thou seest the glowing of such fire / That on the ashes of his youth doth lie . . ." (9-10).

You may omit the page number and supply the line number(s) for the quotation. To prevent confusion with page numbers, precede the numbers with line or lines in the first citation; then use just the numbers. (See pp. 55–57 for a sample paper on a poem.)

c. Verse play or poem divided into parts

Later in Shakespeare's *King Lear* the disguised Edgar says, "The prince of darkness is a gentleman" (3.4.147).

MLA
48a

Omit a page number and cite the appropriate part—act (and scene, if any), canto, book, and so on—plus the line number(s). Use Arabic numerals for parts, including acts and scenes (3.4), unless your instructor specifies Roman numerals (III.iv).

d. Prose play

In Miller's *Death of a Salesman,* Willie Loman's wife, Linda, acknowledges her husband's failings but also the need for him to be treated with dignity: "He's not the finest character that ever lived. But he's a human being, and a terrible thing is happening to him" (56; act 1).

Provide the page number followed by the act and scene, if any.

14. The Bible

When you cite passages of the Bible in parentheses, abbreviate the title of any book longer than four letters—for instance, 1 Sam. (1 Samuel) or Ps. (Psalms). Then give the chapter and verse(s).

According to the Bible, at Babel God "did . . . confound the language of all the earth" (Gen. 11.9).

15. Two or more works in the same citation

When you refer to more than one work in a single parenthetical citation, separate the references with a semicolon.

Two recent articles point out that a computer badly used can be less efficient than no computer at all (Gough and Hall 201; Richards 162).

Footnotes or endnotes in special circumstances

Footnotes or endnotes may supplement parenthetical citations when you cite several sources at once, when you comment on a source, or when you provide information that does not fit easily in the text. Signal a note in your text with a numeral raised above the appropriate line. Then write a note with the same numeral.

Text   So far, no one has confirmed these results.[2]

Note   2. Manter tried repeatedly to replicate the experiment, but he was never able to produce the high temperatures (616).

If the note appears as a footnote, use the footnote feature of your word processor to place it at the bottom of the page on which the citation appears. If the note appears as an endnote, place it in numerical order with the other endnotes on a page between the text and the list of works cited. Double-space all footnotes and endnotes.

48b MLA list of works cited

MLA 48b

In MLA documentation style, your in-text parenthetical citations (discussed in 48a) refer the reader to complete information on your sources in a list you title Works Cited and place at the end of your paper. The list should include all the sources you quoted, paraphrased, or summarized in your paper.

Format of the list of works cited

To format the list of works cited, use the following guidelines. For a complete list of works cited, see pages 275–76.

Arrangement Arrange sources alphabetically by the author's last name. If there is no author, alphabetize by the first main word of the title (excluding *A*, *An*, or *The*).

Spacing Double-space everything in the list.

Indention Begin each entry at the left margin, and indent the second and subsequent lines one-half inch. Your word processor can create this so-called hanging indent automatically.

Elements of works-cited entries

The eighth edition of the *MLA Handbook* simplifies writing works-cited entries by building them on the core, visible elements in sources. In the following description and the box on the next page, these core elements are listed in order of their appearance in a works-cited entry. Few sources include all of the listed elements: as you build works-cited entries, give the elements that you find in your sources. For more information from MLA, go to *style.mla.org*.

Author Begin each entry with the author's last name, a comma, and the author's first name and middle name or initial, if any—for instance, Hohulin, John D. End the author's name with a period. See models 1–6 for how to cite various numbers and kinds of authors.

Title of source After the author, give the full title and any subtitle of the source, separating them with a colon. End the title with a period.

- **Quotation marks for shorter works:** Use quotation marks around titles of works that are part of larger works, such as articles, pages on Web sites, and selections from anthologies: "A Rose for Emily." (See pp. 148–49 for titles to enclose in quotation marks.)
- **Italics for longer works:** Use italics for the titles of longer, independent works such as books and films: Do the Right Thing. Containers (next item) also have italic titles. (See pp. 168–69 for titles to italicize.)
- **Descriptions for untitled works:** For works that do not have titles, such as interviews, give a description of the work after the name of the author. (See models 32, 34, 47, and 50 for examples of descriptions of untitled works.)

Title of container Many sources used in research are shorter works, such as articles and Web pages, that are published in larger works, such as journals and Web sites. In MLA style, the larger publication is called the **container**. In your works-cited entry, give the title of the container in italics, followed by a comma.

Building MLA works-cited entries

Following are the core elements and their order in works-cited entries. Most sources will not contain every element. The colors correspond to the highlight colors in the models on pages 232–64.

Author's last name, First name.

"Title of Shorter Work." or *Title of Longer Work.*

Container 1
Give these elements in this order if they are available. Skip "Title of Container" for self-contained works.

Title of Container 1,

Other contributors,

Version,

Number,

Publisher,

Publication date,

Location.

Container 2
Give these elements in this order if they are available.

Title of Container 2,

Other contributors,

Version,

Number,

Publisher,

Publication date,

Location.

MLA
48b

- **Container 1:** Some works fall in one container. For example, if you are citing an article on a Web site, the container is the Web site (see model 34). If you are citing a short story or a chapter from a print anthology, the container is the anthology (see models 27 and 28).
- **Container 2:** Many sources have more than one container—in essence, the source is inside container 1, which is inside container 2. For example, if you are citing an article from a journal that you found in a database, container 1 is the journal and container 2 is

the database (see pp. 238–39). If your source is an episode of a television series that you watched on *Netflix*, container 1 is the television series and container 2 is *Netflix* (see model 48b).

- **Self-contained works:** Note that some sources are self-contained. These include books such as novels, manuals, works of nonfiction, and the like.

The models beginning on page 232 give examples of many short works in containers such as books, journals, databases, and Web sites, as well as longer, self-contained works such as books, films, Web sites, music albums, and so on.

Other contributors Some sources and some containers, such as anthologies and edited collections, may include the work of people besides the author. If a person's contribution to a work is important to your research, add the contributor's name to your works-cited entry preceded by a description such as adapted by, directed by, edited by, illustrated by, interviewed by, introduction by, narrated by, performance by, or translated by. Follow the name of a contributor with a comma. For examples of works-cited entries showing contributors, see models 16, 17, 19 (books), 48 (television episodes and series), 49 (radio programs), 51 (films and videos), 52 (sound recordings), and 54 (live performances).

Version Books, films, and computer software such as games and apps often appear in updated or revised editions and versions. If your source or its container gives a version or edition, add it to your works-cited entry, followed by a comma—for instance, version 8.1, or 3rd ed., (ed. stands for "edition"). For examples of works-cited entries showing editions and versions, see models 14 (book) and 56 (app).

Number in a sequence Some sources and containers are published in a numbered sequence. Examples include academic journals, which often have volume and issue numbers (models 7 and 8). Some books are published in sets consisting of multiple volumes (model 20). Television series and episodes are typically numbered by season and by episode (model 48). In your works-cited entry, follow a sequence number with a comma—for example, season 1, episode 6, or vol. 32, no. 6, (vol. and no. stand for "volume" and "number," respectively).

Publisher Give the publisher followed by a comma. For instance, the publisher of a book is the company that issued the book (see pp. 244–45), the publisher of a Web site is the organization that sponsors the site (see p. 254), and the publisher of a TV series is generally the main studio that produced the series (see model 48). If the source has more than one publisher, separate the names with a forward slash: Vertigo / DC Comics.

You do not need to list a publisher for some kinds of sources or containers, including periodicals (journals, newspapers, and magazines), databases, self-published works, and Web sites whose titles and publishers are the same.

Publication date Give the date of publication followed by a comma. Publication dates vary considerably depending on the type of source you are citing. To identify and cite the publication date, see the box on pages 233–34 to locate a model that most closely matches your source. Abbreviate all months except May, June, and July. See also model 37 to cite an undated source you find on the Web.

Location Give a location telling where you found the source or its container so that other researchers can find the source, too. Follow the location with a period.

- **Page numbers:** For a source within a container with page numbers, such as a chapter of a book or an article in a periodical, provide the page numbers. Use the abbreviation p. or pp. before the page numbers: p. 72 or pp. 210-13. See pages 238–39, 240, and 243 for examples of page numbers.
- **Digital Object Identifer (DOI):** Many journal articles, books, and other documents have a DOI attached to them, a permanent URL that links to the text and functions as a unique identifier. When a DOI is available, include it at the end of your works-cited entry and follow it with a period: doi:10.1682/JRRD.2010.03.0024. Usually a DOI will follow the title of a container such as a database or a Web site. See pages 238–39 for an example of a DOI.
- **URL:** If a DOI is not available for a source you found in a database or on the Web, copy and paste the URL from your browser into your works-cited entry, deleting "http://"—for instance, harpers.org/archive/2012/10/contest-of-words/. If your source gives a stable URL, such as a *permalink*, give it instead.
- **Name and city:** If you viewed an object in a museum or an archive or attended a performance or lecture, give the name of the institution or venue and the city in which it is located—for instance, DeYoung Museum, San Francisco. For examples, see models 44, 54, and 58.

Models of MLA works-cited entries

Unlike earlier editions of the *MLA Handbook*, which gave numerous examples of works-cited entries organized by the type of source, the eighth edition emphasizes building entries based on the elements described in the preceding section. This chapter blends the two approaches, applying the new guidelines to a wide variety of sources you may encounter during your research. The models here are extensive but not exhaustive, and you will surely come across sources that do not match exactly. For such sources, refer to the list of core elements on page 229 and give whatever information you can find in the source.

The box on the next two pages will help you find appropriate MLA works-cited models for your sources.

Authors

The following models show how to handle authors' names in citing any kind of source.

1. One author

Ehrenreich, Barbara. *Dancing in the Streets: A History of Collective Joy*. Henry Holt,
2006.

Give the author's full name—last name first, a comma, first name, and any middle name or initial. Omit any title, such as *Dr.* or *PhD*. End the name with a period.

2. Two authors

Lifton, Robert Jay, and Greg Mitchell. *Who Owns Death: Capital Punishment, the American
Conscience, and the End of Executions*. William Morrow, 2000.

Give the authors' names in the order provided on the title page. Reverse the first and last names of the first author *only*, not of the other author. Separate the authors' names with a comma and and.

MLA
48b

3. More than two authors

Wilcox, Dennis L., et al. *Think Public Relations*. 2nd ed., Allyn & Bacon, 2013.

Give the name of the first author only, and follow the name with a comma and the abbreviation et al. (for the Latin *et alii*, meaning "and others").

4. The same author(s) for two or more works

Gardner, Howard. *The Arts and Human Development*. John Wiley & Sons, 1973.

---. *Five Minds for the Future*. Harvard Business School P, 2007.

Give the author's name only in the first entry. For the second and any subsequent works by the same author, substitute three hyphens for

MLA works-cited models

MLA
48b

(continued)

MLA works-cited models

MLA
48b

the author's name, followed by a period. Note that the three hyphens may substitute only for *exactly* the same name or names.

5. A corporate author

Corporate authors include associations, committees, institutions, government bodies, companies, and other groups. When a source gives only the name of the organization as author and not an individual's name, the source has a corporate author.

a. Source cited by author

Vault Technologies. *Turnkey Parking Solutions*. Mills, 2016.

When the corporate author and the publisher are different, start with the name of the author.

b. Source cited by title

"Thailand's Campaign for Tobacco Control." *Center for Global Development*, 2015,

 millionssaved.cgdev.org/case-studies/thailands-campaign-for-tobacco-control.

When the corporate author and the publisher are the same, omit the author and start with the title. Omit the publisher as well when its name is the Web site title, as in model b. (For examples of government documents cited in this way, see model 33b.)

6. Author not named (anonymous)

The Dorling Kindersley World Atlas. DK Publishing, 2013.

List a work that names no author—neither an individual nor a group—by its full title. If the work is a book, italicize the title, as above. If the work is a periodical article or other short work, enclose the title in quotation marks:

"Drilling in the Wilderness." *The Economist,* 24 Apr. 2015, p. 32.

Alphabetize the work by the title's first main word, excluding *A, An,* or *The* (*Dorling* in the first example and Drilling in the second).

Articles in journals, newspapers, and magazines

 Articles in scholarly journals, in newspapers, and in magazines appear in print periodicals, in online databases available through your library, and on the Web.

Articles in scholarly journals

 To cite an article in a scholarly journal, give the author and the title of the article. Enclose the title in quotation marks. Then give information about the container(s), depending on what is available. In container 1, give the title of the journal, any volume and issue numbers, the publication date, and the location of the source, such as page numbers of the article or possibly a URL. Add a container 2 if you reached the source electronically—for instance, through a library database—and give the source's location, such as a Digital Object Identifier (DOI) or a URL.

You do not need to give a publisher for articles in academic journals in print, in online databases such as *EBSCOhost* or *ProQuest*, or on Web sites.

7. Article in a scholarly journal with volume and issue numbers

a. Print journal article

Mattingly, Carol. "Telling Evidence: Rethinking What Counts in Rhetoric." *Rhetoric Society Quarterly*, vol. 32, no. 1, Winter 2002, pp. 99-108.

See pages 238–39 for an explanation of this format and where to find the required information in a print journal.

b. Database journal article

Neves, Joshua. "Cinematic Encounters in Beijing." *Film Quarterly*, vol. 67, no. 1, Fall 2013, pp. 27-40. *EBSCOhost,* doi:10.1525/FQ.2.13.67.1.27.

See pages 238–39 for an explanation of this format and where to find the required information in a database. Basically, start with the information for a print article (previous model), and add the information for container 2—the title of the database and the DOI or URL.

c. Web journal article

Zarkin, Michael. "Unconventional Pollution Control Politics: The Reformation of the US Safe Drinking Water Act." *Electronic Green Journal*, vol. 38, no. 1, 2015, escholarship.org/uc/item/69s0f9s0.

For a scholarly article you find in a Web journal, begin with the author and title. Then give available information about the container: the title of the journal, the volume and issue numbers, the publication date, and a URL, as here, or a DOI. If the journal article does not have page numbers, omit them from the works-cited entry.

8. Article in a journal with only issue numbers

Dobozy, Tomas. "The Writing of Trespass." *Canadian Literature,* no. 218, Autumn 2013, pp. 11-28. *EBSCOhost,* web.a.ebscohost.com/ehost/detail/AN=94425037&db=aph.

If a scholarly journal numbers only issues, not volumes, give the issue alone after the journal title.

Articles in newspapers

To cite an article in a newspaper, give the author and the title of the article. Enclose the title in quotation marks. Then give information about the container(s), depending on what is available. In container 1, give the title of the newspaper, the publication date, and the location of the article (generally page numbers or a URL). Add information for a container 2 if you used another source, such as a library database, to reach the article.

You do not need to give a publisher for newspaper articles that appear in print, in online databases such *LexisNexis*, or on Web sites.

9. Article in a national newspaper

a. Print newspaper article

Cieply, Michael. "Film Academy Adds to Ranks to Lift Diversity." *The New York Times,*
   30 June 2016, pp. A1+.

If the newspaper is divided into lettered sections, provide the section designation before the page number when the newspaper does the same: A1+ above. The plus sign indicates that the article continues on a later page.

b. Database newspaper article

Stein, Rob. "Obesity May Stall Trend of Increasing Longevity." *The Washington Post,* 15 Mar.
   2015, p. A2. *LexisNexis Academic,* www.lexisnexis.com/lnacademic/HEADLINE
   (Obesity+may+stall%2C+trend+of+increasing%2C+longevity)%2BDATE%2B2015.

See page 240 for an explanation of this format and where to find the required information in a database. Basically, start with the information for a print article (previous model), and add the information for container 2—the title of the database and the URL or DOI.

c. Web news article

Jarvie, Jenny. "What Life Is Like on $7.25 Per Hour." *Los Angeles Times,* 6 Apr.2016,
   www.latimes.com/nation/la-na-minimum-wage-life-20160405-story.html.

To cite a newspaper article that you find on the open Web, follow the author and title with the information for the container: the title of the newspaper, the publication date (day, month, year), and the URL. To cite a reader's comment on an article, see model 40.

(text continues on p. 241)

Citing journal articles: Print and database

Print journal article

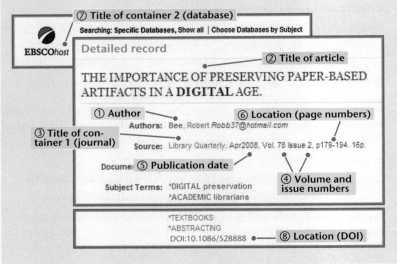

First page of article

THE IMPORTANCE OF PRESERVING PAPER-BASED ARTIFACTS IN A DIGITAL AGE

② **Title of article**

Robert Bee[1] ●—— ① **Author**

The preservation of paper-based ④ **Volume and** ial issue for collection management in academic libraries. I **issue numbers** brary science profession has

③ **Title of container 1 (journal)** ●— [*Library Quarterly*, vol. 78, no. 2, pp. 179–194] ●—— ⑥ **Location (page numbers)**
© 2008 by The University of Chicago. All rights reserved.
0024-2519/2008/7802-0002$10.00

⑤ **Publication date**

179

Database journal article

⑦ **Title of container 2 (database)**

Searching: Specific Databases, Show all | Choose Databases by Subject

EBSCO*host*

Detailed record

② **Title of article**

THE IMPORTANCE OF PRESERVING PAPER-BASED ARTIFACTS IN A **DIGITAL** AGE.

① **Author** ⑥ **Location (page numbers)**

Authors: Bee, Robert *Robb37@hotmail.com*

③ **Title of container 1 (journal)** Source: Library Quarterly. Apr2008, Vol. 78 Issue 2, p179-194. 16p.

Docume ⑤ **Publication date**

④ **Volume and issue numbers**

Subject Terms: *DIGITAL preservation
*ACADEMIC librarians

*TEXTBOOKS
*ABSTRACTING
DOI:10.1086/528888 ●—— ⑧ **Location (DOI)**

MLA 48b

Works-cited entry: Print journal article

① ②
Bee, Robert. "The Importance of Preserving Paper-Based Artifacts in a
③ ④ ⑤ ⑥
Digital Age." *Library Quarterly,* vol. 78, no. 2, Apr. 2008, pp. 179-94.

Works-cited entry: Database journal article

① ②
Bee, Robert. "The Importance of Preserving Paper-Based Artifacts
③ ④ ⑤
in a Digital Age." *Library Quarterly,* vol. 78, no. 2, Apr. 2008,
⑥ ⑦ ⑧
pp. 179-94. *EBSCOhost,* doi:10.1086/528888.

① **Author.** Give the full name—last name first, a comma, first name, and any middle name or initial. Omit *Dr., PhD,* or any other title. End the name with a period.

② **Title of article,** in quotation marks. Give the full title and any subtitle, separating them with a colon. End the title with a period inside the final quotation mark.

③ **Title of container 1 (journal),** in italics. End with a comma.

④ **Volume and issue numbers,** in Arabic numerals, preceded by vol. and no. and followed by commas.

⑤ **Publication date,** preceded by the month or season, if available. Abbreviate all months except May, June, and July. End with a comma.

⑥ **Location (page numbers of the article),** preceded by pp. and ending with a period. Provide only as many digits in the last number as needed for clarity, usually two.

⑦ **Title of container 2 (database),** in italics. End with a comma.

⑧ **Location.** If available, give a Digital Object Identifier (DOI), preceded by doi:. End with a period. If no DOI is available, give the URL without "http://." (For more on DOIs and URLs, see p. 231.)

MLA
48b

Citing a newspaper article: Database

LexisNexis® Academic

⑦ **Location (URL)**

www.lexisnexis.com/lnacademic/?HEADLINE(A+combat+role+and+anguish+too.)%2BDATE%2B2009

⑥ **Title of container 2 (database)**

Results Web News

④ **Publication date**

The New York Times ● — ③ **Title of container 1 (newspaper)**

November 1, 2009 Sunday
Late Edition - Final

② **Title of article**

A Combat Role, and Anguish, Too

① **Author**

BYLINE: By DAMIEN CAVE; Diana Oliva Cave contributed reporting.

SECTION: Section A; Column 0; National Desk; WOMEN AT ARMS; Pg. 1

LENGTH: 3198 words   ⑤ **Location (page number)**

For Vivienne Pacquette, being a combat veteran with post-traumatic stress disorder means avoiding phone calls to her sons, dinner out with her husband and therapy sessions that make her talk about

①
Cave, Damien. ② "A Combat Role, and Anguish, Too." ③ *The New York*
④   ⑤   ⑥
Times, 1 Nov. 2009, p. A1. *LexisNexis Academic,*
⑦
www.lexisnexis.com/lnacademic/?HEADLINE(A+combat+

role+and+anguish+too.)%2BDATE%2B2009.

① **Author.** Give the full name—last name first, a comma, first name, and any middle name or initial. End the name with a period.

② **Title of article,** in quotation marks. Give the full title and any subtitle, separating them with a colon. End the title with a period inside the final quotation mark.

③ **Title of container 1 (newspaper),** in italics. End with a comma.

④ **Publication date,** giving day, month, and year. Abbreviate all months except May, June, and July. End with a comma.

⑤ **Location (page number),** preceded by p. or pp. and ending with a period. (Use pp. if the article runs more than one page.) Include a section designation before the page number, as in A1 here, if the newspaper does.

⑥ **Title of container 2 (database),** in italics. End with a comma.

⑦ **Location (URL).** Give the URL without "http://." End with a period.

(continued from p. 237)

10. Article in a local newspaper

Beckett, Lois. "The Ignored PTSD Crisis: Americans Wounded in Their Own Neighbor-

    hoods." *The Louisiana Weekly* [New Orleans], 17 Feb. 2014, pp. 12-13.

If the city of publication does not appear in the title of a local newspaper, follow the title with the city name in brackets, not italicized.

Articles in magazines

To cite an article in a magazine, give the author and the title of the article. Enclose the title in quotation marks. Then give information about the container(s), depending on what is available. For container 1, give the title of the magazine, the publication date (abbreviate all months except May, June, and July), and the location of the article (page numbers, a URL, or a DOI). Add information for a container 2 if you used another source, such as a library database, to reach the article.

You do not need to give a publisher for magazine articles that appear in print, in online databases such *EBSCOhost,* or on Web sites.

11. Article in a weekly or biweekly magazine

a. Print magazine article

Gonnerman, Jennifer. "Home Free." *The New Yorker,* 20 June 2016, pp. 40-49.

Following the author and title, give information for the container: the title of the magazine, the publication date (day, month, year), and the page numbers.

b. Database magazine article

Barras, Colin. "Hunting for the Greatest of Apes." *New Scientist,* 21 May 2016,

    pp. 34-37. *EBSCOhost,* search.ebscohost.com/s6254798&db=115409746.

See the next page for an explanation of this format and where to find the required information in a database. Basically, start with the information for a print article (previous model). Then add the information for container 2—the title of the database and the URL or a DOI.

c. Web magazine article

Stampler, Laura. "These Cities Have the Most Open-Minded Daters." *Time,* 14 Apr.

    2014, time.com/61947/these-cities-have-the-most-open-minded-daters/.

To cite a magazine article you find on the open Web, follow the author and title with information for the container: the title of the magazine, the publication date (day, month, year), and the URL. To cite a reader's comment on an article, see model 40.

Citing a magazine article: Database

⑥ **Title of container 2 (database)**

Searching: Specific Databases, Show all | Choose Databases by Subject

EBSCO*host*

Detailed record

⑦ **Location (URL)**

𝒫 Permalink   search.ebscohost.com/login.aspx?direct=true&AuthType=s6254798&db=aph&AN=112426

② **Title of article**

BABY DOE.

① **Author** — Authors: LEPORE, JILL (AUTHOR)

⑤ **Location (page numbers)**

Source: New Yorker. 2/1/2016, Vol. 91 Issue 46, p46-57. 12p. 1 Color Photograph, 10 Black and White Photographs.

Document Type: Article

④ **Publication date**

③ **Title of container 1 (magazine)**

ns: *CHILD murder
     *CHILD welfare
     *CHILD abuse – Law & legislation
     *LAW
     *LAW reform
     MASSACHUSETTS

People: GALLISON, Jennifer
         BOND, Bella

① ② ③ ④ ⑤
Lepore, Jill. "Baby Doe." *The New Yorker,* 1 Feb. 2016, pp. 46-57.
⑥ ⑦
EBSCOhost, search.ebscohost.com/login.aspx?direct=

true&AuthType=s6254798&db=aph&AN=112426301.

① **Author.** Give the full name—last name first, a comma, first name, and any middle name or initial. End the name with a period.

② **Title of article,** in quotation marks. Give the full title and any subtitle, separating them with a colon. End the title with a period inside the final quotation mark.

③ **Title of container 1 (magazine),** in italics. End with a comma.

④ **Publication date,** giving day (if available), month, and year. Abbreviate all months except May, June, and July. End with a comma.

⑤ **Location (page numbers),** preceded by pp. and ending with a period. (Use p. if the article runs on a single page.)

⑥ **Title of container 2 (database),** in italics. End with a comma.

⑦ **Location (URL).** Give the URL (without "http://") or DOI (if one is available). End with a period.

12. Article in a monthly or bimonthly magazine

Wong, Kate. "Rise of the Human Predator." *Scientific American,* Apr. 2014, pp. 46-51.

Follow the magazine title with the month and the year of publication. If the date on the magazine spans two months, give both months: Jan.-Feb. 2016.

Books and government publications

Complete books

A complete, stand-alone book is self-contained, so the title of a book is followed by the names of other contributors (if any) and publication information. A book in a library database or on the Web requires information for the container: the name of the database or Web site and a DOI or URL after the publication information.

13. Basic format for a complete book

To cite a book, give the author, the title, the publisher, and the date. When other information is present, give it between the author's name and the title, between the title and the publication information, or at the end of the entry, as in models 14–23.

a. Print book

Shteir, Rachel. *The Steal: A Cultural History of Shoplifting.* Penguin Press, 2011.

See the next two pages for an explanation of this format and where to find the required information in a print book.

b. Database book

Levine, Daniel. *Bayard Rustin and the Civil Rights Movement.* Rutgers UP, 2000. *eBook Collection,* web.a.ebscohost.com/ehost/ebookviewer/ebook/e6967d23-394e-41d9-ab54-d292ebd6287b=2.

See the next two pages for an explanation of this format and where to find the required information in a database. Basically, give any print publication information before the information about the container —the name of the database and a DOI or URL.

c. E-book

Booth, Marilyn. *May Her Likes Be Multiplied: Biography and Gender Politics in Egypt.* Kindle ed., U of California P, 2001.

Give the type of e-book after the title, followed by the publication information. If you do not know the type you consulted, give E-book instead.

MLA
48b

(text continues on p. 246)

Citing books: Print and database

Print book

Title page

like
a man
gone
mad

Poems in a New Century

Samuel Hazo ② Title and subtitle

① Author

③ Publisher

SU

Syracuse University Press

Copyright page

Copyright © 2010 by Syracuse University Press
Syracuse, New York 13244-5290 ④ Publication date

All Rights Reserved

⑥ Location (URL)

https://muse.jhu.edu/book/12959

We cannot verify your location (Log In)

⑤ Title of container (database)

m

PROJECT MUSE

BROWSE OR Search

Like a Man Gone Mad ② Title and subtitle

Poems in a New Century

Samuel Hazo ① Author

Publication Year: 2010 ④ Publication date

Hazo, National Book Award finalist and former State Poet of Pennsylvania, transports the reader with poems of both lament and celebration in his sensual new collection. Like a Man Gone Mad features much of the spare yet precise imagery of his earlier work. Searing portraits, a deft use of allegorical language, and a wry sense of humor are all signatures of Hazo's unique voice.

Published by: Syracuse University Press ③ Publisher

MLA
48b

Works-cited entry: Print book

① ②
Hazo, Samuel. *Like a Man Gone Mad: Poems in a New Century.*
③ ④
    Syracuse UP, 2010.

Works-cited entry: Database book

① ②
Hazo, Samuel. *Like a Man Gone Mad: Poems in a New Century.*
③ ④ ⑤ ⑥
    Syracuse UP, 2010. *Project Muse,* muse.jhu.edu/book/12959.

① **Author.** Give the full name—last name first, a comma, first name, and any middle name or initial. Omit *Dr., PhD,* or any other title. End the name with a period.

② **Title,** in italics. Give the full title and any subtitle, separating them with a colon. Capitalize all significant words of the title even if the book does not. End the title with a period.

③ **Publisher.** Give the name as it appears on the title page or copyright page, followed by a comma. Shorten "University Press" to UP and omit "Company," "Co.," and "Inc." from other publishers' names. If two publisher names are listed on the title or copyright page, determine their relationship: If they are both independent entities, list them both with a forward slash between the names (see model 19). If one is a division of the other (for instance, Scribner is a division of Simon & Schuster), cite only the division.

④ **Publication date.** If the date doesn't appear on the title page, look for it on the next page. End with a period.

⑤ **Title of container (database),** in italics. End with a comma.

⑥ **Location (URL).** Give the URL without "http://," ending with a period. If the database record gives a DOI, provide it instead. (For more on DOIs, see p. 231.)

MLA
48b

(continued from p. 243)

d. Web book

Cather, Willa. *One of Ours*. Alfred A. Knopf, 1922. *Bartleby.com*, 2000, www.bartleby.
   com/1006/1.html.

Print publication information for a book on the Web is not required,
but it can help readers. This example gives the original publisher and
publication date followed by information for the container: the title
of the Web site and the URL. (The title of the Web site and its publisher are the same, so only the Web site is given.)

14. Second or subsequent edition

Bolinger, Dwight L. *Aspects of Language*. 3rd ed., Harcourt Brace Jovanovich, 1981.

For any edition after the first, place the edition number after the title.
Use the designation given in the source, such as Expanded ed., Updated
ed., or 3rd ed., as in the example.

15. Book with an editor

Holland, Merlin, and Rupert Hart-Davis, editors. *The Complete Letters of Oscar Wilde*.
   Henry Holt, 2000.

Handle editors' names like authors' names (models 1–4), but add a
comma and editor or editors after the last editor's name.

16. Book with an author and an editor

Mumford, Lewis. *The City in History*. Edited by Donald L. Miller, Pantheon, 1986.

When citing the work of the author, give the author's name first. After the title, give the editor's name (another contributor) preceded by
Edited by. When citing the work of the editor, use model 15 for a book
with an editor, adding By and the author's name after the title:

Miller, Donald L., editor. *The City in History*. By Lewis Mumford, Mariner Books, 1968.

17. Book with a translator

Alighieri, Dante. *The Inferno*. Translated by John Ciardi, New American Library, 1971.

When citing the work of an author, shown above, give his or her
name first, and give the translator's name (another contributor) after
the title, preceded by Translated by. When citing the work of the translator, give his or her name first, followed by a comma and translator. Follow the title with By and the author's name:

MLA
48b

Ciardi, John, translator. *The Inferno.* By Dante Alighieri, New American Library, 1971.

18. Anthology

Kennedy, X. J., and Dana Gioia, editors. *Literature: An Introduction to Fiction, Poetry, Drama, and Writing.* 13th ed., Pearson, 2016.

Cite an entire anthology only when citing the work of the editor or editors or when your instructor permits cross-referencing like that shown in model 28. Give the name of the editor or editors (followed by editor or editors) and then the title of the anthology.

19. Illustrated book or graphic narrative

Wilson, G. Willow. *Cairo.* Illustrated by M. K. Perker, Vertigo / DC Comics, 2005.

When citing the work of the writer, give the writer's name, the title, Illustrated by, and the illustrator's name (another contributor). This book's two publishers, Vertigo and DC Comics, are separated by a forward slash.

When citing the work of an illustrator, list his or her name first, followed by a comma and illustrator. List the author's name after the title.

Williams, Garth, illustrator. *Charlotte's Web.* By E. B. White, Harper & Brothers, 1952.

20. Multivolume work

Lincoln, Abraham. *The Collected Works of Abraham Lincoln.* Edited by Roy P. Basler, vol. 5, Rutgers UP, 1953. 8 vols.

When the work you cite is one volume in a set of numbered volumes, give the volume number before the publication information (vol. 5 in the example). The total number of volumes at the end of the entry is optional (8 vols. in the example).

If you use two or more volumes of a multivolume work, give the work's total number of volumes before the publication information (8 vols. in the following example). Your in-text citation will indicate which volume you are citing (see p. 225).

Lincoln, Abraham. *The Collected Works of Abraham Lincoln.* Edited by Roy P. Basler, 8 vols., Rutgers UP, 1953.

21. Book in a series

Bergman, Ingmar. *The Seventh Seal.* Simon and Schuster, 1960. Modern Film Scripts Series 12.

When you cite a work in a series, you may give the name of the series, not italicized or in quotation marks, at the end of the entry.

22. Book published before 1900

James, Henry. *The Bostonians*. London, 1886.

Although the city of publication is not required in most works-cited entries, MLA recommends giving the city rather than the publisher for books published before 1900 because such books are usually associated with the cities in which they were published.

23. Republished book

Achebe, Chinua. *Things Fall Apart*. 1958. Anchor Books, 1994.

Many books, especially classic literary works, are republished and reissued by publishers. If the original publication date of a book is important to your use of it, give the date after the title. Then provide the publication information for the source you are using.

24. Sacred works

The Bible: Authorized King James Version with Apocrypha. Edited by Robert Carroll and
    Stephen Prickett, Oxford UP, 2008.

The Koran. Translated by N. J. Dawood, rev. ed., Penguin Books, 2015.

When citing a sacred work, give the edition you consulted, beginning with the title unless you are citing the work of an editor or translator.

25. Book with a title in its title

Eco, Umberto. *Postscript to* The Name of the Rose. Translated by William Weaver, Har-
    court Brace Jovanovich, 1983.

When a book's title contains another book title (here *The Name of the Rose*), do not italicize the second title. When a book's title contains a quotation or the title of a work normally placed in quotation marks, keep the quotation marks and italicize both titles: *Critical Response to Henry James's "The Beast in the Jungle."*

26. Book lacking publication information or pagination

Carle, Eric. *The Very Busy Spider*. Philomel Books, 1984, n. pag.

Some books are not paginated or do not list a publisher or date of publication. Although MLA style no longer requires you to indicate missing information, your instructor may ask you to do so for clarity. These abbreviations are conventional: n.p. if no publisher, n.d. if no publication date, and n. pag. if no page numbers.

Parts of books

Parts of books include selections from anthologies, articles and chapters in scholarly collections and reference works, and the like. Works-cited entries for these short works include the author and title as well as information about the container in which they appear: the title, any other contributors, publication information, and page numbers, if available.

27. Selection from an anthology

Munro, Alice. "How I Met My Husband." *Literature: An Introduction to Fiction, Poetry,*
    Drama, and Writing, edited by X. J. Kennedy and Dana Gioia, 13th ed., Pearson,
    2016, pp. 189-201.

This listing adds to the anthology entry in model 18: author of the selection, title of the selection (in quotation marks), and inclusive page numbers for the selection. If you wish, you may also supply the original date of publication for the work you are citing, after its title (see model 23).

If the work you cite comes from a collection of works by one author that has no editor, use the following form:

Hempel, Amy. "San Francisco." *The Collected Stories of Amy Hempel,* Scribner, 2006,
    pp. 27-28.

28. Two or more selections from the same anthology

Bradstreet, Anne. "The Author to Her Book." Kennedy and Gioia, pp. 657-58.

Kennedy, X. J., and Dana Gioia, editors. *Literature: An Introduction to Fiction,*
    Poetry, Drama, and Writing. 13th ed., Pearson, 2016.

Merwin, W. S. "For the Anniversary of My Death." Kennedy and Gioia, p. 828.

Stevens, Wallace. "Thirteen Ways of Looking at a Blackbird." Kennedy and Gioia,
    pp. 831-33.

When you are citing more than one selection from the same anthology, your instructor may allow you to avoid repetition by giving the anthology information in full (the Kennedy and Gioia entry) and then simply cross-referencing it in entries for the works you used. Thus the Bradstreet, Merwin, and Stevens examples replace full publication information with Kennedy and Gioia and the appropriate pages in that book. Note that each entry appears in its proper alphabetical place among other works cited.

29. Work from a collection of scholarly articles

Molloy, Francis C. "The Suburban Vision in John O'Hara's Short Stories." *Short Story Criticism: Excerpts from Criticism of the Works of Short Fiction Writers,* edited by David Segal, Gale, 1989, pp. 287-92. Originally published in *Critique: Studies in Modern Fiction,* vol. 25, no. 2, 1984, pp. 101-13.

Scholarly articles may be in collections like the one in the example above, *Short Story Criticism*. If the articles were written for the collection, you can follow model 27 for a selection from an anthology. However, if the articles were previously printed elsewhere—for instance, in scholarly journals—your instructor may ask you to provide the information for the earlier publication of articles you cite. Add Originally published in to the end of the entry and then give information for the earlier publication.

30. Article in a reference work

List an article in a reference work by the title if no author is given (models a and b) or by the author (model c). Then give the information for the container.

a. Print reference work

"Fortune." *Encyclopedia of Indo-European Culture,* edited by J. P. Malloy and D. Q. Adams, Fitzroy, 1997, pp. 211-12.

b. Web reference work

"Ming Dynasty." *Encyclopaedia Britannica,* 14 Dec. 2015, www.britannica.com/topic/Ming-dynasty-Chinese-history.

c. CD-ROM or DVD-ROM reference work

Nunberg, Geoffrey. "Usage in the Dictionary." *The American Heritage Dictionary of the English Language,* 4th ed., Houghton Mifflin, 2000.

Single-issue CD-ROMs may be encyclopedias, dictionaries, books, and other resources that are published just once. Cite such sources like print books.

31. Introduction, preface, foreword, or afterword

Quindlen, Anna. Foreword. *A Tree Grows In Brooklyn,* by Betty Smith, HarperCollins, 2011, pp. vii-xv.

Give the author of an introduction, foreword, or afterword followed by the name of the piece, as with Foreword in the example. (If the piece has a title of its own, provide it, in quotation marks, between the name of the author and the title of the book.) Give the page numbers of the part you cite.

When the author of a preface or introduction is the same as the author of the book, give only the last name after the title:

Gould, Stephen Jay. Prologue. *The Flamingo's Smile: Reflections in Natural History,* by

    Gould, W. W. Norton, 1985, pp. 13-20.

32. Published letter

Buttolph, Mrs. Laura E. Letter to Reverend and Mrs. C. C. Jones. 20 June 1857.

    The Children of Pride: A True Story of Georgia and the Civil War, edited by Robert

    Manson Myers, Yale UP, 1972, pp. 334-35.

List a published letter under the writer's name. Give it a descriptive label, specifying that the source is a letter and to whom it was addressed, and give the date of the letter. Do not put this description in quotation marks or italics. Treat the rest of the information like a selection from an anthology (model 27), giving the title of collection, the editor, publication information, and any page numbers.

Government publications

33. Government publication

a. Publication cited by author

Gray, Colin S. *Defense Planning for National Security: Navigation Aids for the*

    Mystery Tour. United States Army War College Press, 2014.

United States, Dept. of Defense, Office of Civil Defense. *Fallout Protection: What to Know*

    and Do about Nuclear Attack. US Government Printing Office, 1961.

If a government publication lists a person as author or editor, treat the source as an authored or edited book (first example). If a publication does not list an author or editor, give the government and the agency as author (second example). If the author and publisher are the same agency, see model b on the next page.

For a congressional publication, give the house and committee involved before the title. Then give the title (in italics) and information for the container: title of the Web site, date, and URL.

United States, Congress, Senate, Committee on Veterans' Affairs. *Post-9/11 Veterans*

    Educational Assistance Improvements Act of 2010. US Government Printing Office,

    2010, www.gpo.gov/fdsys/pkg/BILLS-111s3447.

If you like, after the URL you may include the number and session of Congress, the chamber (House of Representatives or Senate), and the type and number of the publication—for instance, 111th Congress, 2nd session, Senate Bill 3447.

b. Publication cited by title

"Autism Spectrum Disorder." *National Institute of Mental Health,* Sept. 2015,

www.nimh.nih.gov/health/publications/autism-spectrum-disorder-qf-15-5511/

index.shtml.

"A Comprehensive Approach to Bullying Prevention." *Wisconsin Dept. of Public*

Instruction, 24 Feb. 2016, dpi.wi.gov/sspw/safe-schools/bullying-prevention.

MLA style recommends omitting a corporate author when it is the same as the publisher and omitting the publisher when it has the same name as its Web site. The preceding examples begin with the title and then give information for the container: the title of the Web site, the date, and the URL. (For more on corporate authors, see model 5, p. 235.)

Web sources and social media

Web sites and parts of Web sites

The following models encompass pages, essays, articles, stories, poems, plays, and other works that you find on larger Web sites. To cite journal, newspaper, and magazine articles that you find on the open Web, see, respectively, models 7c, 9c, and 11c. To cite books that you find on the open Web, see model 13c. To cite a government document on a Web site, see model 33. To cite a complete Web site, see model 35.

34. Page or work on a Web site

When you cite a page or work on a Web site, treat the Web site as the container of the source. After the author and title, give the title of the Web site, in italics, any other contributors (such as an editor of the site), the publisher (if different from the site title), the publication date, and the location of the source (the URL).

a. Work with an author and a title

Murray, Amanda. "Invention Hot Spot: Birth of Hip-Hop in the Bronx, New York, in the

1970s." *Lemelson Center for the Study of Invention and Innovation,* Smithsonian

Institution, 15 Oct. 2010, invention.si.edu/invention-hot-spot-birth-hip-hop-

bronx-new-york-1970s.

See the next page for an explanation of this format and where to find the required information on a Web site.

Most works on Web sites are brief, and their titles should be placed in quotation marks. However, some works, such as books and plays, are longer, and their titles should be italicized. (See pp. 148–49 and 168–69 for titles to be quoted or italicized.) The work cited below is a collection of poems:

Wheatley, Phillis. *Poems on Various Subjects, Religious and Moral.* London, 1773.

> *Bartleby.com,* www.bartleby.com/150/.

b. Work without an author

"Eliminating Polio in Haiti." *Center for Global Development,* 2015, millionssaved.cgdev.

> org/case-studies/eliminating-polio-in-haiti.

If the work lacks an author, start with the title.

c. Work without a title

Cyberbullying Research Center. Home page. 2016, cyberbullying.org/.

If you are citing an untitled work from a Web site, such as the home page or an untitled blog posting, give the name of the site followed by Home page, Online posting, or another descriptive label. Do not use quotation marks or italics for this label.

d. Work with print publication information

Herodotus. *The Histories.* Translated by A. D. Godley, Harvard UP, 1920. *Perseus Digital*

> *Library,* Tufts U, Dept. of Classics, www.perseus.tufts.edu/hopper/text?doc=

> Perseus:text:1999.01.0126.

If the print information for a source is relevant to your research, give it after the title of the work. In this example, the name of the translator and the publication information identify a specific version of the work. The title of the Web site, the publisher, and the URL follow. For more examples of digital books, see model 13.

35. Entire Web site

a. Web site with an author or an editor

Crane, Gregory, editor. *The Perseus Digital Library.* Tufts U, Dept. of Classics, 1985-2016,

> www.perseus.tufts.edu/hopper/.

When citing an entire Web site, include the name of the editor or author (if available), followed by the title of the site, the publisher, the publication date, and the URL.

Citing a page or work on a Web site

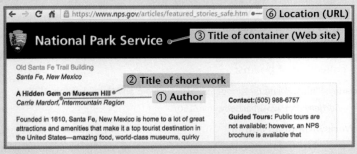

Bottom of page

①
Mardorf, Carrie. ②"A Hidden Gem on Museum Hill." ③*National Park*
④
Service, US Dept. of the Interior, ⑤3 July 2012, ⑥www.nps.

gov/articles/featured_stories_safe.htm.

① **Author.** Give the full name—last name first, a comma, first name, and any middle name or initial. Omit *Dr., PhD*, or any other title. End the name with a period. If no author is listed, begin with the title of the short work.

② **Title of the short work,** in quotation marks. End the title with a period inside the final quotation mark.

③ **Title of container (Web site),** in italics. End with a comma.

④ **Publisher,** followed by a comma. The publisher of a Web site may be at the top of the home page, at the bottom of the home page, or on a page that provides information about the site. If the site title and the publisher are the same, omit the publisher.

⑤ **Publication date.** For dates that include day and month, give the day first, then month, then year. Abbreviate all months except May, June, and July. End with a comma.

⑥ **Location (URL).** Give the URL without "http://." End with a period.

b. Web site without an author or an editor

Center for Financial Security. U of Wisconsin, 2016, cfs.wisc.edu/.

If a Web site lacks an author or an editor (as many do), begin with the title of the site.

36. Wiki

"Podcast." *Wikipedia.* Wikimedia Foundation, 6 Apr. 2016, en.wikipedia.org/
   wiki/Podcast.

To cite an entry from a wiki, give the entry title, the site title, the publisher (if different from the title of the Web site), the publication date, and the URL.

37. Undated Web source

"Clean Cars 101." *Union of Concerned Scientists,* www.ucsusa.org/our-work/clean-
   vehicles/clean-cars-101#.Vwa-KfkrKM8. Accessed 7 Apr. 2016.

MLA style no longer requires access dates for all online sources. However, if the work you cite is undated, or if your instructor requires an access date, give it at the end of the entry preceded by Accessed.

Social Media

38. Post on a blog

Minogue, Kristin. "Diverse Forests Are Stronger against Deer." *Smithsonian
   Insider,* 8 Apr. 2014, insider.si.edu/2014/04/diverse-forests-resist-deer-
   better/2014.

Cite a blog post like a work on a Web site, giving the author, the title of the post, and information about the container. The example gives the title of the blog, the publication date, and the URL. It does not give the name of the publisher because the name is clear from the title of the blog.

   Cite an entire blog as you would cite an entire Web site (see model 35).

39. Post on a social-networking site

Literacy Network. Status update. *Facebook,* 5 Apr. 2016, www.facebook.com/
   LiteracyNetwork/?fref=ts.

Give the name of the author (a person or an organization, as here), the type of post, the title of the site, the publisher (if different from the site title), the date of the post, and the URL.

MLA
48b

40. Comment

Teka. Comment on "When a Feminist Pledges a Sorority." By Jessica Bennett,

The New York Times, 9 Apr. 2016, www.nytimes.com/2016/04/10/fashion/

sorority-ivy-league-feminists.

List the author's name or user name if the author uses a pseudonym (as here). Then give Comment on followed by the title of the article or post the comment responds to and the information for the container. This example includes the author of the article the comment responds to, the title of the site, the article's publication date, and the URL.

41. Tweet

Bittman, Mark. "Eating Less Meat Could Save up to $31 Trillion (and Many Lives)

bit.ly/1UyYxyp." *Twitter*, 21 Mar. 2016, 2:21 p.m., twitter.com/bittman/status/

712026468738404352?lang=en.

Give the author's name or user name if the author uses a pseudonym. Give the entire tweet, using the author's capitalization, in quotation marks. Then give the information for the container: the name of the site (*Twitter*), the date and time of the tweet, and the URL.

42. Post to a discussion group

Williams, Frederick. "Circles as Primitive." *The Math Forum @ Drexel*, Drexel U, 28 Feb.

2016, mathforum.org/kb/thread.jspa?threadID=2583537.

If a discussion-group post does not have a title, say Online posting instead. Then give the information for the container: the title of the discussion group, the publisher, the date, and the URL of the discussion thread.

43. E-mail or text message

Green, Reginald. "Re: Early College Applications." Received by the author, 2 Sept.

2016.

For an e-mail message, use the subject line as the title, in quotation marks, with standard capitalization. Then name the recipient, whether yourself (the author) or someone else. For a text message, give a descriptive label:

Soo, Makenna. Text message to the author. 16 Apr. 2016.

Visual, audio, and other media sources

44. Painting, photograph, or other work of visual art

a. Original artwork

Abbott, Berenice. *Soap Bubbles*. 1946, Museum of Modern Art, New York.

To cite a work of visual art that you see in person, such as in a museum, name the artist and give the title (in italics). Then give the date of creation and the name and location of the place where you saw the work. You may omit the city if the name of the place includes the city.

b. Reproduction of an artwork in a print publication

Graham, David. *Bob's Java Jive, Tacoma, Washington, 1989*. *Only in America: Some Unexpected Scenery*, Alfred A. Knopf, 1991, p. 93.

To cite a reproduction of a work of visual art, give the artist and title of the work followed by information for the container in which you found it. In the example, the container is a print book with title, publisher, publication date, and location (a page number).

c. Work of art on the Web

O'Keefe, Georgia. *It Was Red and Pink*. 1959, *Milwaukee Art Museum*, collection.mam.org/details.php?id=6725.

To cite a work of art that you view on the Web, give the name of the artist or creator, the title of the work, and the date of the work (if any). Then give information for the container: the title of the Web site, the publisher of the Web site (if different from the title), and the location of the work (here, a URL).

d. Artwork in a digital file

Girls on the playground. Personal photograph by the author, 10 Aug. 2015.

To cite an unpublished artwork in a digital file that you are reproducing, such as personal photograph or work of art, give a description of it, the photographer, and the date.

45. Advertisement

a. Advertisement without a title

Apple iPhone 7. Advertisement. *Vogue*, Oct. 2016, p. 3.

To cite an advertisement without a title, start with the name of the company and/or product followed by the description Advertisement.

Then give information for the container of the source, in this case a print magazine: title, date, and location (page number).

b. Advertisement with a title

Honey Maid. "This Is Wholesome." *YouTube*, 10 Mar. 2016, youtu.be/2xeanX6xnRU.

Many companies post titled advertisements on their Web sites and on *YouTube*. To cite such an ad, give the company's name and/or product followed by the title of the ad in quotation marks. Then give information for the container: the site where you viewed the ad, the date, and the URL.

46. Comic strip or cartoon

a. Titled comic strip

Johnston, Lynn. "For Better or Worse." *San Francisco Chronicle*, 22 Aug. 2016, p. E6.

Cite a titled comic strip with the artist's name, the title of the strip (in quotation marks), and the information for the container—here, the title of the newspaper, the date, and the page number.

b. Individual cartoon

Sipress, David. Cartoon. *The New Yorker*, 7 Apr. 2016, www.newyorker.com/
cartoons/daily-cartoon/daily-cartoon-thursday-april-7th/.

To cite a cartoon that is not part of a comic strip, start with the name of the artist. If the cartoon has a title, give it in quotation marks. If it does not have a title, provide the description Cartoon (as in the example), without quotation marks or italics. Then give information for the container of the work—here, the title of the Web site, the date, and the URL.

47. Map, chart, or diagram

List an illustration by its title (model a) unless the creator of the illustration is given on the source (model b). Put the title in italics if it is published independently or in quotation marks if it is contained in another source (model a). If the illustration does not have a title, provide a description in place of the title (model b). End with publication information for the source.

a. Titled map, chart, or diagram

Eastern United States Area Map. H. M. Gousha, 1992.

"Water Cycle Diagram." *Earthguide,* Scripps Institution of Oceanography, 2014,
earthguide.ucsd.edu/earthguide/diagrams/watercyclel/index.html.

b. Untitled map, chart, or diagram

Tufte, Edward R. Diagram. *Envisioning Information,* Graphics Press, 1990, p. 63.

48. Television episode or series

To cite a television series or episode, start with the title (model a) unless you are citing the work of a person or persons (model b). Give the names of contributors if they are important to your project. To cite contributors to specific episodes, give the name(s) after the episode title (model b). To cite contributors to an entire series, give the names(s) after the series title (models c and d).

a. Broadcast TV episode

"Sink or Swim." *Nurse Jackie,* season 6, episode 1, Showtime, 2014.

This example gives the episode title and information for the container: the series title, the season and episode numbers, the name of the network, and the date.

b. Web TV episode

Peretz, Jesse, director. "Sink or Swim." By Clyde Phillips. *Nurse Jackie,* season 6,
    episode 1, Showtime, 2014. *Netflix,* www.netflix.com/watch/80065552.

This example gives the director and title of the episode. The writer is given next because he wrote this episode, not the entire series. Container 1 includes the name of the series, the season, and the episode number. Container 2 gives the streaming service, *Netflix,* and the URL.

c. TV episode on DVD, Blu-ray, or videocassette

"Sink or Swim." *Nurse Jackie Complete Collection,* created by Liz Brixius, Linda Wallem,
    and Evan Dunsky, performance by Edie Falco, season 6, episode 1, Lion's Gate,
    2016, disc 7.

This example gives the episode title followed by the information for the container, a DVD set. The creators of the series and the actor who played the central character are named, followed by the season and episode numbers and publication information about the DVD.

d. TV series

Nurse Jackie. Created by Liz Brixius, Linda Wallem, and Evan Dunsky, Showtime,
    2009-15.

This example gives information on the series as a whole: the title, the creators, the network, and the years during which the series aired.

MLA
48b

49. Radio program

To cite a radio program, start with the title of the program (model a) unless you are citing the work of a person or persons (model b). Then give information about the container: the title of the radio show, any contributors you wish to include (model a), and broadcast or Web publication information. (To cite a podcast, see model 53.)

a. Broadcast radio program

On the Media. Hosted by Brooke Gladstone and Bob Garfield, WNYC, New York,

5 Feb. 2016.

This example gives the name of the radio program, the main contributors, the station that produces the show, and the date.

b. Web radio program

McEvers, Kelly. "Opioid Epidemic Sparks HIV Outbreak in Tiny Indiana Town."

All Things Considered, National Public Radio, 31 Mar. 2016, www.npr.org/2016/

03/31/472577254/opioid-epidemic-sparks-hiv-outbreak-in-tiny-indiana-town.

Radio content streamed from a Web site may give the names of reporters and titles of stories. This example gives the name of the reporter, the title of the story, and information about the container: the name of the program, the publisher (because it is different from the title of the site), the date, and the URL. If instead of listening to the story you consulted the written transcript, add Transcript at the end of the entry, followed by a period.

50. Interview

This section provides models for interviews that you heard or saw. For a published interview that you read, use a format for an article (models 7–12) or for a selection from an anthology (model 27). For an interview you conducted yourself, see model 57.

a. Broadcast interview

Morrison, Toni. Interview. By Terry Gross. *Fresh Air,* National Public Radio, WHYY, Phila-

delphia, 20 Apr. 2015.

Begin with the person interviewed. Follow the name with Interview (not italicized or in quotation marks) in place of a title unless the interview has one. Then give the interviewer's name and information for the container: the title of the program and broadcast information.

b. Web interview

Mosley, Walter. Interview. By Tavis Smiley. *Tavis Smiley,* Public Broadcasting Service, 29

June 2016, www.pbs.org/wnet/tavissmiley/interviews/author-walter-mosley/.

After the name of the person interviewed and Interview, give the interviewer's name and information for the container: the title of the Web site, the publisher (if different from the site title), and the URL.

51. Film or video

Start with the title (model a) unless you are citing the work of a person or a corporation (models b and c). Generally, list the director. You may also cite other contributors and their roles after the title (model b).

a. Film

Chi-Raq. Directed by Spike Lee, Amazon Studios, 2015.

For a film you see in a theater, end with the distributor and the date.

b. DVD, Blu-ray, or videocassette

Balanchine, George. *Serenade*. 1991. Directed by Hilary Bean, performance by the
San Francisco Ballet, PBS Video, 1999.

For a DVD, Blu-ray disc, or videocassette, include the original release date after the title (as here) if it is relevant to your use of the source.

c. Video on the Web

CBS News. "1968 King Assassination Report." 4 Apr. 1968. *YouTube*, 3 Apr. 2008,
youtube/cmOBbxgxKvo.

For a film or video on the Web, give a creator, if available, and a title or a description. Then give information for the container: the title of the Web site, the date the video was uploaded (if available), and the URL. If the video's original publication date is significant, give it after the title, as here.

52. Sound recording

Sound recordings include music on vinyl LPs, CDs, the Web, and other devices. They also include spoken-word recordings.

a. Song

Springsteen, Bruce. "This Life." *Working on a Dream*, Columbia, 2009.

Start with the name of the artist and the title of the song. Treat the album like a container, giving the title, the publisher, and the date. For a song you stream on the Web, treat the streaming service like a second container:

Jackson, Michael. "Billie Jean." *Thriller*, MJJ Productions, 1982. *Spotify*, play.
spotify.com/track/5ORmAhIMRTcisVlB6jShJl.

b. Album

Shocked, Michelle. *Short, Sharp, Shocked.* PolyGram Records, 1988.

Give the name of the artist and the title of the album. Then give information about the container: other contributors if relevant, the recording company (as in the example), and the date of release. For an album on the Web, add the name of the streaming service and a URL, as in the Jackson example on the previous page.

If you are citing a musical work identified by form, number, and key, see model 54.

c. Spoken word

Dunbar, Paul Laurence. "We Wear the Mask." Narrated by Rita Dove. *Poetry Out Loud,*

Poetry Foundation / National Endowment for the Arts, 2014, www.poetryoutloud.

org/poems-and-performance/listen-to-poetry.

Spoken-word performances include readings, recitations, monologues, and the like. This example, of a poem read aloud, gives the author of the poem, the title, the narrator, and the container information: the Web site, the publishers (separated by a slash), the date, and the URL.

53. Podcast

Sedaris, David. "Now We Are Five." *This American Life,* Chicago Public Media, 31 Jan.

2014, www.thisamericanlife.org/podcast/episode/517/day-at-the-beach?act=4.

This podcast lists the author of a story on a radio program, the title of the story (in quotation marks), and information about the container: the title of the program, the publisher, the date of the broadcast, and the URL.

54. Live performance

Beethoven, Ludwig van. Symphony no. 9 in D-minor. Performance by Ricardo Muti and

the Chicago Symphony Orchestra, 8 May 2015, Symphony Center, Chicago.

The New Century. By Paul Rudnick, directed by Nicholas Martin, 6 May 2013, Mitzi E. New-

house Theater, New York.

For a live performance, place the title first (second example) unless you are citing the work of an individual (first example). After the title, provide relevant information about contributors as well as the date of the performance, the performance venue, and the city (if it is not part of the venue's name).

If you are citing a work of classical music identified by form, number, and key (first example), do not use quotation marks or italics for the title.

55. Lecture, speech, address, or reading

Fontaine, Claire. "Economics and Education." 7 June 2016, Museum of Contemporary

Art, North Miami. Address.

Give the speaker's name and the title of the talk (if any), the date of the presentation, the name of the venue, and the city (if it is not part of the venue's name). If the presentation occurred at a sponsored meeting, add the title of the meeting and the sponsor's name before the date. You can also give the type of presentation (Lecture, Speech, Address, Reading) if doing so will help readers understand what you are citing.

To cite a classroom lecture in a course you are taking, adapt the preceding format by giving a description in place of the title:

Cavanaugh, Carol. Class lecture on teaching mentors. Lesley U, 4 Apr. 2016. Lecture.

To cite a video of a lecture or other presentation that you view on the Web, see model 51b.

56. Video game, computer software, or app

Notch Development. *Minecraft: Pocket Edition*. Version 0.14.1, Mojang, 6 Apr.

2016, minecraft.net.

For a video game, computer program, or app, give the name of the developer or author, the title, the version, the publisher, the publication date, and the URL.

Other sources

57. Personal interview

Greene, Matthew. Personal interview. 7 May 2016.

Begin with the name of the person interviewed. For an interview you conducted, give a description of the interview—Personal interview, Telephone interview, or E-mail interview—and then give the date.

See also model 50 to cite a broadcast interview or a video of an interview on the Web.

58. Unpublished or personal letter

a. Unpublished letter

James, Jonathan E. Letter to his sister. 16 Apr. 1970. Jonathan E. James papers,

South Dakota State Archive, Pierre.

For an unpublished letter in the collection of a library or archive, give the writer, a description in place of a title, and the date (if the letter is dated). Then give the information for the container: the title of the archive and the location. See also model 32 to cite a published letter.

b. Personal letter

Murray, Elizabeth. Letter to the author. 6 Apr. 2016.

For a letter you received, give a description in place of the title and the date. To cite an e-mail message, see model 43.

59. Dissertation

McFaddin, Marie Oliver. *Adaptive Reuse: An Architectural Solution for Poverty and Home-lessness.* Dissertation, U of Maryland, 2007. UMI, 2007.

Treat a published dissertation like a book, but after the title insert Dissertation, the name of the degree-granting institution, and the year. Then give the publication information.

60. Pamphlet or brochure

Understanding Childhood Obesity. Obesity Action Network, 2016.

Most pamphlets and brochures can be treated as books. In this example, the pamphlet has no listed author, so the title comes first. If your source has an author, give the name first, followed by the title and publication information.

48c MLA paper format

The MLA's Web site (*style.mla.org*) provides guidelines for the format of a paper, with just a few elements. For guidelines on type fonts, headings, lists, illustrations, and other features that MLA style does not specify, see pages 24–30.

Margins Use one-inch margins on all sides of every page.

Spacing and indentions Double-space throughout. Indent the first lines of paragraphs one-half inch. (See opposite for treatment of poetry and long prose quotations.)

Paging Begin numbering on the first page, and number consecutively through the end (including the list of works cited). Use Arabic numerals (1, 2, 3) positioned in the upper right, about one-half inch from the top. Place your last name before the page number in case the pages later become separated.

Identification and title A title page is not required. In the upper left of the first page, give your name, your instructor's name, the course title, and the date—all double-spaced. Center the title. Do not type it in all-capitals or italics or place it in quotation marks.

Poetry and long prose quotations Treat a single line of poetry like any other quotation, running it into your text and enclosing it in quotation marks. You may run in two or three lines of poetry as well, separating the lines with a slash surrounded by space.

> An example of Robert Frost's incisiveness is in two lines from "Death of the Hired Man": *"*Home is the place where, when you have to go there **/** They have to take you in*"* (119-20).

Always set off from your text a poetry quotation of more than three lines. Use double spacing above and below the quotation and for the quotation itself. Indent the quotation one-half inch from the left margin. *Do not add quotation marks.*

> In "The Author to Her Book," written in 1678, Anne Bradstreet characterizes her book as a child. In these lines from the poem, she captures a parent's and a writer's frustration with the imperfections of her offspring:
>
>> I washed thy face, but more defects I saw,
>> and rubbing off a spot, still made a flaw.
>> I stretched thy joints to make thee even feet,
>> Yet still thou run'st more hobbling than is meet. (13-16)

Also set off a prose quotation of more than four typed lines. *Do not add quotation marks.*

> In the influential *Talley's Corner* from 1967, Elliot Liebow observes that "unskilled" construction work requires more skill than is generally assumed:
>
>> A healthy, sturdy, active man of good intelligence requires from two to four weeks to break in on a construction job. . . . It frequently happens that his foreman or the craftsman he services is not willing to wait that long for him to get into condition or to learn at a glance the difference in size between a rough 2 x 8 and a finished 2 x 10. (62)

48d Sample paper in MLA Style

The paper on the following pages illustrates the content and elements of a research paper that uses MLA style for source citation and paper format. Annotations in blue address format and documentation; the others address content.

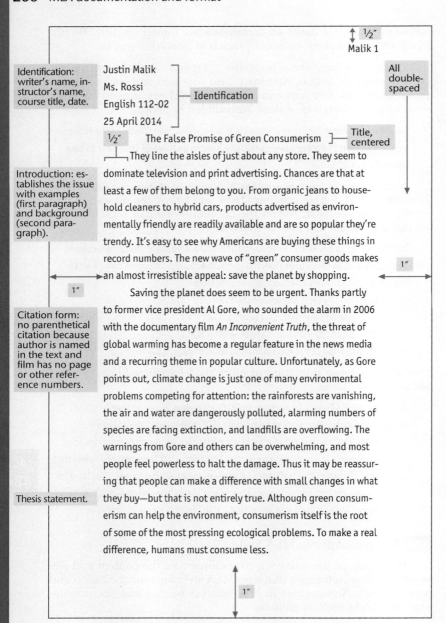

½″

Malik 1

All double-spaced

Identification: writer's name, instructor's name, course title, date.

Justin Malik
Ms. Rossi
English 112-02
25 April 2014

Identification

½″ The False Promise of Green Consumerism

Title, centered

Introduction: establishes the issue with examples (first paragraph) and background (second paragraph).

They line the aisles of just about any store. They seem to dominate television and print advertising. Chances are that at least a few of them belong to you. From organic jeans to household cleaners to hybrid cars, products advertised as environmentally friendly are readily available and are so popular they're trendy. It's easy to see why Americans are buying these things in record numbers. The new wave of "green" consumer goods makes an almost irresistible appeal: save the planet by shopping.

1″

1″

Citation form: no parenthetical citation because author is named in the text and film has no page or other reference numbers.

Saving the planet does seem to be urgent. Thanks partly to former vice president Al Gore, who sounded the alarm in 2006 with the documentary film *An Inconvenient Truth*, the threat of global warming has become a regular feature in the news media and a recurring theme in popular culture. Unfortunately, as Gore points out, climate change is just one of many environmental problems competing for attention: the rainforests are vanishing, the air and water are dangerously polluted, alarming numbers of species are facing extinction, and landfills are overflowing. The warnings from Gore and others can be overwhelming, and most people feel powerless to halt the damage. Thus it may be reassuring that people can make a difference with small changes in what

Thesis statement.

they buy—but that is not entirely true. Although green consumerism can help the environment, consumerism itself is the root of some of the most pressing ecological problems. To make a real difference, humans must consume less.

1″

Malik 2

The market for items perceived as ecologically sound is enormous. Experts estimate that spending on green products already approaches $500 billion a year in the United States (Broder 4). Shoppers respond well to new options, whether the purchase is as minor as a bottle of chemical-free dish soap or as major as a front-loading washing machine. Not surprisingly, companies are responding by offering as many new eco-products as they can. The journalist Rebecca Harris reports in *Marketing Magazine* that the recent "proliferation of green products" has been a revolution for business. She cites a market research report by TerraChoice: in the first decade of this century, the number of new packaged goods labeled as green increased by approximately 75% each year, and now nearly five thousand consumer items claim to be good for the environment. These products are offered for sale at supermarkets and at stores like Walmart, Target, Home Depot, Starbucks, and Pottery Barn. Clearly, green consumerism has grown into a mainstream interest.

Determining whether or not a product is as green as advertised can be a challenge. Claims vary: a product might be labeled as organic, biodegradable, energy efficient, recycled, carbon neutral, renewable, or just about anything that sounds environmentally positive. However, none of these terms carries a universally accepted meaning, and no enforceable labeling regulations exist (Atkinson and Rosenthal 34-35). Some of the new product options offer clear environmental benefits: for instance, LED lightbulbs last fifty times longer than regular bulbs and draw about 15% of the electricity ("LED Lightbulbs" 25), and paper made from recycled fibers saves many trees.

Background on green products (next two paragraphs).

Citation form: author and page number; author not named in the text.

Citation form: no parenthetical citation because author is named in the text and article (in HTML format) has no page numbers.

Common-knowledge examples of stores and products do not require source citations.

Citation form: source with two authors; authors not named in the text.

Citation form: shortened title for anonymous source.

Malik 3

But other "green" products just as clearly do little or nothing to help the environment: a disposable razor made with less plastic is still a disposable razor, destined for a landfill after only a few uses.

Distinguishing truly green products from those that are not so green merely scratches the surface of a much larger issue. The products aren't the problem; it's humans' high rate of consumption that poses the real threat to the environment. People seek what's newer and better—whether cars, clothes, phones, computers, televisions, shoes, or gadgets—and they all require resources to make, ship, and use them. Political scientists Thomas Princen, Michael Maniates, and Ken Conca maintain that overconsumption is a leading force behind several ecological crises, warning that

> ever-increasing pressures on ecosystems, life-supporting
> environmental services, and critical natural cycles are driven
> not only by the sheer number of resource users . . . but also
> by the patterns of resource use themselves. (4)

Those patterns of resource use are disturbing. In just the last century, gross world product (the global output of consumer goods) grew at five times the rate of population growth—a difference explained by a huge rise in consumption per person. (See fig. 1.) Such growth might be good for the economy, but it is bad for the environment. As fig. 1 shows, it is accompanied by the depletion of natural resources, increases in the carbon emissions that cause global warming, and increases in the amount of solid waste disposal.

The first negative effect of overconsumption, the depletion of resources, occurs because the manufacture and distribution of any consumer product depends on the use of water,

---

Margin annotations:

Environmental effects of consumption (next four paragraphs). Writer synthesizes information from half a dozen sources to develop his own ideas.

Quotation over four lines set off without quotation marks.

Ellipsis mark signals omission.

Authors named in text, so not named in parenthetical citation.

Text refers to and discusses figure.

First effect of overconsumption

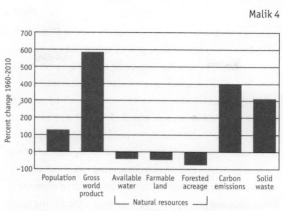

Fig. 1 Global population, consumption, and environmental impacts, 1960-2010. Data from United Nations Development Programme, *Human Development Report: Sustainability and Equity—A Better Future For All, Palgrave,* 2011, pp. 32, 37-38, 165; and from "Data Center," *Earth policy Institute,* 16 Feb. 2014, www.earth-policy.org/?/data_center/C22/.

land, and raw materials such as wood, metal, and oil. Paul Hawken, a respected environmentalist, explains that just in the United States "[i]ndustry moves, mines, extracts, shovels, burns, wastes, pumps, and disposes of *4 million pounds of material* in order to provide one average . . . family's needs for a year" (qtd. in DeGraaf et al. 78; emphasis added). The United Nations Development Programme's 2011 *Human Development Report* warns that many regions in the world don't have enough water, productive soil, or forests to meet the basic needs of their populations (4-5). Additional data from the Web site of the Earth Policy Institute confirm that as manufacturing and per-person consumption continue to rise, the supply of

Figure presents numerical data visually.

Figure caption explains the chart and gives complete source information.

Brackets signal capitalization changed to integrate quotation with writer's sentence.

Citation form: source with more than two authors; "qtd. in" indicates indirect source; "emphasis added" indicates italics were not in original quotation.

Malik 5

resources needed for survival continues to decline ("Data Center"). Thus heavy consumption poses a threat not only to the environment but also to the well-being of the human race.

In addition to using up scarce natural resources, manufacturing and distributing products harm the earth by spewing pollution into the water, soil, and air. The most worrisome aspect of that pollution may be its link to climate change. Al Gore explains the process as it is understood by most scientists: the energy needed to power manufacturing and distribution comes primarily from burning fossil fuels, which releases carbon dioxide and other greenhouse gases into the air; the gases build up and trap heat in the earth's atmosphere; and the rising average temperatures will raise sea levels, expand deserts, and cause more frequent floods and hurricanes around the world. This view is reflected in the bar chart of fig. 1, which shows that carbon emissions, like the production of consumer goods in general, are rising at rates out of proportion with population growth. The more humans consume, the more they contribute to global warming.

As harmful as they are, gradual global warming and the depletion of resources can be difficult to comprehend or appreciate. A more immediate environmental effect of buying habits can be seen in the volumes of trash those habits create. A US government study found that in a single year (2012), US residents and organizations produced 251 million tons of municipal solid waste, amounting to "4.38 pounds per person per day" ("Municipal Solid Waste Generation" 1). Nearly a third of that trash came just from the wrappers, cans, bottles, and boxes used for shipping consumer goods. Yet the mountains of trash left over from

---

Citation form: article cited by title; no page numbers given because online source lacks them.

Second effect of overconsumption

Signal phrase introduces summary, which reduces a lengthy explanation to one sentence.

Citation form: no parenthetical citation because Gore is named in the text and film has no page or other reference numbers.

Writer's own conclusion from preceding data.

Third effect of overconsumption.

Malik 6

consumption are only a part of the problem. In industrial
countries overall, 90% of waste comes not from what gets
thrown out, but from the manufacturing processes of con-
verting natural resources into consumer products (DeGraaf
et al. 192). Nearly everything people buy creates waste in
production, comes in packaging that gets discarded immediately, and ultimately ends up in landfills that are already
overflowing.

Unfortunately, the growing popularity of green products has not reduced the environmental effects of consumption. The journalist David Owen notes that as eco-friendly and
energy-efficient products have become more available, the
"reduced costs stimulate increased consumption" (80). The
author gives the example of home cooling: in the last fifty
years, air conditioners have become much more affordable
and energy efficient, but seven times more Americans now use
them on a regular basis, for a net gain in energy use. At the
same time, per-person waste production in the United States
has risen by more than 20% ("Municipal Solid Waste Generation" 10). Greener products may reduce our cost of consumption and even reduce our guilt about consumption, but they
do not reduce consumption and its effects.

If buying green won't solve the problems caused by
overconsumption, what will? Politicians, environmental-
ists, and economists have proposed an array of far-reaching
ideas, including creating a financial market for carbon
credits and offsets, aggressively taxing consumption and
pollution, offering financial incentives for environmentally
positive behaviors, and even abandoning market capitalism
altogether (de Blas). However, all of these are "top-down"

Citation form: source with more than two authors; authors not named in text.

Environmental effects of green consumption.

Citation form: author is named in the text, so page number only.

Writer's own conclusion from preceding data.

Solutions to problem of consumption (next three paragraphs).

Long-term solutions.

Citation form: author's name only, because scholarly article on the Web has no page numbers.

solutions that require concerted government action. Gaining support for any one of them, putting it into practice, and
getting results could take decades. In the meantime, the
environment would continue to deteriorate. Clearly, short-
term solutions are also essential.

Short-term
solution.

The most promising short-term solution is for individuals to change their own behavior as consumers. The greenest

Common-
knowledge
definition and
writer's own
examples do not
require source
citations.

behavior that individuals can adopt may be precycling, the
term widely used for avoiding purchases of products that involve the use of raw materials. Precycling includes choosing
eco-friendly products made of nontoxic or recycled materials
(such as aluminum-free deodorants and fleece made from discarded soda bottles) and avoiding items wrapped in excessive
packaging (such as printer cartridges sealed in plastic clam-
shells). More important, though, precycling means not buying
new things in the first place. Renting and borrowing, when
possible, save money and resources; so do keeping possessions in good repair and not replacing them until absolutely
necessary. Good-quality used items, from clothing to furniture to electronics, can be obtained for free, or very cheaply,
through online communities like *Craigslist* and *Freecycle,* from
thrift stores and yard sales, or by trading with friends and
relatives. When consumers choose used goods over new, they
can help to reduce the demand for manufactured products
that waste energy and resources, and they can help to keep
unwanted items out of the waste stream.

Avoiding unnecessary purchases brings personal benefits

Primary source:
personal inter-
view by e-mail.

as well. Brenda Lin, an environmental activist, explained in an
e-mail interview that frugal living not only saves money but
also provides pleasure:

Malik 8

You'd be amazed at what people throw out or give
away: perfectly good computers, oriental rugs, barely
used sports equipment, designer clothes, you name
it. . . . It's a game for me to find what I need in other
people's trash or at Goodwill. You should see the
shock on people's faces when I tell them where I got
my stuff. I get almost as much enjoyment from that as
from saving money and helping the environment at the
same time.

Lin's experience relates to research on the personal and
social consequences of consumerism by the sociologist Juliet
B. Schor. In one study, Schor found that the more people buy,
the less happy they tend to feel because of the stress of working longer hours to afford their purchases (*Overspent* 11-12).
Researching the opposite effect, Schor surveyed thousands of
Americans who had drastically reduced their spending so
that they would be less dependent on paid work. For these
people, she discovered, a deliberately lower standard of
living improved their quality of life by leaving them more
time to socialize, get involved with their communities,
and pursue personal interests (*True Wealth* 126-27, 139).
Reducing consumption, it turns out, does not have to trans-
late into sacrifice.

For unavoidable purchases like food and light bulbs,
buying green can make a difference by influencing corporate
decisions. Some ecologists and economists believe that as
more shoppers choose earth-friendly products over their
traditional counterparts—or boycott products that are clearly
harmful to the environment—more manufacturers and retail-
ers will look for ways to limit the environmental effects of

Sidebar annotations:

Quotation of over four lines set off without quotation marks.

Ellipsis mark signals omission from quotation.

Citation form: no parenthetical citation because author is named in the text and inter-view has no page or other reference numbers.

Citation form: shortened titles for one of two works by the same author.

Writer's own conclusion from two sources.

Benefits of green consumerism.

Citation form: two works in the same citation.

their industrial practices and the goods they sell (de Blas; Gore). Indeed, as environmental business consultant Joel Makower and his coauthors point out, Coca-Cola, Walmart, Procter & Gamble, General Motors, and other major companies have already taken up sustainability initiatives in response to market pressure. In the process, the companies

Citation form: authors are named in the text, so page numbers only.

have discovered that environmentally minded practices tend to raise profits and strengthen customer loyalty (5-6). By giving industry solid, bottom-line reasons to embrace ecological goals, consumer demand for earth-friendly products can magnify the effects of individual action.

Conclusion: summary and a call for action.

Careful shopping can help the environment, but green doesn't necessarily mean "Go." All consumption depletes resources, increases the likelihood of global warming, and creates waste, so even eco-friendly products must be used in moderation. Individuals can play small roles in helping the environment—and help themselves at the same time—by not buying anything they don't really need, even if it seems environmentally sound. The sacrifice by each person in reducing his or her personal impact on the earth is a small price for preserving a livable planet for future generations.

MLA 48d

½"

Double-spaced

Works Cited ← Center

Atkinson, Lucy, and Sonny Rosenthal. "Signaling the Green
½" Sell: The Influence of Eco-Label Source, Argument for
Specificity, and Product Involvement on Consumer Trust."
Journal of Advertising, vol. 43, no. 1, 2014, pp. 33-45.
Business Source Premier, doi:10.1080/00913367.2013.
834803.

Broder, John M. "Complaints Abound in 'Green' Certification
Industry." *The New York Times,* 1 June 2013, p. F4.
LexisNexis Academic, www.lexisnexis.com/lnacademic/
HEADLINE(Complaints+abound+green+certification+2C+
industry)%4F2013.

"Data Center." *Earth Policy Institute,* 16 Feb. 2014, www.
earth-policy.org/?/data_center/C22/.

deBlas, Alexandra. "Making the Shift: From Consumerism to
Sustainability." *Ecos,* no. 153, 2010. www.ecos.net/
?paper=EC153p10.

DeGraaf, John, et al. *Affluenza: The All-Consuming Epidemic.*
3rd ed. Berrett-Koehler Publishers, 2014.

Gore, Al. *An Inconvenient Truth.* Paramount, 2006.

Harris, Rebecca. "Greenwashing: Cleaning Up by 'Saving the
World.'" *Marketing Magazine,* 25 Apr. 2013, pp. 37-40.
MasterFILE Premier, www.masterfile.com/marketingmag/
greenwashing-cleaning-up-by-saving-the-world-77259.

"LED Lightbulbs." *Consumer Reports,* Oct. 2010, pp. 26-28.

Lin, Brenda. "Re: Interview about Living Green." Received by
the author, 21 Mar. 2014.

Makower, Joel, et al. "State of Green Business Report 2014."
Greenbiz, Jan. 2014, www.greenbiz.com/research/

New page.
Sources alphabetized by authors' last names.

Article in a scholarly journal that numbers volumes and issues, consulted in a database, with a DOI.

Article in a newspaper consulted in a database.

1"

Web page cited by title: same corporate author, publisher, and site title.

Article in a Web journal that numbers only issues and lacks page numbers.

Book with more than two authors: et al. ("and others") after first author.

Article in a weekly magazine consulted in a database.

Anonymous article listed and alphabetized by title.

Personal interview by e-mail.

Source with more than two authors.

Malik 11

report/2014/01/19/state-green-business-report-2014.

"Municipal Solid Waste Generation, Recycling, and Disposal in the United States: Facts and Figures for 2012." *US Environmental Protection Agency,* Feb. 2014, www3.epa.gov/wastes/nonhaz/municipal/pubs/2012_msw_dat_tbls.pdf.

Owen, David. "The Efficiency Dilemma." *The New Yorker,* 20 Dec. 2010, pp. 78-85. *Points of View Reference Center,* www.ebscohost.com/points-of-view/article=AN159870231.

Princen, Thomas, et al. Introduction. *Confronting Consumption,* edited by Princen et al., MIT P, 2002, pp. 1-20.

Schor, Juliet B. *The Overspent American: Upscaling, Downshifting, and the New Consumer.* Basic Books, 1998.

---. *True Wealth: How and Why Millions of Americans Are Creating a Time-Rich, Ecologically Light, Small-Scale, High-Satisfaction Economy.* Penguin Books, 2011. *Ebrary,* site.ebrary.com/lib/reader.action?docID=10493613.

United Nations Development Programme. *Human Development Report: Sustainability and Equity—A Better Future for All.* Palgrave Macmillan, 2011.

Report cited by title: same corporate author, publisher, and Web site.

Article in a weekly magazine consulted in a database.

Introduction to a print anthology.

Book with one author.

Second source by author of two cited works: three hyphens replace author's name.

Book with a corporate author that is named because it's different from the publisher.

**MLA
48d**

49 APA Documentation and Format

The style guide for psychology and some other social sciences is the *Publication Manual of the American Psychological Association* (6th ed., 2010). The APA provides answers to frequently asked questions at *www.apastyle.org/learn/faqs*. For tips on using bibliography software, see page 220.

In APA documentation style, you acknowledge each of your sources twice:

- In your text, a brief citation adjacent to the borrowed material directs readers to a complete list of all the works you refer to.
- At the end of your paper, the list of references includes complete bibliographical information for every source.

Every entry in the list of references has at least one corresponding citation in the text, and every in-text citation has a corresponding entry in the list of references.

49a APA in-text citations

In APA style, citations within the body of the text refer the reader to a list of sources at the end of the text. See the box below for an index to the models for various kinds of sources.

Note When you cite the same source more than once in a paragraph, APA style does not require you to repeat the date beyond the first citation as long as it's clear what source you refer to. Do give the date in every citation if your source list includes more than one work by the same author(s).

APA in-text citations
1. Author not named in your text *278*
2. Author named in your text *278*
3. Work with two authors *278*
4. Work with three to five authors *278*
5. Work with six or more authors *278*
6. Work with a group author *278*
7. Work with no author or an anonymous work *279*
8. One of two or more works by the same authors(s) *279*
9. Two or more works by different authors *279*
10. Indirect source *279*
11. Electronic or Web source *279*

1. Author not named in your text

One critic of Milgram's experiments questioned whether the researchers behaved morally toward their subjects (Baumrind, 1988).

When you do not name the author in your text, place the author's last name and the date of the source in parentheses. Unless none is available, the APA requires a page or other identifying number for a direct quotation and recommends an identifying number for a paraphrase:

In the view of one critic of Milgram's experiments (Baumrind, 1988), the subjects "should have been fully informed of the possible effects on them" (p. 34).

2. Author named in your text

Baumrind (1988) insisted that the subjects in Milgram's study "should have been fully informed of the possible effects on them" (p. 34).

3. Work with two authors

Bunning and Ellis (2015) revealed significant communication differences between teachers and students.

One study (Bunning & Ellis, 2015) revealed significant communication differences between teachers and students.

4. Work with three to five authors

a. First reference

Pepinsky, Dunn, Rentl, and Corson (2013) demonstrated the biases evident in gestures.

b. Later references

In the work of Pepinsky et al. (2012), the loaded gestures included head shakes and eye contact.

5. Work with six or more authors

One study (McCormack et al., 2013) explored children's day-to-day experience of living with a speech impairment.

6. Work with a group author

The students' later work improved significantly (Lenschow Research, 2016).

Use this model for a work that lists an institution, agency, corporation, or other group as author.

7. Work with no author or an anonymous work

One article ("Leaping the Wall," 2016) examines Internet freedom and censorship in China.

For a work that lists "Anonymous" as the author, use that word in the citation: (Anonymous, 2015).

8. One of two or more works by the same author(s)

At about age seven, most children begin to use appropriate gestures to reinforce their stories (Gardner, 1973a).

(See the reference for this source on p. 283.)

9. Two or more works by different authors

Two studies (Marconi & Hamblen, 2010; Torrence, 2015) found that monthly safety meetings can dramatically reduce workplace injuries.

10. Indirect source

Supporting data appeared in a study by Wong (as cited in Gallivan, 2014).

The phrase as cited in indicates that the reference to Wong's study was found in Gallivan. Only Gallivan then appears in the list of references.

11. Electronic or Web source

Ferguson and Hawkins (2016) did not anticipate the "evident hostility" of the participants (para. 6).

Some electronic and Web sources are missing one or more pieces of information:

APA
49a

- **No page numbers:** When quoting or paraphrasing a source that numbers paragraphs instead of pages, provide the paragraph number preceded by para., as in the preceding example. If the source does not number pages or paragraphs but does include headings, list the heading under which the quotation appears and then (counting paragraphs yourself) the number of the paragraph in which the quotation appears—for example, (Endter & Decker, 2015, Method section, para. 3).
- **No author:** For a source with no listed author, follow model 7.
- **No date:** For a source that is undated, use n.d. ("no date") in place of the date.

49b APA reference list

In APA style, the in-text citations refer readers to the list of sources at the end of the text. Title this list References and include in it the full publication information for every source you cited in your paper. Place the list at the end of the paper, and number its page(s) in sequence with the preceding pages. See page 302 for a complete list of references that illustrates the following features.

Arrangement Arrange sources alphabetically by the author's last name. If there is no author, alphabetize by the first main word of the title.

Spacing Double-space everything in the references unless your instructor requests single spacing. (If you do single-space the entries themselves, always double-space *between* them.)

Indention Begin each entry at the left margin, and indent the second and subsequent lines one-half inch. Your word processor can create this so-called hanging indent automatically.

Punctuation Separate the author, date, title, and publication information with a period and one space. Do not use a final period in references that conclude with a DOI or URL (see opposite).

Authors For works with up to seven authors, list all authors with last name first, separating names and parts of names with commas. Use initials for first and middle names even when names are listed fully on the source itself. Use an ampersand (&) before the last author's name. See model 3, page 283, for the treatment of eight or more authors.

Publication date Place the publication date in parentheses after the author's or authors' names, followed by a period. Generally, this date is the year only, though for some sources (such as magazine and newspaper articles) it includes the month and sometimes the day as well.

Titles In titles of books and articles, capitalize only the first word of the title, the first word of the subtitle, and proper nouns; all other words begin with small letters. In titles of journals, capitalize all significant words (see pp. 166–67 for guidelines). Italicize the titles of books and journals. Do not italicize or use quotation marks around the titles of articles.

City and state of publication For sources that are not periodicals (such as books or government publications), give the city of publication, a comma, the two-letter postal abbreviation of the state, and a colon. Omit the state if the publisher is a university whose name includes the state name, such as University of Arizona.

Publisher's name Also for nonperiodical sources, give the publisher's name after the place of publication and a colon. Shorten names of many publishers (such as Morrow for William Morrow), and omit *Co., Inc.,* and *Publishers*. However, give full names for associations, corporations, and university presses (such as Harvard University Press), and do not omit *Books* or *Press* from a publisher's name.

Page numbers Use the abbreviation p. or pp. before page numbers in books and in newspapers. Do *not* use the abbreviation for journals and magazines. For inclusive page numbers, include all figures: 667-668.

Digital Object Identifier (DOI) or retrieval statement At the end of each entry in the reference list, APA style requires a DOI for print and electronic sources (if one is available) or a retrieval statement for electronic sources.

- **DOI:** A DOI is a permanent URL that links to the text and functions as a unique identifier. When a DOI is available, include it in your citation of any print or electronic source. DOIs appear in one of two formats, as shown in model 7a (p. 284) and model 10 (p. 285). Use the format given in the source.
- **Retrieval statement:** If a DOI is not available for a source you found in a database or on the Web, provide a statement beginning with Retrieved from and then giving the URL of the periodical's or Web site's home page (model 7c, p. 284). You need not include the date you retrieved the source unless it is undated (model 22b, p. 290) or is likely to change (model 29, p. 292). If the source is difficult to find from the home page, you may give the complete URL. If you have questions about whether to include a home-page URL or a complete URL, ask your instructor.

**APA
49b**

Do not add a period after a DOI or a URL. Break a DOI or URL from one line to the next only before punctuation, such as a period or a slash, and do not hyphenate.

Authors

1. One author

Rodriguez, R. (1982). *A hunger of memory: The education of Richard Rodriguez.* Boston, MA: Godine.

APA reference-list models

2. Two to seven authors

Nesselroade, J. R., & Baltes, P. B. (1999). *Longitudinal research in behavioral studies.*
    New York, NY: Academic Press.

With two to seven authors, separate authors' names with commas and use an ampersand (&) before the last author's name.

3. Eight or more authors

Wimple, P. B., Van Eijk, M., Potts, C. A., Hayes, J., Obergau, W. R., Smith, H., . . . Zimmer,
    S. (2001). *Case studies in moral decision making among adolescents.* San Francisco, CA: Jossey-Bass.

List the first six authors' names, insert an ellipsis mark (three spaced periods), and then give the last author's name.

4. Group author

Lenschow Research. (2016). *Trends in curriculum.* Baltimore, MD: Arrow Books.

5. Author not named (anonymous)

Merriam-Webster's collegiate dictionary (11th ed.). (2008). Springfield, MA:
    Merriam-Webster.
Resistance is not futile. (2015, April 5). *New Scientist, 221*(15), 5.

If the author is actually given as "Anonymous," use that word in the author's place and alphabetize it as if it were a name:

Anonymous. (2016). *Teaching research, researching teaching.* New York, NY: Alpine
    Press.

APA
49b

6. Two or more works by the same author(s) published in the same year

Gardner, H. (1973a). *The arts and human development.* New York, NY: Wiley.
Gardner, H. (1973b). *The quest for mind: Piaget, Lévi-Strauss, and the structuralist
    movement.* New York, NY: Knopf.

Articles in journals, magazines, and newspapers

7. Article in a scholarly journal

Some journals number the pages of issues consecutively during a year, so that each issue after the first begins numbering where the previous issue left off—say, at page 132 or 416. For this kind of journal, give the volume number after the title (models a, b, c). Other journals as well as most magazines start each issue with page 1. For these journals and magazines, place the issue number in parentheses and not italicized immediately after the volume number (model 8).

a. Print, database, or Web journal article with a DOI

Hirsh, A. T., Gallegos, J. C., Gertz, K. J., Engel, J. M., & Jensen, M. P. (2010).

   Symptom burden in individuals with cerebral palsy. *Journal of Rehabilitation*

   Research & Development, 47, 860-876. doi:10.1682/JRRD.2010.03.0024

See pages 286–87 for an explanation of this format and the location of the required information on a source. The format is the same for any journal article that has a DOI—print, database, or Web.

b. Print journal article without a DOI

Atkinson, N. S. (2011). Newsreels as domestic propaganda: Visual rhetoric at the dawn

   of the cold war. *Rhetoric and Public Affairs, 14,* 69-105.

If a print journal article does not have a DOI, simply end with the page numbers of the article.

c. Database or Web journal article without a DOI

Maness, D. L., & Khan, M. (2015). Disability evaluations: More than completing a form.

   American Family Physician, 91, 102-109. Retrieved from http://www.aafp.org

   /journals/afp.html

If a journal article you found in a database or on the Web does not have a DOI, use a search engine to find the home page of the journal and give the home-page URL, as above. Give the database name if you cannot find the home page of the journal on the Web:

Smith, E. M. (1926, March). Equal rights! *Life and Labor Bulletin, 4,* 1-2. Retrieved from

   Women and Social Movements in the United States, 1600–2000, database.

8. Article in a magazine

For magazine articles, give the month of publication as well as any day along with the year. If the magazine gives volume and issue numbers, list them after the magazine title. Italicize the volume number and give the issue number, not italicized, in parentheses.

a. Print magazine article

Kluger, J. (2016, February 22). The case for life in space. *Time, 187*(6), 104-107.

b. Database or Web magazine article

Hensch, T. K. (2016, February). The power of the infant brain. *Scientific American, 314*(2), 66-69. Retrieved from http://www.scientificamerican.com

If a magazine article includes a DOI, give it after the page numbers. Otherwise, give the URL of the magazine's home page in a retrieval statement. If you do not find the home page, give the name of the database in which you found the article (see the Smith example on p. 284).

9. Article in a newspaper

For newspaper articles, give the month and day of publication along with the year. Use *The* in the newspaper name if the paper itself does.

a. Print newspaper article

Zimmer, C. (2014, May 4). Young blood may hold key to reversing aging. *The New York Times,* p. C1.

b. Database or Web newspaper article

Angier, N. (2015, July 14). The bicycle and the ride to modern America. *The New York Times.* Retrieved from http://www.nytimes.com

Give the URL of the newspaper's home page in the retrieval statement. If you do not find the home page, give the name of the database in which you found the article (see the Smith example on p. 284).

10. Review

Bond, M. (2008, December 18). Does genius breed success? [Review of the book *Outliers: The story of success,* by M. Gladwell]. *Nature, 456,* 785. http://dx.doi.org/10.1038/456874a

11. Interview

Shaffir, S. (2013). It's our generation's responsibility to bring a genuine feeling of hope [Interview by H. Schenker]. *Palestine-Israeli Journal of Politics, Economics, and Culture, 18*(4). Retrieved from http://pij.org

See model 32 (p. 293) to cite a recorded interview. See model 30 (p. 293) to cite an interview you conduct, which should be treated like a personal communication and cited only in the text.

(text continues on p. 288)

APA
49b

Citing journal articles: Print, database, or Web with DOI

Print journal article

⑤ **Volume number**   ② **Year of publication**   Department of Veterans Affairs

JRRD — Volume 47, Number 9, 2010
Pages 863–876 ●——— ⑥ **Page numbers**
Journal of Rehabilitation Research & Development ●——— ④ **Title of journal**

——— ③ **Title of article**
Symptom burden in individuals with cerebral palsy
——— ① **Authors**

Adam T. Hirsh, PhD;[1]* Juan C. Gallegos, BA;[1] Kevin J. Gertz, BA;[1] Joyce M. Engel, PhD;[2] Mark P. Jensen, PhD[1]
[1]*Department of Rehabilitation Medicine, University of Washington School of Medicine, Seattle, WA;* [2]*Department of Occupational Science and Technology, University of Wisconsin-Milwaukee, Milwaukee, WI*

Abstract—The current study sought to (1) determine the relative frequency and severity of eight symptoms in adults with cerebral palsy (CP), (2) examine the perceived course of these eight ... gressive disorder, research over the past several years has highlighted a number of health conditions and functional declines experienced by individuals with CP as they age

INTRODUCTION

Cerebral palsy (CP) is a neurodevelopmental disorder of movement and posture [1]. The onset of CP occurs very early in life, and although it is described as a nonpro-

*Address all correspondence to Adam T. Hirsh, PhD; Department of Psychology, Indiana University-Purdue University Indianapolis, 402 N Blackford St, LD 124, Indianapolis, IN 46202; 317-274-6942; fax: 317-274-6756. Email: athirsh@iupui.edu
DOI:10.1682/JRRD.2010.03.0024
——— ⑦ **Retrieval information**

Database or Web journal article

Journal of Rehabilitation Research & Development (*JRRD*) ●——— ④ **Title of journal**
——— ⑤ **Volume number**

Volume 47 Number 9, 2010 ●——— ② **Year of publication**
Pages 863 — 876 ●——— ⑥ **Page numbers**   ③ **Title of article**

Symptom burden in individuals with cerebral palsy

Adam T. Hirsh, PhD;[1]* Juan C. Gallegos, BA;[1] Kevin J. Gertz, BA;[1] Joyce M. Engel, PhD;[2] Mark P. Jensen, PhD[1] ●——— ① **Authors**

[1]*Department of Rehabilitation Medicine, University of Washington School of Medicine, Seattle, WA;* [2]*Department of Occupational Science and Technology, University of Wisconsin-Milwaukee, Milwaukee, WI*

Abstract — The current study sought to (1) determine the relative frequency and severity of eight symptoms in adults with cerebral palsy (CP), (2) examine the perceived course of these eight symptoms over time, and (3) determine the associations between the severity of these symptoms and psychosocial functioning. Eighty-three adults with CP completed a measure assessing the frequency, severity, and perceived course of eight symptoms (pain, weakness, fatigue, imbalance, numbness, memory loss, vision loss, and shortness of breath). This study highlighted several common and problematic symptoms experienced by adults with CP. Additional research is needed to identify the most effective treatments for those symptoms that affect community integration and psychological functioning as a way to improve the quality of life of individuals with CP.

*Address all correspondence to Adam T. Hirsh, PhD; Department of Psychology, Indiana University-Purdue University Indianapolis, 402 N Blackford St, LD 124, Indianapolis, IN 46202; 317-274-6942; fax: 317-274-6756. Email: athirsh@iupui.edu
DOI:10.1682/JRRD.2010.03.0024 ●———
——— ⑦ **Retrieval information**

References entry: Print, database, or Web journal article
with DOI

Hirsh, A. T., Gallegos, J. C., Gertz, K. J., Engel, J. M., & Jensen,
①
②   ③
M. P. (2010). Symptom burden in individuals with cerebral
④   ⑤
palsy. *Journal of Rehabilitation Research & Development, 47,*
⑥   ⑦
860–876. doi:10.1682/JRRD.2010.03.0024

① **Author.** Give each author's last name, first initial, and any middle initial. Separate names from initials with commas, and use & before the last author's name. Omit *Dr., PhD,* or any other title. See models 1–6 (pp. 281–83) for how to cite various numbers and kinds of authors.

② **Year of publication,** in parentheses and followed by a period.

③ **Title of article.** Give the full article title and any subtitle, separating them with a colon. Capitalize only the first words of the title and subtitle, and do not place the title in quotation marks.

④ **Title of journal,** in italics. Capitalize all significant words and end with a comma.

⑤ **Volume number,** italicized and followed by a comma. Include just the volume number when all the issues in each annual volume are paginated in one sequence. Include the issue number only when the issues are paginated separately.

⑥ **Inclusive page numbers of article,** without "pp." Do not omit any numerals.

⑦ **Retrieval information.** If the article has a DOI, give it using the format here or as shown in model 10. Do not end with a period. If the article does not have a DOI, see models 7b and 7c. (See p. 281 for more on DOIs and retrieval statements.)

APA
49b

(text continued from p. 285)

12. Supplemental periodical content that appears only online

Anderson, J. L. (2014, May 2). Revolutionary relics [Supplemental material]. *The New Yorker*. Retrieved from www.newyorker.com

13. Abstract of a journal article

Thomas, N. L. (2014). Democracy by design. *Journal of Public Deliberation, 10*(1). Abstract retrieved from http://www.publicdeliberation.net/jpd

Books, government publications, and other independent works

14. Basic format for a book

a. Print book

Ehrenreich, B. (2007). *Dancing in the streets: A history of collective joy*. New York, NY: Holt.

b. Web or database book

Reuter, P. (Ed.). (2015). *Understanding the demand for illegal drugs*. Retrieved from http://books.nap.edu

For a book available on the Web or in an online library or database, replace any print publication information with a DOI if one is available (see model 7a) or with a retrieval statement, as above.

c. E-book

Waltz, M. (2013). *Autism: A social and medical history* [Kindle version]. Retrieved from http://www.amazon.com

For an e-book, give the format in brackets and a retrieval statement.

15. Book with an editor

Dohrenwend, B. S., & Dohrenwend, B. P. (Eds.). (1999). *Stressful life events: Their nature and effects*. New York, NY: Wiley.

16. Book with a translator

Trajan, P. D. (1927). *Psychology of animals* (H. Simone, Trans.). Washington, DC: Halperin.

17. Later edition

Bolinger, D. L. (1981). *Aspects of language* (3rd ed.). New York, NY: Harcourt Brace Jovanovich.

18. Work in more than one volume

a. Reference to a single volume

Lincoln, A. (1953). *The collected works of Abraham Lincoln* (R. P. Basler, Ed.).
(Vol. 5). New Brunswick, NJ: Rutgers University Press.

b. Reference to all volumes

Lincoln, A. (1953). *The collected works of Abraham Lincoln* (R. P. Basler, Ed.). (Vols. 1-8).
New Brunswick, NJ: Rutgers University Press.

19. Article or chapter in an edited book

Paykel, E. S. (1999). Life stress and psychiatric disorder: Applications of the clinical approach. In B. S. Dohrenwend & B. P. Dohrenwend (Eds.), *Stressful life events: Their nature and effects* (pp. 239-264). New York, NY: Wiley.

20. Article in a reference work

Wood, R. (1998). Community organization. In W. A. Swados, Jr. (Ed.), *Encyclopedia of religion and society*. Retrieved from http://hirr.hartsem.edu/ency/commorg.htm

21. Government publication

a. Print publication

Hawaii. Department of Education. (2014). *Kauai district schools, profile 2013–14*.
Honolulu, HI: Author.

Stiller, A. (2012). *Historic preservation and tax incentives*. Washington, DC: U.S.
Department of the Interior.

Give Author as the publisher when the authoring agency is also the publisher.

For legal materials such as court decisions, laws, and testimony at hearings, the APA recommends conventional legal citations. The following example of a congressional hearing includes the full title, the number of the Congress, the page number for the hearing transcript in the official publication, and the date of the hearing.

APA
49b

Medicare payment for outpatient physical and occupational therapy services: Hearing before the Committee on Ways and Means, House of Representatives, 110th Cong. 3 (2007).

b. Web publication

National Institute on Alcohol Abuse and Alcoholism. (2016, July). *Underage drinking* [Fact sheet]. Retrieved from http://pubs.niaaa.nih.gov/publications /UnderageDrinking/Underage_Fact.pdf

22. Report

a. Print report

Gerald, K. (2013). *Medico-moral problems in obstetric care* (Report No. NP-71). St. Louis,
MO: Catholic Hospital Association.

b. Web report

Anderson, J. A., & Rainie, L. (2014, March 11). *Digital life in 2025.* Retrieved from Pew
Research Internet Project website: http://www.pewinternet.org

If the work you cite is undated, use the abbreviation n.d. in place
of the publication date and give the date of your access in the retrieval statement:

U.S. Census Bureau. (n.d.). *Men's marital status: 1950–2014.* Retrieved April 23, 2016,
from https://www.census.gov/hhes/families/files/graphics/MS-1a.pdf

23. Dissertation

a. Dissertation in a commercial database

McFaddin, M. O. (2015). *Adaptive reuse: An architectural solution for poverty and
homelessness* (Doctoral dissertation). Available from ProQuest Dissertations and
Theses database. (ATT 1378764)

b. Dissertation in an institutional database

Chang, J. K. (2013). *Therapeutic intervention in treatment of injuries to the hand and wrist*
(Doctoral dissertation). Retrieved from http://medsci.archive.liasu.edu/61724

Web sources and social media

Specific types of Web sources are covered under their respective
categories, such as articles in periodicals (models 7a, 7c, 8b, 9b),
books (model 14b), and reports (model 22b). When citing URLs, APA
recommends giving the home-page URL unless the source is difficult
to find from the home page. In such a case, provide the complete
URL.

24. Part or all of a Web site

a. Page or document on a Web site

American Psychological Association. (2016). Information for students with disabilities. [Web
page]. Retrieved from http://www.apa.org

See the next page for an explanation of this format and the location
of the required information on a source.

Citing a page or document on a Web site

⑤ **URL of home page for retrieval statement**
① **Author**
③ **Title**

Bottom of page

This page was last updated December 2015 ⑥⎯⎯⎯ ② **Date**

 ①   ②
National Institute on Drug Abuse. (2015, December). Teen opioid
                    ③   ④
   prescriptions raise risk of later opioid misuse. [Web page].
                    ⑤
   Retrieved from http://www.drugabuse.gov

① **Author.** When the author is a government agency, as here, give the group name. In the reference list, alphabetize the source as if the first main word (excluding any *The*, *A*, or *An*) were an author's last name. (See models 1–6, pp. 281–83, for how to cite various numbers and kinds of authors.)

② **Date.** Give the publication date in parentheses and followed by a period. Give n.d. if the Web page is undated.

③ **Title.** Give the full title of the page or document and any subtitle, separating them with a colon. Capitalize only the first words of the title and subtitle, and do not place the title in quotation marks.

④ **Description.** Provide a description of page or document in brackets.

⑤ **Retrieval statement with URL of the home page.** After the words Retrieved from, give the URL of the Web site's home page.

b. Entire Web site

Cite an entire Web site just in the text of your paper, giving the name of the site in your text and the URL in parentheses:

The Web site of the National Institutes of Health (2016) provides reliable information on a wide range of health topics for individuals, healthcare providers, and researchers (https://www.nih.gov).

Although APA does not require you to include entire Web sites in your list of references, some instructors ask for such references. Then you can use the format shown in model 24a, substituting the title of the Web site for the title of the Web page or document.

25. Post to a blog or discussion group

Kristof, N. (2014, March 22). Confronting the netherworld of child pornography [Blog post]. Retrieved from https://kristof.blogs.nytimes.com

Follow the message title with [Blog post], [Electronic mailing list message], or [Online forum comment]. Include the name of the blog or discussion group in the retrieval statement if it isn't part of the URL.

26. Blog comment

Peter. (2014, March 23). Re: Confronting the netherworld of child pornography [Blog comment]. Retrieved from http://kristof.blogs.nytimes.com

27. Post to a social-networking site

Environmental Defense Fund. (2015, May 1). Extreme weather = extreme consequences [Facebook status update]. Retrieved from https://www.facebook.com /EnvDefenseFund?fref=ts

28. Tweet

Bittman, M. [bittman]. (2014, April 1). Almost 90% of fast food workers say they've experienced wage theft: buff.ly/1i18eTb [Tweet]. Retrieved from http://twitter .com/bittman

29. Wiki

Clinical psychology. (2016, February 20). Retrieved April 15, 2016, from Wikipedia: http://en.wikipedia.org/wiki/Clinical_psychology

Give your date of retrieval for sources that are likely to change, such as this wiki.

30. E-mail or other personal communication (text citation)

At least one member of the research team has expressed reservations about the design of the study (L. Kogod, personal communication, February 6, 2016).

Personal e-mail, personal letters, interviews that you conduct yourself, and other communication that is not retrievable by others should be cited only in the text, not in the list of references.

Video, audio, and other media sources

For video, audio, and other media sources, give the medium in brackets after the title: [DVD], [Video file], [Audio podcast], and so on.

31. Film or video recording

a. Motion picture or DVD

American Psychological Association (Producer). (2001). *Ethnocultural psychotherapy* [DVD]. Available from http://www.apa.org/videos

Tyrrell, C. (Director). (2010). *The Joneses* [Motion picture]. United States: Bjort Productions.

b. Video on the Web

CBS News (Producer). (1968, April 4). *1968 King assassination report* [Video file]. Retrieved from http://www.youtube.com/watch?v=cmOBbxgxKvo

32. Recorded interview

Ambar, S. (2015, April 1). Interview by T. Smiley [Video file]. Retrieved from http://www.pbs.org/wnet/tavissmiley

For an interview you see on television or hear in a podcast, adapt the preceding example using model 33b or 35.

33. Television series or episode

APA
49b

a. Television series

Rhimes, S. (Executive producer). (2016). *Grey's anatomy* [Television series]. New York, NY: ABC.

b. Broadcast episode of television program

McKee, S. (Writer), & Wilson, C. (Director). (2014). Do you know? [Television series episode]. In S. Rhimes (Executive producer), *Grey's anatomy*. New York, NY: ABC.

c. Web episode of a television program

Randall, T. (Writer & Director). (2012). How smart can we get? [Television series episode]. In J. Cort (Executive producer), *Nova*. Retrieved from http://www.pbs.org/wgbh/nova

34. Musical recording

Springsteen, B. (2002). Empty sky. On *The rising* [CD]. New York, NY: Columbia.

35. Podcast

Glass, I. (Producer). (2016, February 26). Anatomy of doubt [Audio podcast]. *This American life*. Retrieved from http://www.thisamericanlife.org

36. Visual

Southern Illinois University School of Medicine. (n.d.). Reporting child abuse and neglect [Diagram]. Retrieved from http://www.siumed.edu/oec/Year4/how_to _report_child_abuse.pdf

United Nations Population Fund (Cartographer). (2015). *Percent of population living on less than $1/day* [Demographic map]. Retrieved from http://www.unfpa.org

37. Video game, computer software, or app

Mojang. (2016). Minecraft: Pocket Edition (Version 0.14.0) [Mobile application software]. Retrieved May 7, 2014, from https://minecraft.net

49c APA paper format

Use the following guidelines and samples to prepare a paper in APA format. Check with your instructor for any modifications to this format.

Note See pages 296–302 for a sample paper illustrating these elements. And see pages 24–30 for guidelines on type fonts, lists, tables and figures, and other elements of design.

Margins Use one-inch margins on the top, bottom, and both sides.

Spacing and indentions Double-space everywhere. (The only exception is in tables and figures, where related data, labels, and other elements may be single-spaced.) Indent paragraphs and displayed quotations one-half inch.

Paging Begin numbering on the title page, and number consecutively through the end (including the reference list). Provide a header about one-half inch from the top of every page. The header consists of the page number on the far right and your full or shortened title on the far left. Type the title in all-capital letters. On the title page only, precede the title with the label Running head and a colon. Omit this label on all other pages.

Title page Put the title on the top half of the page, followed by the identifying information, all centered horizontally and double-spaced.

Abstract Put the abstract (maximum 120 words) on a page by itself.

Body The body consists of an introduction (not labeled) and labeled sections devoted to method, results, and discussion. (See pp. 59–60 for more on this structure.)

Headings Label the major sections with centered first-level headings in boldface (**Method**, **Results**, **Discussion**). Use second- and third-level headings as needed. Double-space all headings.

First-Level Heading

Second-Level Heading

Third-level heading. Run this heading into the text paragraph with a standard paragraph indention.

Long quotations Run into your text all quotations of forty words or less, and enclose them in quotation marks. For quotations of more than forty words, set them off from your text by indenting all lines one-half inch, double-spacing throughout.

> Echoing the opinions of other Europeans at the time, Freud (1961) had a poor view of Americans:
>
> > The Americans are really too bad. . . . Competition is much more pungent with them, not succeeding means civil death to every one, and they have no private resources apart from their profession, no hobby, games, love or other interests of a cultured person. And success means money. (p. 86)

Do not use quotation marks around a quotation displayed in this way.

Illustrations Present data in tables, graphs, or charts, as appropriate. (See the sample on p. 300 for a clear table format to follow.) Begin each illustration on a separate page. Number each kind of illustration consecutively and separately from the other (Table 1, Table 2, etc., and Figure 1, Figure 2, etc.). Refer to all illustrations in your text—for instance, (see Figure 3). Generally, place illustrations immediately after the text references to them. (See pp. 24–29 for more on illustrations.)

References Start the list of references on a new page with the heading References.

APA
49c

49d Sample research report in APA style

A sociology report below and on the following pages illustrates the content and elements of a formal research report described on pages 59–60. The report also follows the APA style of source citation and paper format. Annotations in blue address format and documentation; the others address content.

[Title page.]

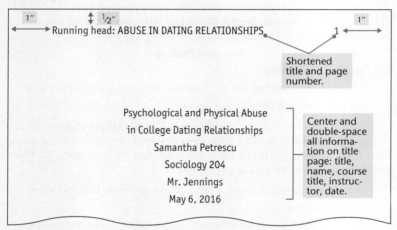

1"   ↕ ½"

Running head: ABUSE IN DATING RELATIONSHIPS   1   1"

Shortened title and page number.

Psychological and Physical Abuse

in College Dating Relationships

Samantha Petrescu

Sociology 204

Mr. Jennings

May 6, 2016

Center and double-space all information on title page: title, name, course title, instructor, date.

[New page.]

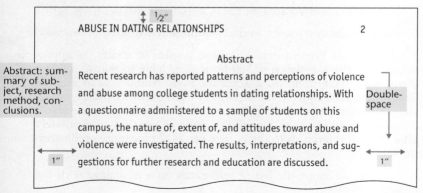

↕ ½"

ABUSE IN DATING RELATIONSHIPS   2

Abstract

Abstract: summary of subject, research method, conclusions.

Recent research has reported patterns and perceptions of violence and abuse among college students in dating relationships. With a questionnaire administered to a sample of students on this campus, the nature of, extent of, and attitudes toward abuse and violence were investigated. The results, interpretations, and suggestions for further research and education are discussed.

Double-space

1"   1"

½″

ABUSE IN DATING RELATIONSHIPS   3

Triple-space

Psychological and Physical Abuse
in College Dating Relationships

Double-space

½″

In recent years, a great deal of attention has been devoted to relationship violence. Numerous studies have been published on spousal abuse and on violence among teenage couples. Violence among college-age dating couples has also been researched, as this study will discuss. Furthermore, published studies indicate that rates of relationship abuse have remained fairly consistent despite public attention to the problem. This study confirms that trend on one college campus.

Advocacy groups have defined dating violence as "a pattern of destructive behaviors used to exert power and control over a dating partner" (Break the Cycle, n.d.). These behaviors include both physical assault, from slapping to sexual coercion, and psychological abuse such as insults and threats. Recent studies have shown that such behavior is not uncommon in dating relationships. Kaura and Lohman (2007) found that 28.76% of respondents at Iowa State University had experienced premarital abuse. Similarly, a national poll revealed that 27% of college students have been subjected to possessive or controlling behaviors from a dating partner (Knowledge Networks, 2011). Another study (Helweg-Larsen, Harding, & Kleinman, 2008) found that so-called date rape, while more publicized, was reported by many fewer respondents (less than 2%) than was other physical violence during courtship (20%).

The purpose of the present study was to survey students on this campus to test whether the incidence of abuse was similar to the patterns reported in published studies.

1″

Margin annotations:

Introduction: presentation of the problem researched by the writer.

Review of published research.

Citation form: undated source by group author, with no page numbers.

Citation form: source with two authors, named in the text.

Citation forms: source with group author and source with three authors.

1″

ABUSE IN DATING RELATIONSHIPS   4

Method

Sample

  I conducted a survey of 200 students (109 females, 91 males) enrolled in an introductory sociology course at a large state university in the northeastern United States. Participants were primarily sophomores (67%) and juniors (18%), with an average age of 20. After I omitted from the analysis both incomplete questionnaires and responses from subjects who indicated they were married or not currently dating, the sample totaled 123 subjects.

The Questionnaire

  A questionnaire exploring the personal dynamics of relationships was approved by the Institutional Review Board and distributed during class with informed consent forms. Questions were answered anonymously at home using a secure online survey system.

  The questionnaire consisted of three sections. The first asked for basic demographic information such as gender, age, and relationship status. The second section required participants to assess aspects of their current dating relationships, such as levels of stress and frustration, communication between partners, and patterns of decision making. These variables were expected to influence the amount of violence in a relationship. The third section asked subjects to identify any psychologically or physically abusive behaviors they had experienced with their dating partner, from yelling to choking.

Results

  The questionnaire revealed significant levels of psychological aggression among unmarried couples, consistent with the published studies. Of the respondents who indicated they were dating, just over half (62 of 123 subjects) reported that they had

---

First- and second-level headings.

"Method" section: discussion of how research was conducted.

"Results" section: summary and presentation of data.

ABUSE IN DATING RELATIONSHIPS   5

experienced verbal abuse at least once. Nearly 18% (22 of 123) had been shouted at by a romantic partner. In addition, almost 14% of respondents (17 of 123) had been threatened with some type of violence. (See Table 1.)

Reference to table on next page.

Rates of physical assault were also consistent with the published research. More than 16% of the study subjects reported being pushed or shoved by a partner, more than 12% had been slapped, and almost 6% had been kicked, bitten, or punched by a partner. Nine respondents (7.3%) indicated that an object had been thrown at them. One subject reported being attacked with a deadly weapon. (See Table 1.)

Discussion

Violence within premarital relationships has been widely acknowledged in the sociological research, and the present study confirms previous findings. On this campus, abuse and force occur among college couples. A high number of respondents indicated that they have been subjected to minor forms of abuse such as verbal aggression. Although the percentages of physical violence are relatively small, so was the sample. Extending the results to the entire campus population would mean significant numbers. For example, if the incidence of being kicked, bitten, or punched is typical at 6%, then 900 students of a 15,000-member student body might have experienced this type of violence.

"Discussion" section: interpretation of data and presentation of conclusions.

As other studies have shown, participation in an abusive relationship can have lasting consequences. Miller (2011) found that those who don't label abusive behavior as such are more likely to perpetuate it and to accept it as victims, while Prather, Dahlen, Nicholson, and Bullock-Yowell (2012) discovered that violence tends to become more severe as relationships become

APA
49d

Citation form: source with four authors, named in the text.

Table on a page by itself.

Table 1

Incidence of courtship violence

Type of violence	Number of students reporting	Percentage of sample
Psychological aggression		
Insulted or swore	62	50.4
Shouted	22	17.8
Threatened	17	13.8
Physical assault		
Pushed or shoved	20	16.3
Slapped	15	12.2
Kicked, bit, or punched	7	5.7
Threw something that could hurt	9	7.3
Used a knife or gun	1	0.8

Table presents data in a clear format.

APA
49d

ABUSE IN DATING RELATIONSHIPS   7

more serious. Cornelius, Shorey, and Beebe (2010) concluded that for young men and women alike, premarital violence is a problem of "highly maladaptive interactional patterns" similar to those that surface in abusive marriages (p. 445).

Citation form: source with three authors, named in the text.

These published studies suggest that a great deal is at stake for the participants in abusive relationships, not only in the present but for the future. This study extended research on this subject by contributing data on violence and abuse among college-age dating couples. The survey results provided an overview of the variables that may contribute to abusive relationships, the rates and types of dating abuse, and perceptions of abusive behaviors. The study found that rates of abuse are similar to those in published studies. If the courtship period sets the stage for later relationships, including marriage, then more attention should be given to educating young people to recognize and stop the behavior.

Conclusion: summary and implications for further research.

APA
49d

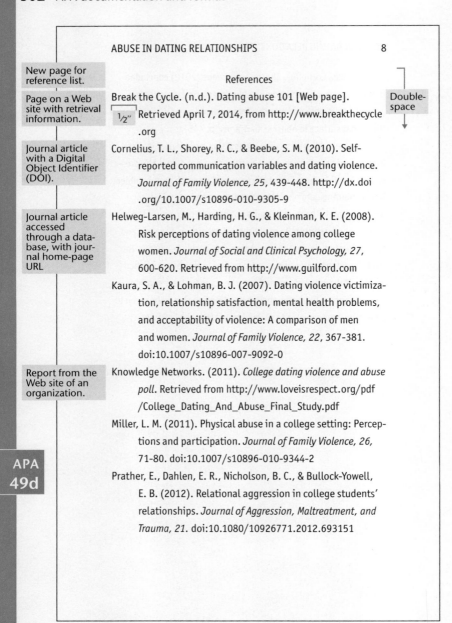

References

Break the Cycle. (n.d.). Dating abuse 101 [Web page].
½″ Retrieved April 7, 2014, from http://www.breakthecycle
.org

Cornelius, T. L., Shorey, R. C., & Beebe, S. M. (2010). Self-
reported communication variables and dating violence.
Journal of Family Violence, 25, 439-448. http://dx.doi
.org/10.1007/s10896-010-9305-9

Helweg-Larsen, M., Harding, H. G., & Kleinman, K. E. (2008).
Risk perceptions of dating violence among college
women. *Journal of Social and Clinical Psychology, 27*,
600-620. Retrieved from http://www.guilford.com

Kaura, S. A., & Lohman, B. J. (2007). Dating violence victimiza-
tion, relationship satisfaction, mental health problems,
and acceptability of violence: A comparison of men
and women. *Journal of Family Violence, 22*, 367-381.
doi:10.1007/s10896-007-9092-0

Knowledge Networks. (2011). *College dating violence and abuse
poll.* Retrieved from http://www.loveisrespect.org/pdf
/College_Dating_And_Abuse_Final_Study.pdf

Miller, L. M. (2011). Physical abuse in a college setting: Perceptions and participation. *Journal of Family Violence, 26*,
71-80. doi:10.1007/s10896-010-9344-2

Prather, E., Dahlen, E. R., Nicholson, B. C., & Bullock-Yowell,
E. B. (2012). Relational aggression in college students'
relationships. *Journal of Aggression, Maltreatment, and
Trauma, 21*. doi:10.1080/10926771.2012.693151

New page for
reference list.

Page on a Web
site with retrieval
information.

Journal article
with a Digital
Object Identifier
(DOI).

Journal article
accessed
through a data-
base, with jour-
nal home-page
URL

Report from the
Web site of an
organization.

Double-
space

APA
49d

Writers in history, art history, philosophy, religion, and other humanities use the note style of documentation from *The Chicago Manual of Style*, 16th ed. (2010), or the student reference adapted from it, *A Manual for Writers of Research Papers, Theses, and Dissertations*, by Kate L. Turabian, 8th ed., revised by Wayne C. Booth et al. (2013).

This chapter explains the Chicago note style (below) and Chicago paper format (p. 315). For tips on using bibliography software, see page 220.

50a Chicago notes and bibliography

In the Chicago note style, raised numerals in the text refer to footnotes (bottoms of pages) or endnotes (end of paper). These notes contain complete source information. A separate bibliography is optional: ask your instructor for his or her preference.

The following examples show the essential elements of a note and a bibliography entry. (See p. 317 for more illustrations.)

Note

6. Martin Gilbert, *Pictorial Atlas of British History* (New York: Dorset Press, 2012), 96.

Bibliography entry

Gilbert, Martin. *Pictorial Atlas of British History*. New York: Dorset Press, 2012.

Treat some features of notes and bibliography entries the same:

- Unless your instructor requests otherwise, single-space each note or entry, and double-space between them.
- Italicize the titles of books and periodicals.
- Enclose in quotation marks the titles of parts of books or articles in periodicals.
- Do not abbreviate publishers' names, but omit "Inc.," "Co.," and similar abbreviations.
- Do not use "p." or "pp." before page numbers.

Treat other features of notes and bibliography entries differently:

Note	Bibliography entry
Start with a number that corresponds to the note number in the text.	Do not begin with a number.
Indent the first line one-half inch.	Indent the second and subsequent lines one-half inch.
Give the author's name in normal order.	Begin with the author's last name.
Use commas between elements such as author's name and title.	Use periods between elements.
Enclose a book's publication information in parentheses, with no preceding punctuation.	Precede a book's publication information with a period, and don't use parentheses.
Include the specific page number(s) you borrowed from, omitting "p." or "pp."	Omit page numbers except for parts of books or articles in periodicals.

You can instruct your computer to position footnotes at the bottoms of appropriate pages. It will also automatically number notes and renumber them if you add or delete one or more.

50b Chicago models

The Chicago models for common sources are indexed on the next page. Notes and bibliography entries appear together for easy reference. Be sure to use the correct form—numbered note or unnumbered bibliography entry.

Note Chicago style generally recommends notes only, not bibliography entries, for personal communication such as e-mail, personal letters, and interviews you conduct yourself. Bibliography entries are shown among the following models in case your instructor requires such entries.

Authors

1. One, two, or three authors

1. Carol Gilligan, *In a Different Voice: Psychological Theory and Women's Development* (Cambridge: Harvard University Press, 1982), 27.

Gilligan, Carol. *In a Different Voice: Psychological Theory and Women's Development.* Cambridge: Harvard University Press, 1982.

1. Dennis L. Wilcox, Phillip H. Ault, and Warren K. Agee, *Public Relations: Strategies and Tactics,* 10th ed. (New York: Pearson, 2011), 182.

Chicago note and bibliography models

Chic
50b

Wilcox, Dennis L., Phillip H. Ault, and Warren K. Agee. *Public Relations: Strategies and Tactics*. 10th ed. New York: Pearson, 2011.

2. More than three authors

2. Geraldo Lopez et al., *China and the West* (Boston: Little, Brown, 2004), 461.

Lopez, Geraldo, Judith P. Salt, Anne Ming, and Henry Reisen. *China and the West*. Boston: Little, Brown, 2004.

The Latin abbreviation et al. in the note means "and others."

3. Author not named (anonymous)

3. *The Dorling Kindersley World Atlas* (London: Dorling Kindersley, 2015), 150-51.

The Dorling Kindersley World Atlas. London: Dorling Kindersley, 2015.

Articles in journals, newspapers, and magazines

4. Article in a scholarly journal

For journals that are paginated continuously through an annual volume, include at least the volume number—or, for greater clarity, add the issue number, if any, or the month or season of publication as in models a and b below. The month or season precedes the year of publication in parentheses. The issue number is required if the journal pages issues separately (no. 1 in models c and d).

a. Print journal article

4. Janet Lever, "Sex Differences in the Games Children Play," *Social Problems* 23 (Spring 1996): 482.

Lever, Janet. "Sex Differences in the Games Children Play." *Social Problems* 23 (Spring 1996): 478-87.

b. Database or Web journal article with DOI

4. Jonathan Dickens, "Social Policy Approaches to Intercountry Adoption," *International Social Work* 52 (September 2014): 600, doi:10.1177/0020872809337678.

Dickens, Jonathan. "Social Policy Approaches to Intercountry Adoption." *International Social Work* 52 (September 2014): 595-607. doi:10.1177/0020872809337678.

A DOI, or Digital Object Identifier, is a unique identifier that many publishers assign to journal articles, books, and other documents. If the article you cite has a DOI, give it in the format shown in the source: preceded by doi, as in the example above, or preceded by http://dx.doi.org/.

c. Database journal article without DOI

4. Nathan S. Atkinson, "Newsreels as Domestic Propaganda: Visual Rhetoric at the Dawn of the Cold War," *Rhetoric and Public Affairs* 14, no. 1 (Spring 2011): 72, Academic Search Complete (60502112).

Atkinson, Nathan S. "Newsreels as Domestic Propaganda: Visual Rhetoric at the Dawn of the Cold War." *Rhetoric and Public Affairs* 14, no. 1 (Spring 2011): 69-100. Academic Search Complete (60502112).

If no DOI is available for an article in a database, give the name of the database and the accession number. Notice that these and the next models include the issue number as well as the volume number because the journal pages each issue separately.

d. Web journal article without DOI

4. Rebecca Butler, "The Rise and Fall of Union Classification," *Theological Librarianship* 6, no. 1 (2013): 21, https://journal.atla.com/ojs/index.php/theolib/article/view/254.

Butler, Rebecca. "The Rise and Fall of Union Classification." *Theological Librarianship* 6, no. 1 (2013): 21-28. https://journal.atla.com/ojs/index.php/theolib/article/view/254.

If no DOI is available for an article you find on the open Web, give the URL.

5. Article in a newspaper

a. Print newspaper article

5. Erica Goode, "Invasive Species Aren't Always Unwanted," *New York Times*, February 29, 2016, national edition, D1.

Goode, Erica. "Invasive Species Aren't Always Unwanted." *New York Times*, February 29, 2016, national edition, D1.

b. Database newspaper article

5. Des Bieler, "These Famous Athletes Are Advocating Marijuana as a Workout Tool," *Washington Post*, March 2, 2016, final edition, D1, LexisNexis Academic.

Bieler, Des. "These Famous Athletes Are Advocating Marijuana as a Workout Tool," *Washington Post*, March 2, 2016, final edition, D1. LexisNexis Academic.

If an accession number is available, give it after the database name, as in model 4c above.

c. Web newspaper article

5. Lauren Zumbach, "As Sales Sag, Department Stores Look to Evolve," *Detroit News*, February 29, 2016, http://www.detroitnews.com/story/business/2016/02/29/department-sales-dip/81124706.

Zumbach, Lauren. "As Sales Sag, Department Stores Look to Evolve." *Detroit News*, February 29, 2016. http://www.detroitnews.com/story/business/2016/02/29/department-sales-dip/81124706.

6. Article in a magazine

a. Print magazine article

6. Matthew Desmond, "Forced Out," *New Yorker*, February 8, 2016, 52.

Desmond, Matthew. "Forced Out," *New Yorker*, February 8, 2016, 50-55.

b. Database magazine article

6. Takao K. Hensch, "The Power of the Infant Brain," *Scientific American*, February 2016, 68, Academic Search Complete (93983067).

Hensch, Takao K. "The Power of the Infant Brain," *Scientific American*, February 2016, 66-69. Academic Search Complete (93983067).

If no accession number is available, give just the database name, as in model 5b.

c. Web magazine article

6. Alice Park, "Alzheimer's from a New Angle," *Time*, February 11, 2016, http://time.com/4217067/alzheimers-from-a-new-angle.

Park, Alice. "Alzheimer's from a New Angle." *Time*, February 11, 2016. http://time.com/4217067/alzheimers-from-a-new-angle.

7. Review

7. John Gregory Dunne, "The Secret of Danny Santiago," review of *Famous All over Town*, by Danny Santiago, *New York Review of Books*, August 16, 1994, 25.

Dunne, John Gregory. "The Secret of Danny Santiago." Review of *Famous All over Town*, by Danny Santiago. *New York Review of Books*, August 16, 1994, 17-27.

Books and government publications

8. Basic format for a book

a. Print book

8. Barbara Ehrenreich, *Dancing in the Streets: A History of Collective Joy* (New York: Henry Holt, 2006), 97-117.

Ehrenreich, Barbara. *Dancing in the Streets: A History of Collective Joy*. New York: Henry Holt, 2006.

b. Database book

8. Daniel Levine, *Bayard Rustin and the Civil Rights Movement* (New Brunswick: Rutgers University Press, 1999), 21-45, eBook Collection (44403).

Levine, Daniel. *Bayard Rustin and the Civil Rights Movement.* New Brunswick: Rutgers
University Press, 1999. eBook Collection (44403).

c. E-book

8. Marilyn Booth, *May Her Likes Be Multiplied: Biography and Gender Politics in
Egypt* (Oakland: University of California Press, 2001), Kindle edition.

Booth, Marilyn. *May Her Likes Be Multiplied: Biography and Gender Politics in Egypt.*
Oakland: University of California Press, 2001. Kindle edition.

d. Web book

8. Jane Austen, *Emma*, ed. R. W. Chapman (1816; Oxford: Clarendon, 1926; Oxford
Text Archive, 2014), chap. 1, http://ota.ahds.ac.uk/Austen/ Emma.1519.

Austen, Jane. *Emma*. Edited by R. W. Chapman. 1816. Oxford: Clarendon, 1926. Oxford
Text Archive, 2014. http://ota.ahds.ac.uk/Austen/Emma.1519.

Provide print publication information, if any.

9. Book with an editor

9. Patricia Rushton, ed., *Vietnam War Nurses: Personal Accounts of Eighteen
Americans* (Jefferson, NC: McFarland, 2013), 70–72.

Rushton, Patricia, ed. *Vietnam War Nurses: Personal Accounts of Eighteen Americans.*
Jefferson, NC: McFarland, 2013.

10. Book with an author and an editor

10. Lewis Mumford, *The City in History,* ed. Donald L. Miller (New York:
Pantheon, 1986), 216-17.

Mumford, Lewis. *The City in History*. Edited by Donald L. Miller. New York:
Pantheon, 1986.

11. Translation

11. Dante Alighieri, *The Inferno,* trans. John Ciardi (New York: New American
Library, 1971), 51.

Alighieri, Dante. *The Inferno*. Translated by John Ciardi. New York: New American
Library, 1971.

12. Later edition

12. Dwight L. Bolinger, *Aspects of Language,* 3rd ed. (New York: Harcourt Brace
Jovanovich, 1981), 20.

Bolinger, Dwight L. *Aspects of Language*. 3rd ed. New York: Harcourt Brace
Jovanovich, 1981.

Chic
50b

13. Work in more than one volume

a. One volume without a title

13. Abraham Lincoln, *The Collected Works of Abraham Lincoln,* ed. Roy P. Basler (New Brunswick: Rutgers University Press, 1953), 5:426-28.

Lincoln, Abraham. *The Collected Works of Abraham Lincoln*. Edited by Roy P. Basler. Vol. 5. New Brunswick: Rutgers University Press, 1953.

b. One volume with a title

13. Linda B. Welkin, *The Age of Balanchine,* vol. 3 of *The History of Ballet* (New York: Columbia University Press, 1999), 56.

Welkin, Linda B. *The Age of Balanchine*. Vol. 3 of *The History of Ballet*. New York: Columbia University Press, 1999.

14. Selection from an anthology

14. Rosetta Brooks, "Streetwise," in *The New Urban Landscape,* ed. Richard Martin (New York: Rizzoli, 2005), 38-39.

Brooks, Rosetta. "Streetwise." In *The New Urban Landscape,* edited by Richard Martin, 37-60. New York: Rizzoli, 2005.

15. Work in a series

15. Ingmar Bergman, *The Seventh Seal,* Modern Film Scripts 12 (New York: Simon and Schuster, 1995), 27.

Bergman, Ingmar. *The Seventh Seal*. Modern Film Scripts 12. New York: Simon and Schuster, 1995.

16. Article in a reference work

As shown in the following examples, use the abbreviation s.v. (Latin *sub verbo*, "under the word") for reference works that are alphabetically arranged. Well-known works (model a) do not need publication information except for the edition number. Chicago style generally recommends notes only, not bibliography entries, for reference works; bibliography models are given here in case your instructor requires such entries.

a. Print reference work

16. *Merriam-Webster's Collegiate Dictionary,* 11th ed., s.v. "reckon."

Merriam-Webster's Collegiate Dictionary. 11th ed. S.v. "reckon."

b. Web reference work

16. *Wikipedia,* s.v. "Wuhan," last modified May 9, 2016, http://en.wikipedia.org/wiki/Wuhan.

Wikipedia. S.v. "Wuhan." Last modified May 9, 2016. http://en.wikipedia.org/wiki/
  Wuhan.

17. Government publication

17. House Comm. on Agriculture, Nutrition, and Forestry, *Food and Energy Act of
2008,* 110th Cong., 2nd Sess., H.R. Doc. No. 884, at 21-22 (2008).

House Comm. on Agriculture, Nutrition, and Forestry. *Food and Energy Act of 2008.*
  110th Cong. 2nd Sess. H.R. Doc. No. 884 (2008).

17. Hawaii Department of Education, *Kauai District Schools, Profile 2015-16*
(Honolulu, 2016), 38.

Hawaii Department of Education. *Kauai District Schools, Profile 2015-16.*
  Honolulu, 2016.

Web sites and social media

18. Page or work on a Web site

18. Justin W. Patchin, "Ban School, Open Facebook," Cyberbullying Research
Center, accessed May 10, 2016, http://cyberbullying.us/021649.

Patchin, Justin W. "Ban School, Open Facebook." Cyberbullying Research Center.
  Accessed May 10, 2016. http://cyberbullying.us/021649.

For Web pages and works that are not dated or are likely to change,
The Chicago Manual suggests giving the date of your access, as here,
or a statement beginning with last modified (model 16).

19. Post on a blog or discussion group

19. Joe Hursey, "Renaissance of Craft Beer," *Smithsonian Collections Blog,*
December 7, 2015, http://si-siris.blogspot.com.

Hursey, Joe. "Renaissance of Craft Beer," *Smithsonian Collections Blog.* December 7,
  2015. http://si-siris.blogspot.com.

20. Comment

20. Tony Drees, April 15, 2015, comment on Nicholas Kristof, "Standing by Our
Veterans," *On the Ground* (blog), *New York Times,* April 12, 2014, http://kristof.blogs
.nytimes.com.

Kristof, Nicholas. *On the Ground* (blog). *New York Times.* http://kristof.blogs
  .nytimes.com.

In a note cite a reader's comment on a blog by the reader's name
(Drees above). However, in the bibliography cite the entire blog by
the blog author's name (Kristof above).

21. E-mail

21. Naomi Lee, "Re: Atlanta," e-mail message to author, May 16, 2016.

Lee, Naomi. "Re: Atlanta." E-mail message to author. May 16, 2016.

Video, audio, and other media sources

22. Work of art

a. Original artwork

22. John Singer Sargent, *In Switzerland,* 1908, Metropolitan Museum of Art, New York.

Sargent, John Singer. *In Switzerland.* 1908. Metropolitan Museum of Art, New York.

b. Print reproduction of an artwork

22. David Graham, *Bob's Java Jive, Tacoma, Washington, 1989,* in *Only in America: Some Unexpected Scenery* (New York: Knopf, 1991), 93.

Graham, David. *Bob's Java Jive, Tacoma, Washington, 1989.* In *Only in America: Some Unexpected Scenery.* New York: Knopf, 1991.

c. Web reproduction of an artwork

22. Jackson Pollock, *Shimmering Substance,* 1946, Museum of Modern Art, New York, http://moma.org/collection/conservation/pollock/ shimmering_substance .html.

Pollock, Jackson. *Shimmering Substance.* 1946. Museum of Modern Art, New York. http://moma.org/collection/conservation/pollock/shimmering_substance .html.

23. Film or video

a. Film, DVD, Blu-ray, or video recording

23. George Balanchine, *Serenade,* San Francisco Ballet, performed February 2, 2000 (New York: PBS Video, 2006), DVD.

Balanchine, George. *Serenade.* San Francisco Ballet. Performed February 2, 2000. New York: PBS Video, 2006. DVD.

b. Video on the Web

23. Leslie J. Stewart, *96 Ranch Rodeo and Barbecue* (1951); 16mm, from Library of Congress, *Buckaroos in Paradise: Ranching Culture in Northern Nevada, 1945-1982,* MPEG, http://memory.loc.gov/cgi-bin/query.

Stewart, Leslie J. *96 Ranch Rodeo and Barbecue.* 1951. 16 mm. From Library of Congress, *Buckaroos in Paradise: Ranching Culture in Northern Nevada, 1945-1982.* MPEG. http://memory.loc.gov/cgi-bin/query.

24. Published or broadcast interview

24. Dexter Filkins, interview by Terry Gross, *Fresh Air,* NPR, June 25, 2014.

Filkins, Dexter. Interview by Terry Gross. *Fresh Air*. NPR. June 25, 2014.

25. Sound recording

a. LP or CD

25. Philip Glass, *String Quartet no. 5,* with Kronos Quartet, recorded 1991, Nonesuch 79356-2, 1995, compact disc.

Glass, Philip. *String Quartet no. 5*. Kronos Quartet. Recorded 1991. Nonesuch 79356-2. 1995. Compact disc.

b. Web recording

25. Ronald W. Reagan, "State of the Union Address," January 26, 1982, Vincent Voice Library, Digital and Multimedia Center, Michigan State University, http://www.lib.msu.edu/vincent/presidents/reagan.html.

Reagan, Ronald W. "State of the Union Address." January 26, 1982. Vincent Voice Library. Digital and Multimedia Center, Michigan State University. http://www.lib.msu.edu/vincent/presidents/reagan.html.

26. Podcast

26. Stephanie Foo, "Here's Looking at You, Kidney," *This American Life,* podcast audio, January 19, 2016, http://www.thisamericanlife.org/radio-archives/episode/580/thats-one-way-to-do-it?act=2.

Foo, Stephanie. "Here's Looking at You, Kidney." *This American Life*. Podcast audio. January 19, 2016. http://www.thisamericanlife.org/radio-archives/episode/580/that's-one-way-to-do-it?act=2.

Other sources

27. Letter

a. Published letter

27. Mrs. Laura E. Buttolph to Rev. and Mrs. C. C. Jones, June 20, 1857, in *The Children of Pride: A True Story of Georgia and the Civil War,* ed. Robert Manson Myers (New Haven, CT: Yale University Press, 1972), 334.

Buttolph, Laura E. Mrs. Laura E. Buttolph to Rev. and Mrs. C. C. Jones, June 20, 1857. In *The Children of Pride: A True Story of Georgia and the Civil War,* edited by Robert Manson Myers. New Haven, CT: Yale University Press, 1972.

b. Personal letter

27. Ann E. Packer, letter to author, June 15, 2016.

Packer, Ann E. Letter to author. June 15, 2016.

28. Personal interview

28. Janelle White, interview by author, December 19, 2015.

White, Janelle. Interview by author. December 19, 2015.

29. Work on CD-ROM or DVD-ROM

29. *The American Heritage Dictionary of the English Language,* 4th ed. (Boston: Houghton Mifflin, 2006), CD-ROM.

The American Heritage Dictionary of the English Language. 4th ed. Boston: Houghton Mifflin, 2006. CD-ROM.

Shortened notes

To streamline documentation, Chicago style recommends shortened notes for sources that are fully cited elsewhere, either in a bibliography or in previous notes. Ask your instructor whether your paper should include a bibliography and, if so, whether you may use shortened notes for first references to sources as well as for subsequent references.

A shortened note contains the author's last name, the work's title (minus any initial *A, An,* or *The*), and the page number. Reduce long titles to four or fewer key words.

Complete note

4. Janet Lever, "Sex Differences in the Games Children Play," *Social Problems* 23 (Spring 1996): 482.

Complete bibliography entry

Lever, Janet. "Sex Differences in the Games Children Play." *Social Problems* 23 (Spring 1996): 478-87.

Shortened note

12. Lever, "Sex Differences," 483.

You may use the Latin abbreviation ibid. (for *ibidem*, meaning "in the same place") when you refer to the same source cited in the preceding note. Give a page number if it differs from that in the preceding note.

12. Lever, "Sex Differences," 483.

13. Gilligan, *In a Different Voice,* 92.

14. Ibid., 93.

15. Lever, "Sex Differences," 483.

Chicago style allows for in-text parenthetical citations when you cite one or more works repeatedly. In the following example, the raised number 2 refers to the source information in a note; the number in parentheses is a page number in the same source.

> British rule, observes Stuart Cary Welch, "seemed as permanent as Mount
> Everest."[2] Most Indians submitted, willingly or not, to British influence in
> every facet of life (42).

50c Chicago paper format

The following guidelines come mainly from Turabian's *Manual for Writers*, which offers more specific advice than *The Chicago Manual* on the format of students' papers. See the next two pages for illustrations of the following elements. And see pages 24–30 for advice on type fonts, lists, headings, illustrations, and other elements of document design.

Margins and spacing Use minimum one-inch margins on all pages of the body. Double-space your own text and between notes and bibliography entries; single-space displayed quotations (see below) and each note and bibliography entry.

Paging Number pages consecutively from the first text page through the end. Use Arabic numerals (1, 2, 3) in the upper right corner.

Title page On an unnumbered title page provide the title of the paper, your name, the course title, your instructor's name, and the date. Double-space between adjacent lines, and add extra space below the title as shown on the next page.

Poetry and long prose quotations Display certain quotations separately from your text: three or more lines of poetry and two or more sentences of prose. Indent a displayed quotation a half inch from the left, single-space the quotation, and double-space above and below it. *Do not add quotation marks*.

> Gandhi articulated the principles of his movement in 1922:
>
> > I discovered that pursuit of truth did not permit violence being inflicted on
> > one's opponent, but that he must be weaned from error by patience and
> > sympathy. For what appears to be truth to one may appear to be error to the
> > other.[6]

50d Sample pages in Chicago style

Title page

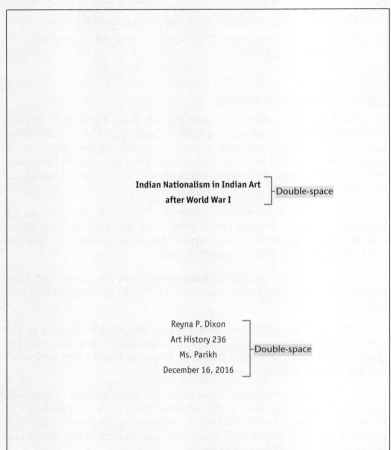

Indian Nationalism in Indian Art
after World War I   ⎤ Double-space

Reyna P. Dixon   ⎤
Art History 236
Ms. Parikh   ⎦ Double-space
December 16, 2016

First page of paper with footnotes

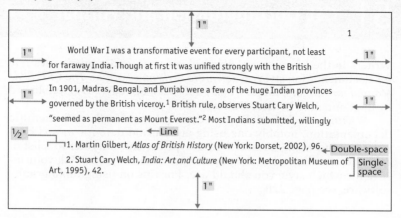

Endnotes

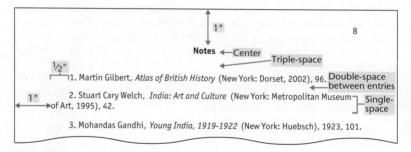

Bibilography

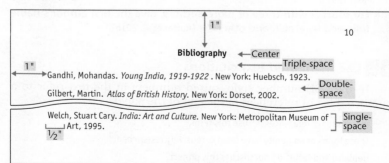

51 CSE Documentation and Format

Writers in the life sciences, physical sciences, and mathematics rely for documentation style on *Scientific Style and Format: The CSE Style Manual for Authors, Editors, and Publishers*, 8th ed. (2014), published by the Council of Science Editors.

Scientific Style and Format details several styles of scientific documentation, notably one using author and date for in-text citations and one using numbers. Both types of citation refer to a list of references at the end of the paper. (See the next page.) Ask your instructor which style you should use. For tips on using bibliography software, see page 220.

51a CSE name-year text citations

In the CSE name-year style, in-text citations provide the last name of the author being cited and the source's year of publication. At the end of the paper, a list of references, arranged alphabetically by authors' last names, provides complete bibliographic information on each source.

The CSE name-year style closely resembles the APA name-year style detailed on pages 277–79. You can use the APA examples for in-text citations, with three differences:

- **Do not use a comma to separate the author's name and the date:** (Baumrind 1968, p. 34).
- **Separate two authors' names with and (not "&"):** (Pepinsky and DeStefano 1997).
- **For sources with three or more authors, give the first author's name followed by et al. ("and others"):** (Rutter et al. 2016).

51b CSE numbered text citations

In the CSE number style, raised numbers in the text refer to a numbered list of references at the end of the paper.

Two standard references[1, 2] use this term.

These forms of immunity have been extensively researched.[3]

Hepburn and Tatin[2] do not discuss this project.

Assignment of numbers The number for each source is based on the order in which you cite the source in the text: the first cited source is 1, the second is 2, and so on.

Reuse of numbers When you cite a source that you have previously cited and numbered, use the original number again (see the last example opposite, which reuses the number 2 from an earlier example).

This reuse is the key difference between the CSE numbered citations and numbered references to footnotes or endnotes. In the CSE style, each source has only one number, determined by the order in which the source is cited. With notes, in contrast, the numbering proceeds in sequence, so that each source has as many numbers as it has citations in the text.

Citation of two or more sources When you cite two or more sources at once, arrange their numbers in sequence and separate them with a comma and a space, as in the first example on the previous page.

51c CSE reference list

For both the name-year and the number styles of in-text citation, provide a list, titled References, of all sources you have cited. Center this heading about an inch from the top of the page, and double-space beneath it.

The following examples show the differences and similarities between the name-year and number styles:

Name-year style

Hepburn PX, Tatin JM. 2015. Human physiology. New York (NY): Columbia University Press.

Number style

2. Hepburn PX, Tatin JM. Human physiology. New York (NY): Columbia University Press; 2015.

CSE
51c

Spacing In both styles, single-space each entry and double-space between entries.

Arrangement In the name-year style, arrange entries alphabetically by authors' last names. In the number style, arrange entries in numerical order—that is, in order of their citation in the text.

Format In the name-year style, type all lines of entries at the left margin—do not indent. In the number style, begin the first line of each entry at the left margin and indent subsequent lines as shown above.

Authors In both styles, list each author's name with last name first, and initials for first and middle names. Do not use a comma between the last name and initials, and do not use periods or spaces with the initials. Do use a comma to separate authors' names.

Placement of dates In the name-year style, the date follows the author's or authors' names. In the number style, the date follows the publication information (for a book) or the periodical title (for a journal, magazine, or newspaper).

Journal titles In both styles, do not italicize or underline journal titles. For titles of two or more words, abbreviate words of six or more letters (without periods) and omit most prepositions,° articles,° and conjunctions.° Capitalize each word. For example, *Journal of Chemical and Biochemical Studies* becomes J Chem Biochem Stud, and *Hospital Practice* becomes Hosp Pract.

Book and article titles In both styles, do not italicize, underline, or use quotation marks around a book or an article title. Capitalize only the first word and any proper nouns.

Publication information for journal articles The name-year and number styles differ in the placement of the publication date (see above). However, after the journal title both styles give the journal's volume number, any issue number in parentheses, a colon, and the inclusive page numbers of the article, run together without space: 28:329-30 or 62(2):26-40. See model 6 on page 322.

The box opposite lists the CSE models. The models themselves include examples of both a name-year reference and a number reference for each type of source.

Authors

1. One author

Gould SJ. 1987. Time's arrow, time's cycle. Cambridge (MA): Harvard University Press.

1. Gould SJ. Time's arrow, time's cycle. Cambridge (MA): Harvard University Press; 1987.

2. Two to ten authors

Hepburn PX, Tatin JM, Tatin JP. 2015. Human physiology. New York (NY): Columbia University Press.

2. Hepburn PX, Tatin JM, Tatin JP. Human physiology. New York (NY): Columbia University Press; 2015.

°Defined in "Grammar Terms," page 340.

CSE reference-list models

Authors

1. One author *320*
2. Two to ten authors *320*
3. More than ten authors *321*
4. Author not named *321*
5. Two or more cited works by the same author(s) published in the same year *321*

Articles in journals, newspapers, and magazines

6. Article in a journal *322*
   a. Print *322*
   b. Database or Web *322*
7. Article in a newspaper *322*
8. Article in a magazine *322*

Books

9. Basic format for a book *322*
   a. Print *322*
   b. Web *323*

10. Book with an editor *323*
11. Selection from a book *323*

Web sites and social media

12. Web site *323*
13. Blog post *323*
14. Personal communication *323*

Other sources

15. Report written and published by the same organization *324*
16. Report written and published by different organizations *324*
17. Audio or visual recording *324*
18. Document on CD-ROM or DVD-ROM *324*

3. More than ten authors

Evans RW, Bowditch L, Dana KL, Drumond A, Wildovitch WP, Young SL, Mills P, Mills RR, Livak SR, Lisi OL, et al. 2013. Organ transplants: ethical issues. Ann Arbor (MI): University of Michigan Press.

3. Evans RW, Bowditch L, Dana KL, Drummond A, Wildovitch WP, Young SL, Mills P, Mills RR, Livak SR, Lisi OL, et al. Organ transplants: ethical issues. Ann Arbor (MI): University of Michigan Press; 2013.

4. Author not named

Health care for children with diabetes. 2016. New York (NY): US Health Care.

4. Health care for children with diabetes. New York (NY): US Health Care; 2016.

5. Two or more cited works by the same author(s) published in the same year

Gardner H. 1973a. The arts and human development. New York (NY): Wiley.

Gardner H. 1973b. The quest for mind: Piaget, Lévi-Strauss, and the structuralist movement. New York (NY): Knopf.

(The number style does not require such forms.)

Articles in journals, newspapers, and magazines

6. Article in a journal

a. Print article

Campos JJ, Walle EA, Dahl A, Main A. 2011. Reconceptualizing emotion regulation. Emotion Rev. 3(1):26-35.

6. Campos JJ, Walle EA, Dahl A, Main A. Reconceptualizing emotion regulation. Emotion Rev. 2011;3(1):26-35.

b. Database or Web article

Grady GF. 2014. New research on immunizations. Today's Med. [accessed 2016 Dec 10]; 10(3):45-49. http://www.fmrt.org/todaysmedicine/Grady050389.pdf8. doi:10.1087/262534887.

6. Grady GF. New research on immunizations. Today's Med. 2014 [accessed 2016 Dec 10]; 10(3):45-49. http://www.fmrt.org/todaysmedicine/Grady050389.pdf8. doi:10.1087/262534887.

Give the date of your access after the journal title (first example) or after the publication date (second example). If the article has no page, paragraph, or other reference numbers, give your calculation of its length in brackets—for instance, [about 15 p.] or [20 paragraphs]. Conclude with the source's URL and the DOI (Digital Object Identifier) if one is available. (See p. 281 for more on DOIs.)

7. Article in a newspaper

Goode, E. 2016 Feb 29. Invasive species aren't always unwanted. New York Times (National Ed.). Sect. D:1 (col. 1).

7. Goode, E. Invasive species aren't always unwanted. New York Times (National Ed.). 2016 Feb 29; Sect. D:1 (col. 1).

8. Article in a magazine

Gordon, DM. 2016 Feb. Collective wisdom of ants. Scientific American. 44-47.

8. Gordon, DM. Collective wisdom of ants. Scientific American. 2016 Feb; 44-47.

Books

9. Basic format for a book

a. Print book

Wilson EO. 2004. On human nature. Cambridge (MA): Harvard University Press.

9. Wilson EO. On human nature. Cambridge (MA): Harvard University Press; 2004.

b. Web book

Ruch BJ, Ruch DB. 2013. New research in medicine and homeopathy. New York (NY): Albert Einstein College of Medicine; [accessed 2016 Jan 25]. http://www.einstein .edu/medicine/books/ruch&ruch.pdf.

9. Ruch BJ, Ruch DB. New research in medicine and homeopathy. New York (NY): Albert Einstein College of Medicine; 2013 [accessed 2016 Jan 25]. http://www.einstein .edu/medicine/books/ruch&ruch.pdf.

10. Book with an editor

Jonson P, editor. 2016. Anatomy yearbook 2016. Los Angeles (CA): Anatco.

10. Jonson P, editor. Anatomy yearbook 2016. Los Angeles (CA): Anatco; 2016.

11. Selection from a book

Kriegel R, Laubenstein L, Muggia F. 2005. Kaposi's sarcoma. In: Ebbeson P, Biggar RS, Melbye M, editors. AIDS: a basic guide for clinicians. 2nd ed. Philadelphia (PA): Saunders. p. 100-126.

11. Kriegel R, Laubenstein L, Muggia F. Kaposi's sarcoma. In: Ebbeson P, Biggar RS, Melbye M, editors. AIDS: a basic guide for clinicians. 2nd ed. Philadelphia (PA): Saunders; 2005. p. 100-126.

Web sites and social media

12. Web site

American Medical Association. c1995-2016. Chicago (IL): American Medical Association; [accessed 2016 Nov 22]. http://ama-assn.org/ama.

12. American Medical Association. Chicago (IL): American Medical Association; c1995-2016 [accessed 2016 Nov 22]. http://ama-assn.org/ama.

If you are unable to determine the most recent update to a Web site, give the copyright date, typically found at the bottom of the home page, preceded by c: c1995-2016 in the preceding examples.

CSE
51c

13. Blog post

Tenenbaum, LF. 2016 Feb 9. The real ice sheet of Antarctica. [blog post]. Earth Right Now. [accessed 2014 Mar 2]. http://climate.nasa.gov/blog/2396.

13. Tenenbaum, LF. The real ice sheets of Antarctica. [blog post]. Earth Right Now. 2016, Feb 9. [accessed 2014 Mar 2]. http://climate.nasa.gov/blog/2396.

14. Personal communication (text citation)

One member of the research team has expressed reservation about the study design (personal communication from L. Kogod, 2016 Feb 6; unreferenced).

A personal letter or e-mail message should be cited in your text, not in your reference list. The format is the same for both the name-year and the number styles.

Other sources

15. Report written and published by the same organization

Warnock M. 2012. Report of the Committee on Fertilization. Waco (TX): Baylor University Department of Embryology. Report No.: BU/DE.4261.

15. Warnock M. Report of the Committee on Fertilization. Waco (TX): Baylor University Department of Embryology; 2012. Report No.: BU/DE.4261.

16. Report written and published by different organizations

Hackney, JD (Rancho Los Amigos Hospital, Downey, CA). 2012. Effect of atmospheric pollutants on human physiologic function. Washington (DC): Environmental Protection Agency (US). Report No.: R-801396.

16. Hackney, JD (Rancho Los Amigos Hospital, Downey, CA). Effect of atmospheric pollutants on human physiologic function. Washington (DC): Environmental Protection Agency (US); 2012. Report No.: R-801396.

17. Audio or visual recording

Cell mitosis [DVD–ROM]. 2014. White Plains (NY): Teaching Media.

17. Cell mitosis [DVD-ROM]. White Plains (NY): Teaching Media; 2014.

18. Document on CD-ROM or DVD-ROM

Reich WT, editor. c2015. Encyclopedia of bioethics [DVD-ROM]. New York (NY): Co-Health. 1 DVD.

18. Reich WT editor. Encyclopedia of bioethics [DVD-ROM]. New York (NY): Co-Health; c2015. 1 DVD.

51d Formatting a paper in CSE style

The CSE guide *Scientific Style and Format* is not specific about margins, spacing for headings, and other elements of paper format. Unless your instructor specifies otherwise, you can use the format of the APA (pp. 294–95). The CSE exception to this style is the list of references, which is described on pages 319–20.

Because you will be expected to share your data with your readers, most of your writing in the sciences is likely to require illustrations to present the data in concise, readable form. Tables usually summarize raw data (see p. 327 for an example), whereas figures such as charts, graphs, and diagrams recast the data to show noteworthy comparisons or changes. See pages 24–30 for guidelines on tables and figures as well as type fonts, headings, and other elements of document design.

51e Sample lab report in CSE style

The following lab report for a biology course illustrates the CSE number style for documenting sources. On page 328, passages from the paper and a reformatted list of references show the name-year style. Annotations in blue address format and documentation; the others address content.

Except for the in-text citations and references, the paper is formatted in APA style because CSE does not specify a format. See pages 294–95 for more on APA paper format, and consult your instructor for any modifications.

This paper illustrates the title page and major sections of a lab report: abstract, introduction, method, results, and discussion. See pages 60–61 for more on the content of each section and the annotations in the margins of the report.

A laboratory report: CSE number style

[Title page.]

Exercise and Blood Pressure

Liz Garson

Biology 161

Ms. Traversa

December 13, 2015

Title and identifying information, double-spaced and centered on the top half of the page.

[New page.]

Abstract

The transient elevation of blood pressure following exercise was demonstrated by pressure measurements of twenty human subjects before and after exercise.

Abstract: summary of subject, research method, conclusions.

[New page.]

Exercise and Blood Pressure

The purpose of this experiment was to verify the changes in blood pressure that accompany exercise, as commonly reported.[1, 2] A certain blood pressure is necessary for the blood to supply nutrients to the body tissues. Baroreceptors near the heart monitor pressure by determining the degree to which blood stretches the wall of the blood vessel.

Introduction: presentation of the topic researched by the writer.

Sources cited in CSE number style.

[The introduction continues.]

During exercise, the metabolic needs of the muscles override the influence of the baroreceptors and result in an increase in blood pressure. This increase in blood pressure is observed uniformly (irrespective of sex or race), although men demonstrate a higher absolute systolic pressure than do women.[3] During strenuous exercise, blood pressure can rise to 40 percent above baseline.[1]

Method

The subjects for this experiment were twenty volunteers from laboratory classes, ten men and ten women. All pressure measurements were performed using a standard sphygmomanometer, which was tested for accuracy. To ensure consistency, the same sphygmomanometer was used to take all readings. In addition, all measurements were taken by the same person to avoid discrepancies in method or interpretation.

The first pressure reading was taken prior to exercise as the subject sat in a chair. This pressure was considered the baseline for each subject. All subsequent readings were interpreted relative to this baseline.

In the experiment, the subjects ran up and down stairs for fifteen minutes. Immediately after exercising, the subjects returned to the laboratory to have their pressure measured. Thirty minutes later, the pressure was measured for the final time.

Results

Table 1 contains the blood pressure measurements for the male and female subjects. With the exception of subjects 3 and 14, all subjects demonstrated the expected post-exercise increase in blood pressure, with a decline to baseline or near baseline thirty minutes after exercise. The data for subjects 3 and 14 were invalid because the subjects did not perform the experiment as directed.

Discussion

As expected, most of the subjects demonstrated an increase in blood pressure immediately after exercise and a decline to near baseline levels thirty minutes after exercise. The usual pressure increase was 20-40 mmHg for the systolic pressure and 5-10 mmHg for the diastolic pressure.

Margin notes:

Second reference to first source.

Method section: discussion of how experiment was conducted.

Reference to table.

Results section: summary and presentation of data.

Discussion section: interpretation of data and presentation of conclusions.

[Table on a page by itself.]

Table 1.   Blood pressure measurements for all subjects (mmHg)

Table presents data in a clear format.

Subject	Baseline[a]	Post-exercise	30-minute reading
Male			
1	110/75	135/80	115/75
2	125/80	140/90	135/85
3	125/70	125/70	125/70
4	130/85	170/100	140/90
5	120/80	125/95	120/80
6	115/70	135/80	125/75
7	125/70	150/80	130/70
8	130/80	145/85	130/80
9	140/75	180/85	155/80
10	110/85	135/95	115/80
Female			
11	110/60	140/85	115/60
12	130/75	180/85	130/75
13	125/80	140/90	130/80
14	90/60	90/60	90/60
15	115/65	145/70	125/65
16	100/50	130/65	110/50
17	120/80	140/80	130/80
18	110/70	135/80	120/75
19	120/80	140/90	130/80
20	110/80	145/90	120/80

[a]Normal blood pressure at rest: males, 110-130/60-90; females, 110-120/50-80.

In the two cases in which blood pressure did not elevate with exercise (subjects 3 and 14), the subjects simply left the laboratory and returned fifteen minutes later without having exercised. The experimental design was flawed in not assigning someone to observe the subjects as they exercised.

[New page.]

New page for reference list.

References

1. Guyton AC. Textbook of medical physiology. Philadelphia (PA): Saunders; 2010.

2. Rowell LB. Blood pressure regulation during exercise. Ann Med. 2004;28:329-333.

Sources in the order they appear in the paper.

3. Gleim GW, Stachenfeld NS. Gender differences in the systolic blood pressure response to exercise. Am Heart J. 2001;121:524-530.

A laboratory report: CSE name-year style

These excerpts from the preceding paper show documentation in CSE name-year style:

Sources cited by author's last name and year of publication.

The purpose of this experiment was to verify the changes in blood pressure that accompany exercise, as commonly reported (Guyton 2010; Rowell 2004).

This increase in blood pressure is observed uniformly (irrespective of sex or race), although men demonstrate a higher absolute systolic pressure than do women (Gleim and Stachenfeld 2001). During strenuous exercise, blood pressure can rise to 40 percent above baseline (Guyton 2010).

References

Sources in alphabetical order.

Gleim GW, Stachenfeld NS. 2001. Gender differences in the systolic blood pressure response to exercise. Am Heart J. 121:524-530.

Guyton AC. 2010. Textbook of medical physiology. Philadelphia (PA): Saunders.

Rowell LB. 2004. Blood pressure regulation during exercise. Ann Med. 28:329-333.

Commonly Misused Words

This section provides notes on words or phrases that often cause problems for writers. The recommendations for standard written English are based on current dictionaries and usage guides. Items labeled *nonstandard* should be avoided in final drafts of academic and business writing. Those labeled *colloquial* and *slang* appear in some informal writing and may occasionally be used for effect in more formal academic and career writing. (Words and phrases labeled *colloquial* include those labeled *informal* by many dictionaries.) See Chapter 15 for more on levels of language.

a, an   Use *a* before words beginning with consonant sounds: *a historian, a one-o'clock class, a university*. Use *an* before words that begin with vowel sounds, including silent *h*'s: *an organism, an L, an honor*.

Using *a* or *an* before an abbreviation depends on how the abbreviation is read: *She was once an AEC aide* (*AEC* is read as three separate letters); *Many Americans opposed a SALT treaty* (*SALT* is read as one word, *salt*).

See also pp. 121–23 on the uses of *a/an* versus *the*.

accept, except   *Accept* is a verb° meaning "to receive." *Except* usually means "but for" or "other than"; when it is used as a verb, it means "to leave out." *I can accept all your suggestions except the last one. I'm sorry you excepted my last suggestion from your list.*

advice, advise   *Advice* is a noun,° and *advise* is a verb.° *Take my advice; do as I advise you.*

affect, effect   Usually *affect* is a verb° meaning "to influence," and *effect* is a noun° meaning "result": *The drug did not affect his driving; in fact, it seemed to have no effect at all.* (Note that *effect* occasionally is used as a verb meaning "to bring about": *Her efforts effected a change.* And *affect* is used in psychology as a noun meaning "feeling or emotion": *One can infer much about affect from behavior.*)

aggravate   *Aggravate* should not be used in its colloquial meaning of "irritate" or "exasperate" (for example, *We were aggravated by her constant arguing*). *Aggravate* means "make worse": *The President was irritated by the Senate's indecision because he feared any delay might aggravate the unrest in the Middle East.*

all, always, never, no one   These absolute words often exaggerate a situation in which *many, often, rarely,* or *few* is more accurate.

Words

all ready, already *All ready* means "completely prepared," and *already* means "by now" or "before now": *We were all ready to go to the movie, but it had already started.*

all right *All right* is always two words. *Alright* is an error.

all together, altogether *All together* means "in unison," or "gathered in one place." *Altogether* means "entirely." *It's not altogether true that our family never spends vacations all together.*

allusion, illusion An *allusion* is an indirect reference, and an *illusion* is a deceptive appearance: *Paul's constant allusions to Shakespeare created the illusion that he was an intellectual.*

a lot *A lot* is always two words, used informally to mean "many." *Alot* is a common misspelling.

always See *all, always, never, no one*.

among, between In general, use *between* only for relationships of two and *among* for more than two.

amount, number Use *amount* with a singular noun that names something not countable (a noncount noun°): *The amount of food varies.* Use *number* with a plural noun that names more than one of something countable (a count noun°): *The number of calories must stay the same.*

and/or *And/or* indicates three options: one or the other or both (*The decision is made by the mayor and/or the council*). If you mean all three options, *and/or* is appropriate. Otherwise, use *and* if you mean both, *or* if you mean either.

anxious, eager *Anxious* means "nervous" or "worried" and is usually followed by *about*. *Eager* means "looking forward" and is usually followed by *to*. *I've been anxious about getting blisters. I'm eager* [not *anxious*] *to get new cross-training shoes.*

anybody, any body; anyone, any one *Anybody* and *anyone* are indefinite pronouns°; *any body* is a noun° modified by *any*; *any one* is a pronoun° or adjective° modified by *any*. *How can anybody communicate with any body of government? Can anyone help Amy? She has more work than any one person can handle.*

any more, anymore *Any more* means "no more"; *anymore* means "now." Both are used in negative constructions: *He doesn't want any more. She doesn't live here anymore.*

anyways, anywheres Nonstandard for *anyway* and *anywhere*.

are, is Use *are* with a plural subject° (*books are*), *is* with a singular subject (*book is*). See pp. 107–08.

as *As* may be unclear when it substitutes for *because, since,* or *while*: *As we were stopping to rest, we decided to eat lunch.* (Does *as* mean "while" or "because"?) *As* should never be used as a substitute for *whether* or *who*.

°Defined in "Grammar Terms," page 340.

I'm not sure whether [not *as*] *we can make it. That's the man who* [not *as*] *gave me directions.*

as, like   See *like, as.*

at this point in time   Wordy for *now, at this point,* or *at this time.*

awful, awfully   Strictly speaking, *awful* means "inspiring awe." As intensifiers meaning "very" or "extremely" (*He tried awfully hard*), *awful* and *awfully* should be avoided in formal speech or writing.

a while, awhile   *Awhile* is an adverb°; *a while* is an article° and a noun.° *I will be gone awhile* [not *a while*]. *I will be gone for a while* [not *awhile*].

bad, badly   In formal speech and writing, *bad* should be used only as an adjective°; the adverb° is *badly. He felt bad because his tooth ached badly.* In *He felt bad,* the verb *felt* is a linking verb° and the adjective *bad* modifies the subject° *he,* not the verb *felt.* See also p. 119.

being as, being that   Colloquial for *because,* the preferable word in formal speech or writing: *Because* [not *Being as*] *the world is round, Columbus never did fall off the edge.*

beside, besides   *Beside* means "next to," while *besides* means "except," "in addition to," or "in addition": *Besides, several other people besides you want to sit beside Dr. Christensen.*

between, among   See *among, between.*

bring, take   Use *bring* only for movement from a farther place to a nearer one and *take* for any other movement. *First, take these books to the library for renewal, then take them to Mr. Daniels. Bring them back to me when he's finished.*

but, hardly, scarcely   These words are negative in their own right; using *not* with any of them produces a double negative (see p. 120). *We have but* [not *haven't got but*] *an hour before our plane leaves. I could hardly* [not *couldn't hardly*] *make out her face.*

can, may   Strictly, *can* indicates capacity or ability, and *may* indicates permission: *If I may talk with you a moment, I believe I can solve your problem.*

climatic, climactic   *Climatic* comes from *climate* and refers to weather: *Recent droughts may indicate a climatic change. Climactic* comes from *climax* and refers to a dramatic high point: *During the climactic duel between Hamlet and Laertes, Gertrude drinks poisoned wine.*

complement, compliment   To *complement* something is to add to, complete, or reinforce it: *Her yellow blouse complemented her black hair.* To *compliment* something is to make a flattering remark about it: *He complimented her on her hair. Complimentary* can also mean "free": *complimentary tickets.*

°Defined in "Grammar Terms," page 340.

conscience, conscious *Conscience* is a noun° meaning "a sense of right and wrong"; *conscious* is an adjective° meaning "aware" or "awake." *Though I was barely conscious, my conscience nagged me.*

contact Avoid using *contact* imprecisely as a verb instead of a more exact word such as *consult, talk with, telephone,* or *write to.*

continual, continuous *Continual* means "constantly recurring": *Most movies on television are continually interrupted by commercials. Continuous* means "unceasing": *Some cable channels present movies continuously without commercials.*

could of See *have, of.*

criteria The plural of *criterion* (meaning "standard for judgment"): *Our criteria are strict. The most important criterion is a sense of humor.*

data The plural of *datum* (meaning "fact"). Though *data* is often used with a singular verb, many readers prefer the plural verb and it is always correct: *The data fail [not fails] to support the hypothesis.*

device, devise *Device* is the noun,° and *devise* is the verb:° *Can you devise some device for getting his attention?*

different from, different than *Different from* is preferred: *His purpose is different from mine.* But *different than* is widely accepted when a construction using *from* would be wordy: *I'm a different person now than I used to be* is preferable to *I'm a different person now from the person I used to be.*

disinterested, uninterested *Disinterested* means "impartial": *We chose Pete, as a disinterested third party, to decide who was right. Uninterested* means "bored" or "lacking interest": *Unfortunately, Pete was completely uninterested in the question.*

don't *Don't* is the contraction for *do not,* not for *does not*: *I don't care, you don't care,* and *he doesn't [not don't] care.*

due to *Due* is an adjective° or noun;° thus *due to* is always acceptable as a subject complement:° *His gray hairs were due to age.* Many object to *due to* as a preposition° meaning "because of" (*Due to the holiday, class was canceled*). A rule of thumb is that *due to* is always correct after a form of the verb *be* but questionable otherwise.

eager, anxious See *anxious, eager.*

effect See *affect, effect.*

elicit, illicit *Elicit* means "bring out" or "call forth." *Illicit* means "unlawful." *The crime elicited an outcry against illicit drugs.*

emigrate, immigrate *Emigrate* means "to leave one place and move to another": *The Chus emigrated from Korea. Immigrate* means "to move into a place where one was not born": *They immigrated to the United States.*

°Defined in "Grammar Terms," page 340.

enthused   Avoid using colloquially to mean "showing enthusiasm." Prefer *enthusiastic*: *The coach was* <u>*enthusiastic*</u> [not <u>*enthused*</u>] *about the team's prospects.*

et al., etc.   Use *et al.,* the Latin abbreviation for "and other people," only in source citations: *Jones* <u>*et al.*</u> Avoid *etc.,* the Latin abbreviation for "and other things," in formal writing, and do not use it to refer to people or to substitute for precision, as in *The government provides health care,* <u>*etc.*</u>

everybody, every body; everyone, every one   *Everybody* and *everyone* are indefinite pronouns:° <u>*Everybody*</u> [or <u>*Everyone*</u>] *knows Tom steals. Every one* is a pronoun° modified by *every,* and *every body* is a noun° modified by *every.* Both refer to each thing or person of a specific group and are typically followed by *of*: *The game commissioner has stocked* <u>*every body*</u> *of fresh water in the state with fish, and now* <u>*every one*</u> *of our rivers is a potential trout stream.*

everyday, every day   *Everyday* is an adjective° meaning "used daily" or "common"; *every day* is a noun° modified by *every*: <u>*Everyday*</u> *problems tend to arise* <u>*every day*</u>.

everywheres   Nonstandard for *everywhere.*

except   See *accept, except.*

explicit, implicit   *Explicit* means "stated outright": *I left* <u>*explicit*</u> *instructions. Implicit* means "implied, unstated": *We had an* <u>*implicit*</u> *understanding.*

farther, further   *Farther* refers to additional distance (*How much* <u>*farther*</u> *is it to the beach?*), and *further* refers to additional time, amount, or other abstract matters (*I don't want to discuss this any* <u>*further*</u>).

feel   Avoid this word in place of *think* or *believe*: *She* <u>*thinks*</u> [not <u>*feels*</u>] *that the law should be changed.*

fewer, less   *Fewer* refers to individual countable items (a plural count noun°), *less* to general amounts (a noncount noun,° always singular): *Skim milk has* <u>*fewer*</u> *calories than whole milk. We have* <u>*less*</u> *milk left than I thought.*

further   See *farther, further.*

get   *Get* is easy to overuse; watch out for it in expressions such as *it's getting better* (substitute *improving*), *we* <u>*got done*</u> (substitute *finished*), and *the mayor* <u>*has got to*</u> (substitute *must*).

good, well   *Good* is an adjective,° and *well* is nearly always an adverb:° *Larry's a* <u>*good*</u> *dancer. He and Linda dance* <u>*well*</u> *together. Well* is properly used as an adjective only to refer to health: *You look* <u>*well*</u>. (*You look* <u>*good*</u>, in contrast, means "Your appearance is pleasing.") See also p. 119.

hanged, hung   Though both are past-tense forms° of *hang, hanged* is used to refer to executions and *hung* is used for all other meanings: *Tom*

Dooley was hanged [not hung] from a white oak tree. I hung [not hanged] the picture you gave me.

hardly   See *but, hardly, scarcely.*

have, of   Use *have,* not *of,* after helping verbs° such as *could, should, would, may, must,* and *might: You should have [not should of] told me.*

he, she; he/she   Convention has allowed the use of *he* to mean "he or she," but most writers today consider this usage inaccurate and unfair because it excludes females. The construction *he/she,* one substitute for *he,* is awkward and objectionable to many readers. The better choice is to recast the sentence in the plural, to rephrase, or to use *he or she.* For instance: *After infants learn to creep, they progress to crawling. After learning to creep, the infant progresses to crawling. After the infant learns to creep, he or she progresses to crawling.* See also pp. 85–87 and 114.

herself, himself   See *myself, herself, himself, yourself.*

hisself   Nonstandard for *himself.*

hopefully   *Hopefully* means "with hope": *Freddy waited hopefully.* The use of *hopefully* to mean "it is to be hoped," "I hope," or "let's hope" is now very common; but try to avoid it in writing because many readers continue to object strongly to the usage.

idea, ideal   An *idea* is a thought or conception. An *ideal* (noun°) is a model of perfection or a goal. *Ideal* should not be used in place of *idea: The idea [not ideal] of the play is that our ideals often sustain us.*

if, whether   For clarity, use *whether* rather than *if* when you are expressing an alternative: *If I laugh hard, people can't tell whether I'm crying.*

illicit   See *elicit, illicit.*

illusion   See *allusion, illusion.*

immigrate   See *emigrate, immigrate.*

implicit   See *explicit, implicit.*

imply, infer   Writers or speakers *imply,* meaning "suggest": *Jim's letter implies he's having a good time.* Readers or listeners *infer,* meaning "conclude": *From Jim's letter I infer he's having a good time.*

irregardless   Nonstandard for *regardless.*

is, are   See *are, is.*

is when, is where   These are faulty constructions in sentences that define: *Adolescence is a stage [not is when a person is] between childhood and adulthood. Socialism is a system in which [not is where] government owns the means of production.*

its, it's   *Its* is the pronoun° *it* in the possessive case:° *That plant is losing its leaves. It's* is a contraction for *it is* or *it has: It's [It is] likely to die. It's [It has] got a fungus.* See also p. 146.

°Defined in "Grammar Terms," page 340.

kind of, sort of, type of In formal speech and writing, avoid using *kind of* or *sort of* to mean "somewhat": *He was rather* [not *kind of*] *tall. Kind, sort,* and *type* are singular and take singular adjectives and verbs: *This kind of dog is easily trained.* Agreement errors often occur when the singular *kind, sort,* or *type* is combined with the plural adjectives *these* and *those: These kinds* [not *kind*] *of dogs are easily trained. Kind, sort,* and *type* should be followed by *of* but not by *a: I don't know what type of* [not *type* or *type of a*] *dog that is.*

Use *kind of, sort of,* or *type of* only when the word *kind, sort,* or *type* is important: *That was a strange* [not *strange sort of*] *statement.*

lay, lie *Lay* means "put" or "place" and takes a direct object:° *We could lay the tablecloth in the sun.* Its main forms are *lay, laid, laid. Lie* means "recline" or "be situated" and does not take an object: *I lie awake at night. The town lies east of the river.* Its main forms are *lie, lay, lain.*

less See *fewer, less.*

lie, lay See *lay, lie.*

like, as In formal speech and writing, *like* should not introduce a main clause.° The preferred choice is *as* or *as if: The plan succeeded as* [not *like*] *we hoped.* Use *like* only before a word or phrase: *Other plans like it have failed.*

literally This word means "actually" or "just as the words say," and it should not be used to intensify expressions whose words are not to be taken at face value. The sentence *He was literally climbing the walls* describes a person behaving like an insect, not a person who is restless or anxious. For the latter meaning, *literally* should be omitted.

lose, loose *Lose* means "mislay": *Did you lose a brown glove? Loose* usually means "unrestrained" or "not tight": *Ann's canary got loose.*

lots, lots of Avoid these colloquialisms in college or business writing. Use *very many, a great many,* or *much* instead.

may, can See *can, may.*

may be, maybe *May be* is a verb,° and *maybe* is an adverb° meaning "perhaps": *Tuesday may be a legal holiday. Maybe we won't have classes.*

may of See *have, of.*

media *Media* is the plural of *medium* and takes a plural verb.° *All the news media are increasingly visual.* The singular verb is common, even in the media, but many readers prefer the plural verb and it is always correct.

might of See *have, of.*

must of See *have, of.*

myself, herself, himself, yourself, ourselves, themselves, yourselves Avoid using the *-self* pronouns° in place of personal pronouns°: *No one except me* [not *myself*] *saw the accident. Michiko and I* [not *myself*]

°Defined in "Grammar Terms," page 340.

Words

planned the ceremony. The *-self* pronouns have two uses: they emphasize a noun or other pronoun (*Paul did the work himself. He himself said so.*), or they indicate that the sentence subject also receives the action of the verb: *I drove myself to the hospital.*

never, no one   See *all, always, never, no one.*

nowheres   Nonstandard for *nowhere.*

number   See *amount, number.*

of, have   See *have, of.*

OK, O.K., okay   All three spellings are acceptable, but avoid this colloquial term in formal speech and writing.

peak, peek, pique   *Peak* means "a highest or greatest point" or "to reach a highest or greatest point": *Voter participation had its peak* [or *peaked*] *in 2008. Peek* means "a secretive look" or "to take a secretive look": *The child stole a peek* [or *peeked*] *behind the curtain. Pique* usually means "to cause interest or curiosity": *Emma's anthropology course piqued her interest in Africa.* But *pique* also means "irritation" or "to feel irritated": *I sensed her pique. She was clearly piqued by my nosy question.*

people, persons   Except when emphasizing individuals, prefer *people* to *persons*: *We the people of the United States . . . ; Will the person or persons who saw the accident please notify. . . .*

percent (per cent), percentage   Both these terms refer to fractions of one hundred. *Percent* always follows a number (*40 percent of the voters*), and the word is often used instead of the symbol (*%*) in nontechnical writing. *Percentage* usually follows an adjective (*a high percentage*).

persons   See *people, persons.*

phenomena   *Phenomena* is the plural of *phenomenon* (meaning "perceivable fact" or "unusual occurrence"): *Many phenomena are not recorded. One phenomenon is attracting attention.*

pique   See *peak, peek, pique.*

plus   *Plus* is standard as a preposition° meaning "in addition to": *His income plus mine is sufficient.* But *plus* is colloquial as a transitional expression°: *Our organization is larger than theirs; moreover* [not *plus*], *we have more money.*

precede, proceed   *Precede* means "come before": *My name precedes yours in the alphabet. Proceed* means "move on": *We were told to proceed to the waiting room.*

prejudice, prejudiced   *Prejudice* is a noun°; *prejudiced* is an adjective.° Do not drop the *-d* from *prejudiced*: *I knew that my grandparents were prejudiced* [not *prejudice*].

principal, principle   *Principal* is an adjective° meaning "foremost" or "major," a noun° meaning "chief official," or, in finance, a noun meaning

---

°Defined in "Grammar Terms," page 340.

"capital sum." *Principle* is a noun only, meaning "rule" or "axiom." *Her principal reasons for confessing were her principles of right and wrong.*

proceed, precede   See *precede, proceed.*

raise, rise   *Raise* means "lift" or "bring up" and takes a direct object°: *The Kirks raise cattle.* Its main forms are *raise, raised, raised. Rise* means "get up" and does not take an object: *They must rise at dawn.* Its main forms are *rise, rose, risen.*

real, really   In formal speech and writing, *real* should not be used as an adverb°; *really* is the adverb and *real* an adjective.° *Popular reaction to the announcement was really* [not *real*] *enthusiastic.*

reason is because   Although colloquially common, this construction should be avoided in formal speech and writing. Use a *that* clause after *reason is*: *The reason he is absent is that* [not *is because*] *he is sick.* Or: *He is absent because he is sick.*

respectful, respective   *Respectful* means "full of (or showing) respect": *Be respectful of other people. Respective* means "separate": *The two teams sat in their respective dugouts.*

rise, raise   See *raise, rise.*

scarcely   See *but, hardly, scarcely.*

sensual, sensuous   *Sensual* suggests sexuality; *sensuous* means "pleasing to the senses." *Stirred by the sensuous scent of meadow grass and flowers, Sophia and James found their thoughts turning sensual.*

set, sit   *Set* means "put" or "place" and takes a direct object°: *He sets the pitcher down.* Its main forms are *set, set, set. Sit* means "be seated" and does not take an object: *She sits on the sofa.* Its main forms are *sit, sat, sat.*

shall, will   *Will* is a helping verb for all person: *I will go, you will go, they will go.* The main use of *shall* is for first-person questions requesting an opinion or consent: *Shall I order a pizza? Shall we dance? Shall* can also be used for the first person when a formal effect is desired (*I shall expect you around three*), and it is occasionally used with the second or third person to express the speaker's determination (*You shall do as I say*).

should of   See *have, of.*

since   *Since* mainly relates to time: *I've been waiting since noon.* But *since* can also mean "because": *Since you ask, I'll tell you.* Revise sentences in which the word could have either meaning, such as *Since you left, my life is empty.*

sit, set   See *set, sit.*

so   Avoid using *so* alone or as a vague intensifier: *He was so late. So* needs to be followed by *that* and a statement of the result: *He was so late that I left without him.*

°Defined in "Grammar Terms," page 340.

somebody, some body; someone, some one *Somebody* and *someone* are indefinite pronouns°; *some body* is a noun° modified by *some*; and *some one* is a pronoun° or an adjective° modified by *some*. *Somebody ought to invent a shampoo that will give hair <u>some body</u>. <u>Someone</u> told James he should choose <u>some one</u> plan and stick with it.*

somewheres Nonstandard for *somewhere*.

sort of, sort of a See *kind of, sort of, type of*.

supposed to, used to In both these expressions, the *-d* is essential: *I <u>used to</u> [not <u>use to</u>] think so. He's <u>supposed to</u> [not <u>suppose to</u>] meet us.*

sure and, sure to; try and, try to *Sure to* and *try to* are the correct forms: *Be <u>sure to</u> [not <u>sure and</u>] buy milk. <u>Try to</u> [not <u>Try and</u>] find some decent tomatoes.*

take, bring See *bring, take*.

than, then *Than* is a conjunction° used in comparisons, *then* an adverb° indicating time: *Holmes knew <u>then</u> that Moriarty was wilier <u>than</u> he had thought.*

that, which *That* introduces an essential element: *We should use the lettuce <u>that Susan bought</u>* (*that Susan bought* limits the lettuce to a particular lettuce). *Which* can introduce both essential elements and nonessential elements, but many writers reserve *which* only for nonessential elements: *The leftover lettuce, <u>which is in the refrigerator</u>, would make a good salad* (*which is in the refrigerator* simply provides more information about the lettuce we already know of). Essential elements (with *that* or *which*) are not set off by commas; nonessential elements (with *which*) are. See also pp. 136–37.

that, who, which Use *that* to refer to most animals and to things: *The animals <u>that</u> escaped included a zebra. The rocket <u>that</u> failed cost millions.* Use *who* to refer to people and to animals with names: *Dorothy is the girl <u>who</u> visits Oz. Her dog, Toto, <u>who</u> accompanies her, gives her courage.* Use *which* only to refer to animals and things: *The river, <u>which</u> runs a thousand miles, empties into the Indian Ocean.*

their, there, they're *Their* is the possessive° form of *they*: *Give them <u>their</u> money. There* indicates place (*I saw her standing <u>there</u>*) or functions as an expletive° (*<u>There</u> is a hole behind you*). *They're* is a contraction° for *they are*: *<u>They're</u> going fast.*

theirselves Nonstandard for *themselves*.

then, than See *than, then*.

these, this *These* is plural; *this* is singular. *<u>This</u> pear is ripe, but <u>these</u> pears are not.*

these kind, these sort, these type, those kind See *kind of, sort of, type of*.

thru   A colloquial spelling of *through* that should be avoided in all academic and business writing.

to, too, two   *To* is a preposition°; *too* is an adverb° meaning "also" or "excessively"; and *two* is a number. *I too have been to Europe two times.*

toward, towards   Both are acceptable, though *toward* is preferred. Use one or the other consistently.

try and, try to   See *sure and, sure to*; *try and, try to*.

type of   See *kind of, sort of, type of*.

uninterested   See *disinterested, uninterested*.

unique   *Unique* means "the only one of its kind" and so cannot sensibly be modified with words such as *very* or *most*: *That was a unique* [not *a very unique* or *the most unique*] *movie*.

used to   See *supposed to, used to*.

weather, whether   The *weather* is the state of the atmosphere. *Whether* introduces alternatives. *The weather will determine whether we go or not*.

well   See *good, well*.

whether, if   See *if, whether*.

which, that   See *that, which*.

who, which, that   See *that, who, which*.

who, whom   *Who* is the subject of a sentence or clause°: *We know who will come*. *Whom* is the object° of a verb° or preposition°: *We know whom we invited*.

who's, whose   *Who's* is the contraction° of *who is* or *who has*: *Who's* [*Who is*] *at the door? Jim is the only one who's* [*who has*] *passed. Whose* is the possessive° form of *who*: *Whose book is that?*

will, shall   See *shall, will*.

would be   *Would be* is often used instead of *is* or *are* to soften statements needlessly: *One example is* [not *would be*] *gun-control laws*.

would have   Avoid this construction in place of *had* in clauses that begin *if*: *If the tree had* [not *would have*] *withstood the fire, it would have been the oldest in town*.

would of   See *have, of*.

you   In all but very formal writing, *you* is generally appropriate as long as it means "you, the reader." In all writing, avoid indefinite uses of *you*, such as *In one ancient tribe your first loyalty was to your parents*.

your, you're   *Your* is the possessive° form of *you*: *Your dinner is ready*. *You're* is the contraction° of *you are*: *You're late for dinner*.

yourself   See *myself, herself, himself, yourself*.

Words

°Defined in "Grammar Terms," page 340.

This section defines the terms and concepts of basic English grammar, including every term marked ° in the text.

absolute phrase   A phrase that consists of a noun° or pronoun° plus the *-ing* or *-ed* form of a verb° (a participle°): *Our accommodations arranged, we set out on our trip. They will hire a local person, other things being equal.*

active voice   The verb form° used when the sentence subject° names the performer of the verb's action: *The drillers used a rotary blade.* For more, see *voice.*

adjective   A word used to modify a noun° or pronoun:° *beautiful morning, ordinary one, good spelling.* Contrast *adverb.* Nouns, word groups, and some verb° forms may also serve as adjectives: *book sale; sale of old books; the sale, which occurs annually; increasing profits.*

adverb   A word used to modify a verb,° an adjective,° another adverb, or a whole sentence: *warmly greet* (verb), *only three people* (adjective), *quite seriously* (adverb), *Fortunately, she is employed* (sentence). Word groups may also serve as adverbs: *drove by a farm, plowed the field when the earth thawed.*

agreement   The correspondence of one word to another in person,° number,° or gender.° Mainly, a verb° must agree with its subject° (*The chef orders eggs*), and a pronoun° must agree with its antecedent° (*The chef surveys her breakfast*). See also pp. 104–08 and 112–15.

antecedent   The word a pronoun° refers to: *Jonah, who is not yet ten, has already chosen the college he will attend* (*Jonah* is the antecedent of the pronouns *who* and *he*).

appositive   A word or word group appearing next to a noun° or pronoun° that renames or identifies it and is equivalent to it: *My brother Michael, the best horn player in town, won the state competition* (*Michael* identifies which brother is being referred to; *the best horn player in town* renames *My brother Michael*).

article   The words *a, an,* and *the.* A kind of determiner,° an article always signals that a noun follows. See p. 329 for how to choose between *a* and *an.* See pp. 121–23 for the rules governing *a/an* and *the.*

auxiliary verb   See *helping verb.*

case   The form of a pronoun° or noun° that indicates its function in the sentence. Most pronouns have three cases. The **subjective case** is for

°Defined in this section.

subjects° and subject complements°: *I, you, he, she, it, we, they, who, whoever.* The **objective case** is for objects°: *me, you, him, her, it, us, them, whom, whomever.* The **possessive case** is for ownership: *my/mine, your/yours, his, her/hers, its, our/ours, their/theirs, whose.* Nouns use the subjective form (*dog, America*) for all cases except the possessive (*dog's, America's*).

clause   A group of words containing a subject° and a predicate.° A main clause can stand alone as a sentence: *We can go to the movies.* A subordinate clause cannot stand alone as a sentence: *We can go if Bridget gets back on time.* For more, see *subordinate clause.*

collective noun   A word with singular form that names a group of individuals or things: for instance, *team, army, family, flock, group.* A collective noun generally takes a singular verb and a singular pronoun: *The army is prepared for its role.* See also pp. 106 and 114.

comma splice   A sentence error in which two sentences (main clauses°) are separated by a comma without *and, but, or, nor,* or another coordinating conjunction.° Splice: *The book was long, it contained useful information.* Revised: *The book was long; it contained useful information.* Or: *The book was long, and it contained useful information.* See pp. 130–32.

comparison   The form of an adjective° *or* adverb° that shows its degree of quality or amount. The **positive** is the simple, uncompared form: *gross, clumsily.* The **comparative** compares the thing modified to at least one other thing: *grosser, more clumsily.* The **superlative** indicates that the thing modified exceeds all other things to which it is being compared: *grossest, most clumsily.* The comparative and superlative are formed either with the endings *-er/-est* or with the words *more/most* or *less/least.*

complement   See *subject complement.*

complex sentence   See *sentence.*

compound-complex sentence   See *sentence.*

compound construction   Two or more words or word groups serving the same function, such as a **compound subject**° (*Harriet and Peter poled their barge down the river*), **compound object** (*John writes stories and screenplays*), **compound predicate**° (*The scout watched and waited*), or parts of a predicate (*She grew tired and hungry*), and compound sentence° (*He smiled, and I laughed*). **Compound words** include nouns (*roommate, strip-mining*) and adjectives (*two-year-old, downtrodden*).

compound sentence   See *sentence.*

conditional statement   A statement expressing a condition contrary to fact and using the subjunctive mood° of the verb: *If she were mayor, the unions would cooperate.*

°Defined in this section.

conjunction A word that links and relates parts of a sentence. See *coordinating conjunction* (*and, but,* etc.), *correlative conjunction* (*either . . . or, both . . . and,* etc.), and *subordinating conjunction* (*because, if,* etc.).

conjunctive adverb A type of transitional expression° that can relate two main clauses° in a single sentence: *We had hoped to own a house by now; however, prices are still too high.* The main clauses are separated by a semicolon or a period. Some common conjunctive adverbs: *accordingly, also, anyway, besides, certainly, consequently, finally, further, furthermore, hence, however, in addition, incidentally, indeed, instead, likewise, meanwhile, moreover, namely, nevertheless, next, nonetheless, now, otherwise, rather, similarly, still, then, thereafter, therefore, thus, undoubtedly.*

contraction A condensed expression, with an apostrophe replacing the missing letters: for example, *doesn't* (*does not*), *we'll* (*we will*).

coordinating conjunction A word linking words or word groups serving the same function: *The dog and cat sometimes fight, but they usually get along.* The coordinating conjunctions are *and, but, or, nor, for, so, yet.*

coordination The linking of words or word groups that are of equal importance, usually with a coordinating conjunction.° *He and I laughed, but she was not amused.* Contrast *subordination.*

correlative conjunction Two or more connecting words that work together to link words or word groups serving the same function: *Both Michiko and June signed up, but neither Stan nor Carlos did.* The correlatives include *both . . . and, just as . . . so, not only . . . but also, not . . . but, either . . . or, neither . . . nor, whether . . . or, as . . . as.*

count noun A word that names a person, place, or thing that can be counted (and so may appear in plural form): *camera/cameras, river/rivers, child/children.*

dangling modifier A modifier that does not sensibly describe anything in its sentence. Dangling: *Having arrived late, the concert had already begun.* Revised: *Having arrived late, we found that the concert had already begun.* See p. 125.

determiner A word such as *a, an, the, my,* and *your* that indicates that a noun follows. See also *article.*

direct address A construction in which a word or phrase indicates the person or group spoken to: *Have you finished, John? Farmers, unite.*

direct object A noun° or pronoun° that identifies who or what receives the action of a verb°: *Education opens doors.* For more, see *object* and *predicate.*

direct question A sentence asking a question and concluding with a question mark: *Do they know we are watching?* Contrast *indirect question.*

direct quotation Repetition of what someone has written or said, using the exact words of the original and enclosing them in quotation marks: *Feinberg writes, "The reasons are both obvious and sorry."*

°Defined in this section.

Terms

double negative   A nonstandard form consisting of two negative words used in the same construction so that they effectively cancel each other: *I don't have no money*. Rephrase as *I have no money* or *I don't have any money*. See also p. 120.

ellipsis   The omission of a word or words from a quotation, indicated by the three spaced periods of an **ellipsis mark**: *"all . . . are created equal."* See also pp. 154–56.

essential element   A word or word group that is necessary to the meaning of the sentence because it limits the word it refers to: removing it would leave the meaning unclear or too general. Essential elements are *not* set off by commas: *Dorothy's companion the Scarecrow lacks a brain. The man who called about the apartment said he'd try again*. Contrast *nonessential element*. See also pp. 136–37.

expletive construction   A sentence that postpones the subject° by beginning with *there* or *it* and a form of *be*: *It is impossible to get a ticket. There are no more seats available*.

first person   See *person*.

fused sentence (run-on sentence)   A sentence error in which two complete sentences (main clauses°) are joined with no punctuation or connecting word between them. Fused: *I heard his lecture it was dull*. Revised: *I heard his lecture; it was dull*. See pp. 130–32.

future perfect tense   The verb tense expressing an action that will be completed before another future action: *They will have heard by then*. For more, see *tense*.

future tense   The verb tense expressing action that will occur in the future: *They will hear soon*. For more, see *tense*.

gender   The classification of nouns° or pronouns° as masculine (*he, boy*), feminine (*she, woman*), or neuter (*it, computer*).

generic *he*   *He* used to mean *he or she*. Avoid *he* when you intend either or both genders. See pp. 85–87 and 114.

generic noun   A noun° that does not refer to a specific person or thing: *Any person may come. A student needs good work habits. A school with financial problems may shortchange its students*. A singular generic noun takes a singular pronoun° (*he, she,* or *it*). See also *indefinite pronoun* and p. 114.

gerund   A verb form that ends in *-ing* and functions as a noun°: *Working is all right for killing time*. For more, see *verbals and verbal phrases*.

gerund phrase   See *verbals and verbal phrases*.

helping verb (auxiliary verb)   A verb° used with another verb to convey time, possibility, obligation, and other meanings: *You should write a letter. You have written other letters*. The modals are the following: *be able to,*

Terms

°Defined in this section.

be supposed to, can, could, had better, had to, may, might, must, ought to, shall, should, used to, will, would. The other helping verbs are forms of *be, have,* and *do.* See also pp. 93–95.

idiom An expression that is peculiar to a language and that may not make sense if taken literally: for example, *bide your time, by and large,* and *put up with.*

imperative See *mood.*

indefinite pronoun A word that stands for a noun° and does not refer to a specific person or thing. A few indefinite pronouns are plural (*both, few, many, several*) or may be singular or plural (*all, any, more, most, none, some*). But most are only singular: *anybody, anyone, anything, each, either, everybody, everyone, everything, neither, nobody, no one, nothing, one, somebody, someone, something.* The singular indefinite pronouns take singular verbs and are referred to by singular pronouns: *Something makes its presence felt.* See also *generic noun* and pp. 106 and 113–14.

indicative See *mood.*

indirect object A noun° or pronoun° that identifies to whom or what something is done: *Give them the award.* For more, see *object* and *predicate.*

indirect question A sentence reporting a question and ending with a period: *Writers wonder whether their work must always be lonely.* Contrast *direct question.*

indirect quotation A report of what someone has written or said, but not using the exact words of the original and not enclosing the words in quotation marks. Quotation: *"Events have controlled me."* Indirect quotation: *Lincoln said that events had controlled him.*

infinitive A verb form° consisting of the verb's dictionary form plus *to: to swim, to write.* For more, see *verbals and verbal phrases.*

infinitive phrase See *verbals and verbal phrases.*

interjection A word standing by itself or inserted in a construction to exclaim: *Hey! What the heck did you do that for?*

interrogative pronoun A word that begins a question and serves as the subject° or object° of the sentence. The interrogative pronouns are *who, whom, whose, which,* and *what. Who received the flowers? Whom are they for?*

intransitive verb A verb° that does not require a following word (direct object°) to complete its meaning: *Mosquitoes buzz. The hospital may close.* For more, see *predicate.*

irregular verb See *verb forms.*

linking verb A verb that links, or connects, a subject° and a word that renames or describes the subject (a subject complement°): *They are*

Terms

golfers. You seem lucky. The linking verbs are the forms of *be,* the verbs of the senses (*look, sound, smell, feel, taste*), and a few others (*appear, become, grow, prove, remain, seem, turn*). For more, see *predicate.*

main clause   A word group that contains a subject° and a predicate,° does not begin with a subordinating word, and may stand alone as a sentence: *The president was not overbearing.* For more, see *clause.*

main verb   The part of a verb phrase° that carries the principal meaning: *had been walking, could happen, was chilled.* Contrast *helping verb.*

misplaced modifier   A modifier whose position makes unclear its relation to the rest of the sentence. Misplaced: *The children played with firecrackers that they bought illegally in the field.* Revised: *The children played in the field with firecrackers that they bought illegally.*

modal   See *helping verb.*

modifier   Any word or word group that limits or qualifies the meaning of another word or word group. Modifiers include adjectives° and adverbs° as well as words and word groups that act as adjectives and adverbs.

mood   The form of a verb° that shows how the speaker views the action. The **indicative mood,** the most common, is used to make statements or ask questions: *The play will be performed Saturday. Did you get tickets?* The **imperative mood** gives a command: *Please get good seats. Avoid the top balcony.* The **subjunctive mood** expresses a wish, a condition contrary to fact, a recommendation, or a request: *I wish George were coming with us. If he were here, he'd come. I suggested that he come. The host asked that he be here.*

noncount noun   A word that names a person, place, or thing and that is not considered countable in English (and so does not appear in plural form): *confidence, information, silver, work.* See p. 122 for a longer list.

nonessential element   A word or word group that does not limit the word it refers to and that is not necessary to the meaning of the sentence. Nonessential elements are usually set off by commas: *Sleep, which we all need, occupies a third of our lives. His wife, Patricia, is a chemist.* Contrast *essential element.* See also pp. 136–37.

nonrestrictive element   See *nonessential element.*

noun   A word that names a person, place, thing, quality, or idea: *Maggie, Alabama, clarinet, satisfaction, socialism.* See also *collective noun, count noun, generic noun, noncount noun,* and *proper noun.*

noun clause   See *subordinate clause.*

number   The form of a word that indicates whether it is singular or plural. Singular: *I, he, this, child, runs, hides.* Plural: *we, they, these, children, run, hide.*

°Defined in this section.

object   A noun° or pronoun° that receives the action of or is influenced by another word. A **direct object** receives the action of a verb° or verbal° and usually follows it: *We watched the stars*. An **indirect object** tells for or to whom something is done: *Reiner bought us tapes*. An **object of a preposition** usually follows a preposition°: *They went to New Orleans*.

objective case   The form of a pronoun° when it is the object° of a verb° (*call him*) or the object of a preposition° (*for us*). For more, see *case*.

object of preposition   See *object*.

parallelism   Similarity of form between two or more coordinated elements: *Rising prices and declining incomes left many people in bad debt and worse despair*. See also pp. 76–78.

parenthetical expression   A word or construction that interrupts a sentence and is not part of its main structure, called *parenthetical* because it could (or does) appear in parentheses: *Mary Cassatt (1845–1926) was an American painter. Her work, incidentally, is in the museum.*

participial phrase   See *verbals and verbal phrases*.

participle   See *verbals and verbal phrases*.

particle   A preposition° or adverb° in a two-word verb: *catch on, look up*.

parts of speech   The classes of words based on their form, function, and meaning: nouns, pronouns, verbs, adjectives, adverbs, conjunctions, prepositions, and interjections. See separate entries for each part of speech.

passive voice   The verb form° used when the sentence subject° names the receiver of the verb's action: *The mixture was stirred*. For more, see *voice*.

past participle   The *-ed* form of most verbs°: *fished, hopped*. The past participle may be irregular: *begun, written*. For more, see *verbals and verbal phrases* and *verb forms*.

past perfect tense   The verb tense expressing an action that was completed before another past action: *No one had heard that before*. For more, see *tense*.

past tense   The verb tense expressing action that occurred in the past: *Everyone laughed*. For more, see *tense*.

past-tense form   The verb form used to indicate action that occurred in the past, usually created by adding *-d* or *-ed* to the verb's dictionary form (*smiled*) but created differently for most irregular verbs (*began, threw*). For more, see *verb forms*.

perfect tenses   The verb tenses indicating action completed before another specific time or action: *have walked, had walked, will have walked*. For more, see *tense*.

°Defined in this section.

person   The form of a verb° or pronoun° that indicates whether the subject is speaking, spoken to, or spoken about. In the first person the subject is speaking: *I am, we are.* In the second person the subject is spoken to: *you are.* In the third person the subject is spoken about: *he/she/it is, they are.*

personal pronoun   *I, you, he, she, it, we,* or *they*: a word that substitutes for a specific noun° or other pronoun. For more, see *case.*

phrase   A group of related words that lacks a subject° or a predicate° or both: *She ran into the field. She tried to jump the fence.* See also *absolute phrase, prepositional phrase, verbals and verbal phrases.*

plain form   The dictionary form of a verb: *buy, make, run, swivel.* For more, see *verb forms.*

plural   More than one. See *number.*

positive form   See *comparison.*

possessive case   The form of a noun° or pronoun° that indicates its ownership of something else: *men's attire, your briefcase.* For more, see *case.*

possessive pronoun   A word that replaces a noun° or other pronoun° and shows ownership: *The cat chased its tail.* The possessive pronouns are *my, our, your, his, her, its, their, whose.*

predicate   The part of a sentence that makes an assertion about the subject.° The predicate may consist of an intransitive verb° (*The earth trembled*), a transitive verb° plus direct object° (*The earthquake shook buildings*), a linking verb° plus subject complement° (*The result was chaos*), a transitive verb plus indirect object° and direct object (*The government sent the city aid*), or a transitive verb plus direct object and object complement (*The citizens considered the earthquake a disaster*).

preposition   A word that forms a noun° or pronoun° (plus any modifiers) into a prepositional phrase°: *about love, down the steep stairs.* The common prepositions: *about, above, according to, across, after, against, along, along with, among, around, as, at, because of, before, behind, below, beneath, beside, between, beyond, by, concerning, despite, down, during, except, except for, excepting, for, from, in, in addition to, inside, in spite of, instead of, into, like, near, next to, of, off, on, onto, out, out of, outside, over, past, regarding, since, through, throughout, till, to, toward, under, underneath, unlike, until, up, upon, with, within, without.*

prepositional phrase   A word group consisting of a preposition° and its object.° Prepositional phrases usually serve as adjectives° (*We saw a movie about sorrow*) or as adverbs° (*We went back for the second show*).

present participle   The *-ing* form of a verb°: *swimming, flying.* For more, see *verbals and verbal phrases.*

present perfect tense   The verb tense expressing action that began in the past and is linked to the present: *Dogs have buried bones here before.* For more, see *tense.*

°Defined in this section.

Terms

present tense   The verb tense expressing action that is occurring now, occurs habitually, or is generally true: *Dogs bury bones here often.* For more, see *tense.*

principal parts   The three forms of a verb from which its various tenses are created: the plain form° (*stop, go*), the past-tense form° (*stopped, went*), and the past participle° (*stopped, gone*). For more, see *tense* and *verb forms.*

progressive tenses   The verb tenses that indicate continuing (progressive) action and use the *-ing* form of the verb: *A dog was barking here this morning.* For more, see *tense.*

pronoun   A word used in place of a noun,° such as *I, he, everyone, who,* and *herself.* See also *indefinite pronoun, interrogative pronoun, personal pronoun, possessive pronoun, relative pronoun.*

proper adjective   A word formed from a proper noun° and used to modify a noun° or pronoun°: *Alaskan winter.*

proper noun   A word naming a specific person, place, or thing and beginning with a capital letter: *Jimmy Kimmel, Mt. Rainier, Alaska, US Congress.*

regular verb   See *verb forms.*

relative pronoun   A word that relates a group of words to a noun° or another pronoun.° The relative pronouns are *who, whom, whoever, whomever, which,* and *that. Ask the woman who knows all. This may be the question that stumps her.* For more, see *case.*

restrictive element   See *essential element.*

run-on sentence   See *fused sentence.*

-s form   See *verb forms.*

second person   See *person.*

sentence   A complete unit of thought, consisting of at least a subject° and a predicate° that are not introduced by a subordinating word. A **simple sentence** contains one main clause°: *I'm leaving.* A **compound sentence** contains at least two main clauses: *I'd like to stay, but I'm leaving.* A **complex sentence** contains one main clause and at least one subordinate clause°: *If you let me go now, you'll be sorry.* A **compound-complex sentence** contains at least two main clauses and at least one subordinate clause: *I'm leaving because you want me to, but I'd rather stay.*

sentence fragment   An error in which an incomplete sentence is set off as a complete sentence. Fragment: *She was not in shape for the race. Which she had hoped to win.* Revised: *She was not in shape for the race, which she had hoped to win.* See pp. 127–29.

series   Three or more items with the same function: *We gorged on ham, eggs, and potatoes.*

°Defined in this section.

simple sentence   See *sentence*.

simple tenses   See *tense*.

singular   One. See *number*.

split infinitive   The usually awkward interruption of an infinitive° and its marker *to* by a modifier: *We chose to not go*. See pp. 124–25.

squinting modifier   A modifier that could modify the words on either side of it: *The plan we considered seriously worries me*.

subject   In grammar, the part of a sentence that names something and about which an assertion is made in the predicate°: *The quick, brown fox jumped lazily* (simple subject); *The quick, brown fox jumped lazily* (complete subject).

subject complement   A word that renames or describes the subject° of a sentence, after a linking verb.° *The stranger was a man* (noun°). *He seemed gigantic* (adjective°).

subjective case   The form of a pronoun° when it is the subject° of a sentence (*I called*) or a subject complement° (*It was I*). For more, see *case*.

subjunctive   See *mood*.

subordinate clause   A word group that consists of a subject° and a predicate,° begins with a subordinating word such as *because* or *who,* and is not a question: *They voted for whoever cared the least because they mistrusted politicians*. Subordinate clauses may serve as adjectives° (*The car that hit Edgar was blue*), as adverbs° (*The car hit Edgar when it ran a red light*), or as nouns° (*Whoever was driving should be arrested*). Subordinate clauses are *not* complete sentences.

subordinating conjunction   A word that turns a complete sentence into a word group (a subordinate clause°) that can serve as an adverb° or a noun.° *Everyone was relieved when the meeting ended*. Some common subordinating conjunctions: *after, although, as, as if, as long as, as though, because, before, even if, even though, if, if only, in order that, now that, once, rather than, since, so that, than, that, though, till, unless, until, when, whenever, where, whereas, wherever, while*.

subordination   Deemphasizing one element in a sentence by making it dependent on rather than equal to another element. Through subordination, *I left six messages; the doctor failed to call* becomes *Although I left six messages, the doctor failed to call* or *After six messages, the doctor failed to call*.

superlative   See *comparison*.

tag question   A question attached to the end of a statement and composed of a pronoun,° a helping verb,° and sometimes the word *not*: *It isn't raining, is it? It is sunny, isn't it?*

tense   The verb form that expresses time, usually indicated by endings and by helping verbs. See the next page for the tense forms of a regular verb. See also *verb forms*.

°Defined in this section.

Terms

Present Action that is occurring now, occurs habitually, or is generally true

Simple present Plain form or -*s* form	**Present progressive** *Am, is,* or *are* plus -*ing* form
I *walk.*	I *am walking.*
You/we/they *walk.*	You/we/they *are walking.*
He/she/it *walks.*	He/she/it *is walking.*

Past Action that occurred before now

Simple past Past-tense form	**Past progressive** *Was* or *were* plus -*ing* form
I/he/she/it *walked.*	I/he/she/it *was walking.*
You/we/they *walked.*	You/we/they *were walking.*

Future Action that will occur in the future

Simple future *Will* plus plain form	**Future progressive** *Will be* plus -*ing* form
I/you/he/she/it/we/they *will walk.*	I/you/he/she/it/we/they *will be walking.*

Present perfect Action that began in the past and is linked to the present

Present perfect *Have* or *has* plus *past participle*	**Present perfect progressive** *Have been* or *has been* plus -*ing* form
I/you/we/they *have walked.*	I/you/we/they *have been walking.*
He/she/it *has walked.*	He/she/it *has been walking.*

Past perfect Action that was completed before another past action

Past perfect *Had* plus past participle	**Past perfect progressive** *Had been* plus -*ing* form
I/you/he/she/it/we/they *had walked.*	I/you/he/she/it/we/they *had been walking.*

Future perfect Action that will be completed before another future action

Future perfect *Will have* plus past participle	**Future perfect progressive** *Will have been* plus -*ing* form
I/you/he/she/it/we/they *will have walked.*	I/you/he/she/it/we/they *will have been walking.*

third person See *person.*

transitional expression A word or phrase that shows the relations between sentences or between clauses° within a sentence. Transitional expressions can signal various relationships (examples in parentheses): addition or sequence (*also, besides, finally, first, furthermore, in addition, last*); comparison (*also, similarly*); contrast (*even so, however, in contrast, still*); examples (*for example, for instance, that is*); intensification (*basically,*

°Defined in this section.

indeed, in fact, of course); place (*below, elsewhere, here, nearby, to the east*); time (*afterward, at last, earlier, immediately, meanwhile, simultaneously*); repetition or summary (*in brief, in other words, in short, in summary, that is*); and cause and effect (*as a result, consequently, hence, therefore, thus*).

transitive verb   A verb° that requires a following word (a direct object°) to complete its meaning: *We repaired the roof.* For more, see *predicate.*

verb   A word that expresses an action (*bring, change*), an occurrence (*happen, become*), or a state of being (*be, seem*). A verb is the essential word in a predicate,° the part of a sentence that makes an assertion about the subject.° With endings and helping verbs,° verbs can indicate tense,° mood,° voice,° number,° and person.° For more, see separate entries for each of these aspects as well as *verb forms.*

verbals and verbal phrases   **Verbals** are verb forms used as adjectives,° adverbs,° or nouns.° They form **verbal phrases** with objects° and modifiers.° A **present participle** adds *-ing* to the dictionary form of a verb (*living*). A **past participle** usually adds *-d* or *-ed* to the dictionary form (*lived*), although irregular verbs work differently (*begun, swept*). A participle or **participial phrase** usually serves as an adjective: *Strolling shoppers fill the malls.* A **gerund** is the *-ing* form of a verb used as a noun. Gerunds and **gerund phrases** can do whatever nouns can do: *Shopping satisfies needs.* An **infinitive** is the verb's dictionary form plus *to: to live.* Infinitives and **infinitive phrases** may serve as nouns (*To design a mall is a challenge*), as adverbs (*Malls are designed to make shoppers feel safe*), or as adjectives (*The mall supports the impulse to shop*).

A verbal *cannot* serve as the only verb in a sentence. For that, it requires a helping verb°: *Shoppers were strolling.*

verb forms   Verbs have five distinctive forms. The **plain form** is the dictionary form: *A few artists live in town today.* The **-s form** adds *-s* or *-es* to the plain form: *The artist lives in town today.* The **past-tense form** usually adds *-d* or *-ed* to the plain form: *Many artists lived in town before this year.* Some verbs' past-tense forms are irregular, such as *began, fell, swam, threw, wrote.* The past participle is usually the same as the past-tense form, although, again, some verbs' **past participles** are irregular (*begun, fallen, swum, thrown, written*). The **present participle** adds *-ing* to the plain form: *A few artists are living in town today.*

Regular verbs are those that add *-d* or *-ed* to the plain form for the past-tense form and past participle. **Irregular verbs** create these forms in irregular ways (see above).

verb phrase   A verb° of more than one word that serves as the predicate° of a sentence: *The movie has started.*

voice   The form of a verb° that tells whether the sentence subject° performs the action or is acted upon. In the **active voice** the subject acts: *The city controls rents.* In the **passive voice** the subject is acted upon: *Rents are controlled by the city.* See also pp. 103–04.

Terms

°Defined in this section.

Credits

Text and Illustrations

Page 18: Mayer, Lawence A. "The Confounding Enemy of Sleep." *Fortune*, June 1974.

Page 19: Woolf, Virginia. *The Waves*. Harcourt, 1931.

Page 20: Ehrenreich, Barbara. *Fear of Falling: The Inner Life of the Middle Class*. HarperCollins, 1989.

Page 22: Schor, Juliet B. *The Overworked American*. Basic Books. 1992.

Page 25: Everett Collection.

Page 26 (middle): *MyPlate*, a graphic representation of daily food portions recommended for a healthy diet. From *ChooseMyPlate.gov*, US Dept. of Agriculture, 2011; Web; 8 July 2014.

Page 26 (bottom): NASA/Johnson Space Center.

Page 27 (top): Marital status in 2014 of adults age 18 and over. Data from Pew Research Center, 4 Nov. 2014, www.pewresearch.org/data-trend/society-and-demographics/marriage/.

Page 27 (middle): Lifetime prevalence of use of alcohol, compared with other drugs, among twelfth graders in 2015. Data from *Monitoring the Future: A Continuing Study of American Youth*, U of Michigan, 12 Dec. 2015, www.monitoringthefuture.org/data/2015data-drugs.

Page 27 (bottom): Unemployment rates of high school graduates and college graduates, 1998–2016. Data from *Economics News Release*, US Dept. of Labor, Bureau of Labor Statistics, 1 Apr. 2016, http://www.bls.gov/news.release/empsit.t04.htm.

Pages 35 and 40: Teach.org and the Ad Council.

Page 36: Campbell, Neil A., and Jane B. Reece. *Biology*. 7th ed. Pearson Education.

Page 55: Ali, Agha Shadid. "Postcard from Kashmir." *The Half-Inch Himalayas*. Wesleyan UP, 1987. © 1987 by Agha Shahid Ali. Reprinted by permission.

Page 63: Bill Aron/PhotoEdit.

Page 148: Allen, Woody. "My Philosophy." *Getting Even*. Vintage Books, 1978.

Page 148: Greene, Graham. *The Man Within*. Penguin Classics. New York: Penguin Random House, 2005.

Page 150: Friedan, Betty. *The Feminine Mystique*. W. W. Norton and Co. Copyright © 1963.

Page 156: Frost, Robert. "Stopping by Woods on a Snowy Evening." *New Hampshire*. Henry Holt and Company, LLC. Copyright © 1923.

Page 181: Wilson, Edward O. Excerpt from "Is Humanity Suicidal?" from *The New York Times*, 30 May, 1993. Copyright © 1993.

Answers to Selected Exercises

Coordination and subordination for emphasis, pp. 72–73
Possible revision

Sir Walter Raleigh personified the Elizabethan Age, the period of Elizabeth I's rule of England, in the last half of the sixteenth century. Raleigh was a courtier, a poet, an explorer, and an entrepreneur. Supposedly, he gained Queen Elizabeth's favor by throwing his cloak beneath her feet at the right moment, just as she was about to step over a puddle.

Concise writing, p. 76
Possible revision

If sore muscles after exercising are a problem for you, there are things you can do to ease the discomfort. Avoid heat for the first day of soreness because applying heat within the first twenty-four hours can increase muscle soreness and stiffness. In contrast, applying cold immediately will reduce inflammation.

Parallelism, p. 78
Possible revision

1 The ancient Greeks celebrated four athletic contests: the Olympic Games at Olympia, the Isthmian Games near Corinth, the Pythian Games at Delphi, and the Nemean Games at Cleonae. 2 Each day the games consisted of either athletic events or ceremonies and sacrifices to the gods. 3 Competitors ran sprints, participated in spectacular chariot and horse races, and ran long distances while wearing full armor.

Variety, p. 81
Possible revision

After being dormant for many years, the Italian volcano Vesuvius exploded on August 24 in the year AD 79. The ash, pumice, and mud from the volcano buried two towns—Herculaneum and the more famous Pompeii—which lay undiscovered until 1709 and 1748, respectively.

Appropriate words, pp. 87–88
Possible answers

1 Vaccinations to prevent serious diseases have been very important for public health since they became widely available in the 1920s. 2 Diseases such as polio, measles, and whooping cough that used to sicken and kill many children have been largely eliminated.
3 However, measles is returning because some parents do not vaccinate their children. 4 Measles is a serious and highly contagious disease, causing patients to exhibit multiple symptoms including high fever, cough, vomiting, diarrhea, and full-body rash. 5 Despite extensive evidence to the contrary, some parents claim that the measles vaccine, which is combined with vaccines for mumps and rubella, causes autism.

Exact words, p. 90

1 The acclaimed writer Maxine Hong Kingston cites her mother's stories about ancestors and ancient Chinese customs as the sources of her first two books, *The Woman Warrior* and *China Men*. 2 One of her mother's tales [or stories], about a pregnant aunt who was ostracized by villagers, had a great effect on the young Kingston. 3 The aunt gained vengeance by drowning herself in the village water supply. 4 Kingston made the aunt famous by giving her immortality in *The Woman Warrior*.

Verb forms, p. 98

1 In less than a decade, the world population has grown by two-thirds of a billion people. 2 Recently it broke the 7.4 billion mark.
3 Population experts have painted pictures of a crowded future, predicting that the world population may hit 9.6 billion by the year 2050.
4 The supply of food, clean water, and land is of particular concern.
5 Even though the food supply rose in the last decade, the share to each person fell. 6 At the same time the water supply sank in size and quantity. 7 Changes in land use ran nomads and subsistence farmers off their fields, while the overall number of species on the earth shrank by 20%.

Verb tenses, pp. 100–01

1 The 1960 presidential race between Richard M. Nixon and John F. Kennedy was the first to feature a televised debate. [Sentence

correct.] 2 Despite his extensive political experience, Nixon perspired heavily and looked haggard and uneasy in front of the camera. 3 By contrast, Kennedy projected cool poise and provided crisp answers that made him seem fit for the office of President.

Verb mood, p. 102

1 If John Hawkins had known of all the dangerous side effects of smoking tobacco, would he have introduced the plant to England in 1565? 2 In promoting tobacco, Hawkins noted that if a Florida Indian man were to travel for several days, he would smoke tobacco to satisfy his hunger and thirst.

Verb voice, p. 104

Possible revision

1 Many factors determine water quality. 2 All natural waters contain suspended and dissolved substances. 3 The environment controls the amounts of the substances. 4 Pesticides produce some dissolved substances. 5 Fields, livestock feedlots, and other sources deposit sediment in water.

Agreement of subject and verb, p. 108

1 The Siberian tiger is the largest living cat in the world, much bigger than its relative the Bengal tiger. 2 It grows to a length of nine to twelve feet, including its tail, and to a height of about three and a half feet. 3 It can weigh over six hundred pounds. 4 This carnivorous hunter lives in northern China and Korea as well as in Siberia. 5 During the long winter of this Arctic climate, the yellowish striped coat gets a little lighter in order to blend with the snow-covered landscape. 6 The coat also grows quite thick because the tiger has to withstand temperatures as low as –50°F.

Pronoun forms, pp. 111–12

1 Written four thousand years ago, *The Epic of Gilgamesh* tells the story of Gilgamesh and his friendship with Enkidu. [Sentence correct.] 2 Gilgamesh was a bored king who his people thought was too harsh. [Sentence correct.] 3 Then he met Enkidu, a wild man who had lived with the animals in the mountains. 4 Immediately, he and Gilgamesh wrestled to see who was more powerful. 5 After hours of struggle, Enkidu admitted that Gilgamesh was stronger than he.

6 Now the friends needed adventures worthy of them, the two strongest men on earth. [Sentence correct.]

Agreement of pronoun and antecedent, p. 115
Possible revision

1 Despite their extensive research and experience, neither child psychologists nor parents have yet figured out how children become who they are. [Sentence correct.] 2 Of course, the family has a tremendous influence on the development of a child in its midst. 3 Each member of the immediate family exerts a unique pull on the child. 4 Other relatives, teachers, and friends can also affect the child's view of the world and of himself or herself.

Pronoun reference, p. 118
Possible revision

1 "Life begins at forty" is a cliché many people live by, and this saying may or may not be true. 2 Whether one agrees or not with the cliché, there are many examples of people whose public lives began at forty. 3 For instance, when Pearl Buck was forty, her novel *The Good Earth* won the Pulitzer Prize. 4 Kenneth Kanuda, past president of Zambia, was elected to the presidency in 1964, when he was forty.

Adjectives and adverbs, p. 123

1 Americans often argue about which professional sport is best: basketball, football, or baseball. 2 Basketball fans contend that their sport offers more action because the players are constantly running and shooting. 3 Because it is played indoors in relatively small arenas, basketball allows fans to be closer to the action than the other sports do. 4 Football fanatics say they hardly stop yelling once the game begins. 5 They cheer when their team executes a complicated play well.

Misplaced and dangling modifiers, p. 126
Possible answers

1 As evening falls in the Central American rain forests, the tungara frogs begin their croaking chorus. 2 Croaking loudly at night, male tungara frogs sing "songs" to attract female frogs. 3 When they hear the croaking, predators such as bullfrogs and bats gather to feast on the frogs. 4 The frogs hope only to mate [*or* only hope to mate], but their nightly chorus can result in death instead.

Sentence fragments, p. 129

Possible answers

People generally avoid eating mushrooms except those they buy in stores. But in fact many varieties of mushrooms are edible. Mushrooms are members of a large group of vegetation called nonflowering plants, including algae, mosses, ferns, and coniferous trees, even the giant redwoods of California. Most of the nonflowering plants prefer moist environments such as forest floors, fallen timber, and still water. Mushrooms, for example, prefer moist, shady soil. Algae grow in water.

Comma splices and fused sentences, p. 132

Possible answers

What many call the first genocide of modern times occurred during World War I, when the Armenians were deported from their homes in Anatolia, Turkey. The Turkish government assumed that the Armenians were sympathetic to Russia, with whom the Turks were at war. Many Armenians died because of the hardships of the journey, and many were massacred. The death toll was estimated at between 600,000 and 1 million.

The comma, pp. 139–40

1 Ellis Island, New York, reopened for business in 1990, but now the customers are tourists, not immigrants. 2 This spot, which lies in New York Harbor, was the first American soil seen or touched by many of the nation's immigrants. 3 Though other places also served as ports of entry for foreigners, none has the symbolic power of Ellis Island. 4 Between its opening in 1892 and its closing in 1954, over 20 million people, about two-thirds of all immigrants, were detained there before taking up their new lives in the United States. 5 Ellis Island processed over 2000 [*or* 2,000] newcomers a day when immigration was at its peak between 1900 and 1920.

The semicolon, p. 142

The set, sounds, and actors in the movie captured the essence of horror films. The set was ideal: dark, deserted streets; trees dipping their branches over the sidewalks; mist hugging the ground and creeping up to meet the trees; looming shadows of unlighted, turreted houses. The sounds, too, were appropriate; especially terrifying was the hard, hollow sound of footsteps echoing throughout the film.

Colons and semicolons, pp. 143–44

1 Sunlight is made up of three kinds of radiation: visible rays; infrared rays, which we cannot see; and ultraviolet rays, which are also invisible. [Sentence correct.] 2 Infrared rays are the longest, measuring 700 nanometers and longer, while ultraviolet rays are the shortest, measuring 400 nanometers and shorter. 3 Especially in the ultraviolet range, sunlight is harmful to the eyes. 4 Ultraviolet rays can damage the retina; furthermore, they can cause cataracts on the lens.

The apostrophe, p. 147

1 People whose online experiences include blogging, Web cams, and social-networking sites are often used to seeing the details of other people's private lives. 2 Many are also comfortable sharing their own opinions, photographs, and videos with family, friends, and even strangers. 3 However, they need to realize that employers and even the government can see their information, too. 4 Employers commonly search for applicants' names on social-networking Web sites such as *Twitter* and *Facebook*. [Sentence correct.]

Quotation marks, pp. 150–51

1 In a history class we talked about a passage from Abraham Lincoln's *Gettysburg Address*, delivered on November 19, 1863: [Sentence correct.]

2 Four score and seven years ago our fathers brought forth on this continent, a new nation, conceived in Liberty, and dedicated to the proposition that all men are created equal. 3 Now we are engaged in a great civil war, testing whether that nation, or any nation so conceived and so dedicated, can long endure. [Sentences correct; no quotation marks around a block quotation.]

4 "What was Lincoln referring to in the first sentence?" the teacher asked. 5 "Perhaps we should define *score* first."

End punctuation, p. 152

When visitors first arrive in Hawaii, they often encounter an unexpected language barrier. Standard English is the language of business and government, but many of the people speak Pidgin English. Instead of an excited "Aloha!" the visitors may be greeted with an excited Pidgin "Howzit!" or asked if they know "how fo' find one good hotel."

Punctuation, pp. 156–57

1 Brewed coffee is the most widely consumed beverage in the world. 2 It's believed that coffee cultivation and trade began on the Arabian Peninsula in the fifteenth century. 3 By the middle or late sixteenth century, travelers had introduced the beverage to the Europeans, who at first resisted it because of its strong flavor and effect as a mild stimulant. 4 The French, Italians, and other Europeans incorporated coffee into their diets by the mid-seventeenth century; the English, however, preferred tea, which they were then importing from India. 5 Only after the Boston Tea Party (1773) did Americans begin drinking coffee in large quantities. 6 Now, though, the United States is one of the top coffee-consuming countries. 7 More than 150,000,000 Americans drink at least one cup of coffee each day.

Spelling, pp. 164–65

1 Science affects many important aspects of our lives, though many people have a poor understanding of the role of scientific breakthroughs in their health. 2 Many people believe that doctors, more than science, are responsible for improvements in health care. 3 But scientists in the laboratory have made crucial steps in the search for knowledge about health and medicine. 4 For example, one scientist whose discoveries have affected many people is Ulf Von Euler. 5 In the 1950s Von Euler's discovery of certain hormones led to the invention of the birth control pill.

Capital letters, pp. 167–68

1 San Antonio, Texas, is a thriving city in the Southwest that has always offered much to tourists interested in the roots of Spanish settlement in the New World. 2 Most visitors stop at the Alamo, one of five Catholic missions built by priests to convert Native Americans and to maintain Spain's claims in the area. 3 The Alamo is famous for being the site of an 1836 battle that helped to create the Republic of Texas. 4 San Antonio has grown tremendously in recent years. [Sentence correct.] 5 The Hemisfair Plaza and the San Antonio River link tourist and convention facilities.

Index

Index

Index

in-text citations, 315
models, 304–15
notes: format of, 303–04; models of, 304–15
numbering of notes, 304
page numbers: notes and bibliographies, 304; paper format, 315
paper format, 315
print sources, 306, 308, 310, 312
punctuation, 303, 304, 315
quotation marks: notes and bibliography, 303; paper format, 315
quotations, 315
sample paper, 316–17
shortened notes, 314–15
spacing, 303
title page, paper format, 315
titles of books and periodicals, 303, 310
Web sites, 306–13
child, agreement with pronoun, 113
Claims, of arguments, 42–43, 44, 45, 47
Clauses
adjective and adverb, 349
commas with, 130, 135
conciseness of, 74
coordinating conjunctions with, 71, 130
defined, 341
main. *See* Main (independent) clauses
semicolons with, 71, 131, 140–41
subordinate. *See* Subordinate (dependent) clauses
transitional expressions with, 71, 131, 349–50
Clichés
avoiding, 90
exercises, 90
climatic, climactic, 331
Close antecedents, 116
Coherence in academic writing, 15, 18
Collections. *See* Anthologies or collections
Collective nouns
agreement of pronouns and, 114–15
agreement of verbs and, 106
defined, 341

Colloquial language, in informal writing, 83–84, 329
Colons
at end of main clauses, 143
exercises, 143–44
for introductions, 142–43
not inside main clauses, 143
quotation marks with, 149–50
quotations with complete sentences at beginning, 139
with salutations of business letters, titles and subtitles, and divisions of time, 143
Color, selecting for readers with vision loss, 29
Combining sentences for conciseness, 75
Comic strips. *See* Illustrations and artworks
Commands (imperative mood). *See* Imperative mood
Commas, 135–39
with *and, but, or, nor, for, so, yet,* 135
with absolute phrases, 137
with concluding elements, 136–37
with coordinating conjunctions, 71, 135, 137
with dates, addresses, place names, numbers, 138–39
with direct address, 137
between equal adjectives, 138
exercises, 139
with interrupting elements, 136–37
with introductory elements, 135
between items in series, 137–38
missing, watching for, 83
with nonessential (nonrestrictive) elements, 136, 345
not with essential (restrictive) elements, 136
vs. parentheses, 153
with parenthetical expressions, 137
with phrases of contrast, 137
quotation marks with, 149
with signal phrases and quotations, 139
with transitional expressions (*however, for example,* etc.), 131, 137, 141
with *yes* and *no,* 137

Index

Index

Index

Index

ESL Guide

Throughout this handbook, the symbol **ESL** signals topics for students whose first language is not standard American English. These topics can be tricky because they arise from rules in standard English that are quite different in other languages. Many of the topics involve significant cultural assumptions as well.

Whatever your language background, as a college student you are learning the culture of US higher education and the language that is used and shaped by that culture. The process is challenging, even for native speakers of standard American English. It requires not just writing clearly and correctly but also mastering conventions of developing, presenting, and supporting ideas. The challenge is greater if, in addition, you are trying to learn standard English and are accustomed to other conventions. Several habits can help you succeed:

- **Read.** Besides course assignments, read newspapers, magazines, and books in English. The more you read, the more fluently and accurately you'll write.
- **Write.** Keep a journal in which you practice writing in English every day.
- **Talk and listen.** Take advantage of opportunities to hear and use English.
- **Ask questions.** Your instructors, tutors in the writing center, and fellow students can clarify assignments and help you identify and solve writing problems.
- **Don't try for perfection.** No one writes perfectly, and the effort to do so can prevent you from expressing yourself fluently. View mistakes not as failures but as opportunities to learn.
- **Revise first; then edit.** Focus on each essay's ideas, support, and organization before attending to grammar and vocabulary. See the checklist for revising academic writing on page 15.
- **Set editing priorities.** Check first for errors that interfere with clarity, such as problems with word order or subject-verb agreement. The following index can help you identify the topics you need to work on and can lead you to appropriate text discussions.

ESL

Detailed Contents